DEAD CENTER

DEAD CENTER

The Shocking True Story
of a Murder on Snipe Mountain

Frank J. Daniels

New Horizon Press
Far Hills, New Jersey

Frank J. Daniels
      Dead Center: The Shocking True Story of a Murder on Snipe Mountain

Cover Design: Robert Aulicino
Interior Design: Susan M. Sanderson

Library of Congress Control Number: 2003105756

ISBN: 0-88282-238-1
New Horizon Press

Manufactured in the U.S.A.

2007   2006   2005   2004   2003   /   5   4   3   2   1

Author's Note

This book is based on the experiences and work of Frank J. Daniels and reflects his perceptions of the past, present and future. The personalities, events, actions and conversations portrayed within the story have been taken from his memories, extensive court documents, interviews, testimony, research, letters, personal papers, press accounts and the memories of some participants.

In an effort to safeguard the privacy of certain people, some individuals' names and identifying characteristics have been altered. Events involving the characters happened as described. Only minor details have been changed.

Table of Contents

Foreword

This is a true story. I came upon this tale of greed, lust and violent death through my duties as District Attorney for Colorado's Twenty-first Judicial District in western Colorado. I was called upon to head the investigation. The death happened quickly, taking perhaps fifteen seconds. The investigation spanned better than four years and resulted in eleven thousand pages of investigative reports. Though the story has remained in my memory, for the purposes of this tale, I painstakingly went through all the evidence again, including the reports, page by page, line by line, repeatedly, to distill and repair, so that as I reconstructed the story, only relevant evidence would be included. As with any major investigation, there were many avenues pursued that led nowhere. I have endeavored to keep intact the essence of the investigation, of which I was a part, while bringing out what was meaningful to the course of the prosecution I pursued or influenced the case as it unfolded. Some of the time periods have been condensed and information on investigative leads which may have come out at different points have been connected to make the narrative flow more smoothly. Some, but not all, of the grammar in reports, interviews and conversations were spruced up a bit. In addition, I have reconstructed the dialogue from the memory of participants, court testimony and police reports.

I wrote the book for two reasons: first and foremost, this was the most engrossing and intriguing case in which I ever have been involved; second, this is an excellent example of how an investigation progresses from the prosecution perspective, complete with a complex and interesting set of forensic evidence analyses and results. My intent was to put together a book that makes an enthralling read as well as an educational study of a murder unraveled (or at least as unraveled as we could get it).

Introduction

Looming red sandstone cliffs to the southwest are bathed in early morning light which, reflected from the bottom edges of high clouds to the east, imparts a warm pinkish glow. I begin my journey to Shreveport, Louisiana, a respite to which I have been looking forward for a very long time. I am intrigued, as always, by the geologic marvel evidenced in the cliffs at the northern edge of the Uncompahgre Plateau, composed at the base of black Precambrian gneiss and schist underlying bright red Triassic mudstones and clays that support sheer cliffs of Jurassic Wingate sandstone. Twelve thousand million years of rock are missing between the Precambrian and Triassic strata, evidently due to ancient erosion. This valley, the Grand Valley of Western Colorado, is a geologic wonder. When I first moved to this region, the cliffs were just cliffs and the rocks just rocks, but the longer I've lived here the more these awesome formations of nature became a part of my spirit. I moved here from Boulder, having just graduated law school at the University of Colorado, to take a job as Deputy District Attorney. That was eighteen years ago. For the past eight years, I have held the position of elected District Attorney.

My interest in geology sprung from my interest in petrified wood. When I first started working as a deputy DA, a part-time investigator named Vince Jones, who had been a special agent in the FBI for thirty years, worked in the office. Many times Vince talked about collecting petrified wood. I became intrigued.

I began to collect some pieces of the wood and when I attended my first gem and mineral show, I quickly learned that these shows were a great place to find top-quality specimens of petrified wood. Dealers from all over the world bring gems, minerals and fossils to sell and display, especially at the huge winter shows in Tucson and Quartzsite, Arizona. There, one will find dealers from all the inhabited continents. Previously unknown material shows up every year. Quartzsite would be nothing more than a hot bump on Interstate 10 in the middle of nowhere without the show, which draws hundreds of thousands of visitors annually. It is in the middle of a rocky desert wasteland and comprises a vast network of tents and recreational vehicles. It was at the Quartzsite show that I met Mr. E. P. Akin of Shreveport, Louisiana, purveyor of the world's finest petrified Louisiana palm wood.

Mr. Akin first began setting up as a rock dealer in Quartzsite after retiring from operating a successful nursery business in Shreveport. That was thirty-five years ago. A true southern gentleman who celebrated his ninety-fourth birthday this year, he is a man with broad knowledge in a variety of subject matters, ranging from human nature to horticulture and minerals. His knowledge of gem-quality Louisiana palm wood is unparalleled. So when he wrote to me in February that a friend of his in Shreveport was selling the finest collection of fossil palm wood ever assembled, I very much wanted to see it. However, when I received Mr. Akin's letter, I was still engrossed in the most difficult, complicated and fascinating case I had ever come across. Now that it was over, I badly needed to get away and decided to take up Akin's kind offer.

There are a number of ways to get from Grand Junction to Shreveport. I allowed myself a week to get there and back. I thought, given my interest in adding both to my knowledge and collection of petrified wood, I could finally stop thinking about the strange death of Bruce Dodson. It has preoccupied me for the last four years. However, though this was my objective, since I have been on the road driving, thoughts of Bruce and my involvement in bringing the truth about his death to light have been flooding my consciousness. I still cannot let it all go; perhaps I never will...

Hunting Season

The evening before the opening day of hunting season, Janice Dodson, an experienced hunter, and her new husband, Bruce Dodson, who had never hunted before, were driving in separate vehicles along dark, dusty roads toward camp, rather frustratingly behind schedule. Periodically they caught a glimmer of lantern light through the trees ahead and as they sped past could see the silhouettes of hunters busily readying their campsites for the morning's hunt. There were quite a few other hunters on the road in their pickups and four-wheelers. Like much of the West, the Uncompahgre Plateau in hunting season becomes something of an armed encampment.

Janice planned on finding the spot at which she had camped in years past with her ex-husband. She had visited the place just a few weeks earlier on a grouse hunting and scouting trip. Her destination was a remote location on the 1.2 million acre plateau. While prime campsites can be hard to find during hunting season, there is ample room for all and no need for campers to cluster together. Janice and Bruce finally arrived close to 9:00 P.M.

In the pitch-black night they maneuvered their vehicles through the sharp curve from the main road back toward the spot

Janice had selected for their campsite. Both vehicles made a racket as they traversed the rough terrain from the road to the clearing where they would camp, a few hundred yards off Brushy Ridge Trail. As they curved around the clearing their headlights illuminated two small tents and a pickup truck with Texas plates. Janice drove past the tents and parked at a level spot about sixty yards farther along. Bruce followed. They set up their tents and settled in for a quiet evening.

It is not uncommon to run into a Texas hunter in western Colorado. Much of Colorado was once part of the Republic of Texas and many Texans still treat the area as if they owned it. As it turned out, the hunters from Texas camped near Bruce and Janice were law enforcement officers from East Texas, the same general vicinity where Janice and her first husband were born and settled. One of these Texas hunters was Brent Branchwater, thirty seven years old, six-foot-six, skinny as a rail and a mild-mannered speaker with a quick sense of humor. Branchwater was a captain with the County Sheriff's department based in Titus, Texas.

At about seven the second morning after Bruce and Janice arrived, Branchwater heard one shot close to camp, followed by some "hoopin' and hollerin'." Then he heard two more shots in rapid succession "a minute or two later." He assumed someone shot a deer and the deer got up and was shot at twice more, so he didn't think anymore about it at the time. After Branchwater "fooled around" his camp for a while, he began to skin the deer he shot the previous afternoon. Looking up, he saw an attractive woman with long, silky hair come over a nearby hill and pass between Branchwater's camp and the one set up next to his. She walked over to a Bronco truck, opened the tailgate and placed a rifle into a gun case. Branchwater went back to work on his deer, but a few minutes later the woman he saw earlier walked over to his camp and struck up a conversation.

"That's a nice forky," she said, obviously knowing hunter's lingo for the term for a buck with two antler points on each side.

"Thanks," Branchwater said.

The woman introduced herself. Branchwater thought she said her name was Denise. They talked for a few minutes, then Branchwater told her, "My buddy, who is still out hunting, and I are planning to go into town later to get some ice."

When he told her that, the woman asked, "Would you bring back some water for us? We didn't bring enough."

"Sure, no problem. Do you go hunting often?" he asked.

"I do, but my husband hasn't before. We've been married for three months and today is our anniversary."

"Well, congratulations."

The woman smiled and walked back to her campsite. Captain Branchwater finished skinning and butchering his deer. He was sacking the meat, the radio was on and it must have been around 9:30 when he thought he heard an elk bugling. He turned off the radio to be able to hear better and followed the sound over toward the woman's camp. Suddenly, he realized the sound he had heard was someone screaming. He strode over to the front of the vehicles parked at the site, which were facing away from his camp. Branchwater looked around and then spotted the form of someone lying on the ground in the distance. The woman he had spoken to earlier was screaming and swinging an orange safety vest and hitting the ground with it. She then picked up a rifle which had been lying on the ground near the stricken person's right hand and threw it across the body. When Branchwater started toward her, she saw him and came running over, screaming for help.

Quickly he followed her. Reaching the victim, Branchwater went into police officer mode and carefully surveyed the scene. He noted that the man was lying on his stomach, facing to the left with both arms raised and his hands near his head. The woman cried out,

"His name is Bruce." Standing over him Branchwater saw Bruce's mouth contract and thought perhaps he was trying to speak.

He yelled, "Bruce, can you hear me?" There was no answer. When he touched the injured man, Branchwater felt that Bruce was cold and saw that his eyes were fixed, his skin blue. Next, Captain Branchwater checked for and found no carotid pulse. He picked up Bruce's right hand and pulled off the brown cloth glove to feel for a radial pulse; again there was no sign of life. The woman picked up two spent shell casings by Bruce's right hand and tossed them across the body where she had thrown the rifle.

Captain Branchwater turned to her. "I'm sorry, but I think he's gone."

She yelled back, "No, I saw his mouth move! He's trying to talk. We've got to get some help!"

Not wanting to upset her further, Branchwater asked, "Are your keys in the Bronco?"

"Yes, I think so."

"Stay here, I'll take your truck to get some help."

Branchwater ran up the trail to the top of the low ridge to the Bronco, started it, and headed out to the road to find help. He went south down the trail to where he knew there were some other hunting camps set up. He saw a truck and flagged it down. The driver was a man named George Wright from Arkansas and he had a cell phone. Branchwater quickly told Wright about the shooting victim, emphasizing the fact that he could not find the injured man's pulse. Wright immediately dialed 911.

"911. What is the nature of your emergency?" the operator asked.

In a heavy Arkansas accent Wright said, "I'm off the Divide Road, at the Brushy Ridge Trail. A man's been shot up here."

"Today?"

"Yeah. A while ago."

"There was a man shot up there?"

"Yes."

"Where are you at, sir?"

"I just told you," Wright said with obvious impatience. "Off the Divide Road on the Brushy Ridge Trail."

"Just a minute." There was a pause. "What's your name, sir?"

"George Wright, W-R-I-G-H-T."

"Are you in Montrose or Delta County?"

"I don't know. Probably Delta."

"Okay. We have quite a few Divide Roads. Is this twenty-five Mesa Road?"

"It's up on top of the Uncompahgre."

"That would be twenty-five Mesa Road, I'm thinking… probably…There's a couple of Divide Roads up there."

Wright's face grew red at the operator's confusion, but he kept at it. "Okay. Do you know where the Cold Springs ranger station is?"

"Coal Springs ranger station?"

"Okay. We're past that. Go down to the Dominguez Trail; turn on that left; go up to the Brushy Ridge Trail, and…"

"The Brushy Ridge Trail?"

"Yes."

"Boy, I'm not sure if you're in Delta or Montrose County. There was a guy who was shot up there?"

"Yes."

"When did this happen, sir?"

"I don't know." Wright said. "I'm just up here and a guy came driving up here in a Bronco and said down in his camp there's someone…a guy…was shot through the chest."

"Like suicide?"

"We don't know. The guy said there was two spent rounds beside the man who's shot and his wife's there and she's going crazy."

"Okay. Where did you go from? Did you go from Delta or did you go from Montrose?"

"We came from Grand Junction."

"And to get up on the Divide Road, did you go from...?"

"141," Wright replied with a heavy sigh.

"141. Did you go up between Delta and Grand Junction and go up Debeque Canyon?"

"Yes."

"Off Highway 50 you went up Debeque Canyon. Okay, sir, I'm going to get my map out. Uh, but what's the number you're calling from?"

"I'm on my cell phone, 208-555-7242."

"Okay, I think I'm getting another call on this shooting. Hold on just a minute. Okay, so he is dead then?"

"I don't know for sure. I'm talking to a guy here who says he's a policeman from Texas. Says he was down there at the camp with the lady. We were hunting up above. He is just trying to find some help."

"Sir, gosh. The other dispatcher's getting a call on it. She's getting more directions."

"Well, I'm gonna sign off then," Wright said thinking he'd finally gotten through to her.

"No," the dispatcher's voice rose. "I'd like to keep you on the line, because I need to get the information from you."

Wright had had enough. "Well, let me let you talk to the guy that was down there."

The Delta County operator's sigh was heavier than Wright's had been. "Okay. That would be great."

A discouraged George Wright handed the phone to Captain Branchwater. It is hard to describe how to get to a place in the middle of nowhere. Just trying to determine what county the shot man was in was a substantial hurdle. The call would have been potentially tragic, but for the fact that it seemed clear Bruce would not have benefited from more timely medical assistance.

While it is probably unfair to expect the dispatcher in Delta County to be familiar with every dirt road in Mesa County, it is easy to see how Mr. Wright soon wished he had not become involved in this situation. Part of the problem was the dispatcher suggesting that Wright had driven up Debeque Canyon when he actually came up Unaweep Canyon, a far different part of the county. Brent Branchwater now attempted to communicate their location and get some help.

"Hello, ma'am," Branchwater said in his thick East Texas accent.

"Just a minute." Pause. "Okay."

"My name is Brent Branchwater. These people were camped behind us. And I was cleaning a deer when I heard a woman screaming. I went to see what was happening and the woman came running up telling me her husband was shot."

"Do you have a name of the victim or the wife?"

"I'm in her truck. I'm in her Bronco."

"Can you give me the license off that vehicle, sir?"

"Edward George Victor 0-8-2, Colorado. Is there somebody on the way up? I could meet them down on Divide Road at the Dominguez Trail."

"Sir, right now we're kinda trying to find out what jurisdiction you're in…if you're in Mesa County or if you're in Delta County. The other guy we talked to went up Debeque Canyon to get there. So it kinda sounds like you must be in Mesa County. Okay, so she come runnin' up and she said he was dead?"

"I heard her screamin' down there and she came runnin' up hollerin' 'Help, help.' I met her about halfway there. She took me back down to where he was at."

"Okay, you're by the Coal Springs ranger station, is that right?"

"Yes, Ma'am. Just past there. Is the Ranger Station manned all the time?"

"I don't have that information. The female, do you have a name for her?"

"I think she said her name is Denise. I just talked to her briefly this morning. Would it help if I ...."

"Just a minute."

"Would it help if I met someone at the Divide Road? I'm not that close to it. I probably need to drive five or six miles to get to it."

"Sir, I'm going to run the vehicle. And is the lady still there?"

"She's with the body right now."

"When did this happen? Do you know?"

"Sometime around daylight as far as I know."

"Daylight this morning?"

"Yes, ma'am."

"So he is dead and we don't need to worry about getting an ambulance?" The operator seemed unsure of the situation.

"As far as I can tell. I could feel no pulse. His face was blue and all I could see was a couple of contractions of his jaw."

"Okay, and the plates are Edward George Victor 0-8-2?"

"Yes, Ma'am."

"Okay, Dodson?"

"I don't know their name."

"Okay, okay. Right now, what we're trying to do is find out where you're located at. Can you tell me exactly how you got there?"

"We came in from Delta on 50 toward Grand Junction. We turned south on 141 at Whitewater. We came down 141 in Unaweep Canyon and turned on Divide Road forest service access. And that bisects the Uncompahgre Plateau."

"So do you happen to know if you're in Mesa County or Delta County?"

"No, ma'am."

The sound of crinkling paper came through the cell phone earpiece. The Delta County 911 operator was obviously flipping through a book of maps trying to find the hunters' location. Several minutes passed.

"Okay, sir. We think we've confirmed that you are in Mesa County. I'm going to go ahead and notify Grand Junction. Let me put you on hold."

More time passed while the disappointment of the two men at the delay grew.

The Delta County operator next called State Patrol Dispatch in Grand Junction. They told her this was not a State-Patrol-type situation since it was not a traffic accident. So, she hung up and called the Mesa County Sheriff's Department main line and they put her through to Mesa County Dispatch.

"This is Mesa County Dispatch. May I help you?"

The Delta County 911 operator still seemed confused. "I have a couple of reports of a man who shot himself. I guess it's going to be in Mesa County, just past the Coal Springs forest station."

"Cold Springs ranger station?"

"I guess it's Coal, C-O-A-L, like a coal mine."

"Okay."

"Have you guys heard of this?"

"Not that I'm aware of. We're not aware of it here."

"Apparently, a man has shot himself this morning. He is dead. Don't know how it happened ... if he committed suicide or what. I have the two guys on hold on the other line now. The vehicle comes back to John Bruce Dodson out of Cedaredge. This is apparently the guy who shot himself."

Do not ask how the 911 operator determined from these conversations that the death was a suicide. In addition, it was "Cold Springs" Ranger Station, not "Coal Springs." At any rate, she spoke again to Captain Branchwater on George Wright's cell phone. Captain Branchwater once again offered to meet the responding police

officers out on Divide Road. In what seemed a very long delay to the
two men trying to do their duties and report a crime, an officer
finally came.

Deputy Kevin Patrick, a fit, handsome man in his mid-forties who has an adventurous streak and races stock cars in his spare
time, walked up to the two men. Patrick followed Branchwater back
to the camps. Once things settled down a bit, Deputy Patrick asked
him a few questions, then a few more later and even more later.

Deputy Patrick followed Captain Branchwater in Bruce
Dodson's Bronco to the death scene, where he found a young man
with the woman Branchwater called Denise, who appeared to be
lending her comfort and support. After enough backup officers
arrived so that someone could look after the victim's wife, Deputy
Patrick had the opportunity to take a statement from the genial
twenty-five year old whose name was Larry Coller.

Larry told Deputy Patrick that he and his younger brother
were visiting from Wisconsin. They had been hunting up on Snipe
Mountain that morning and, on their way back to camp after an
unsuccessful hunt, they saw a woman heading up a hill toward
them. Their truck was headed west and was just up the road about
two hundred yards from the turnoff to the campsite when they saw
her. When they got closer, they could see that she was out of breath.
Her sandals had slipped off her feet and were hanging around her
ankles as if she had run right out of them. Larry said, "The lady was
hysterical, waving her arms and yelling, 'My husband's been shot!
My husband's been shot!'" They stopped, put her into the truck and
she showed them the way. After driving a short distance farther west,
the distraught woman gestured to a track off the road to the north
towards the camps. As they traversed the rough trail and the crest of
a small hill, Larry could see the body in the distance. They drove
down to get a bit closer.

Larry told the deputy, "The woman and I got out of the
truck and my younger brother, Fred, left to find a man who had

been talking on a cell phone in a red and white Bronco we had passed down the road." Larry went on, "When I got to the victim the man was lying kind of on his right side, but face down with his right arm underneath him." He paused and shook his head. "I felt his wrist and couldn't find a pulse. The man's cheeks were white and his ears and forehead were somewhat blue. The eyes were open and the pupils dilated." Larry said that after he'd finished he just attempted to keep the woman calm, because he knew the man was dead. He tried to make small talk with her to get her mind off her husband. She told him her name was Janice and that she and her husband had separated while hunting that morning. He was hunting the ridge and she was hunting the valley. They had agreed to meet back in camp at 9:30 for breakfast. When she returned to camp and was not joined by her husband, she went looking for him. According to Janice, they had been married for three months and today was their anniversary. Moreover, this was her husband's first time deer hunting. Larry went on, "I rolled the body over onto its back while checking for a pulse." He saw Janice replace her husband's right glove, which was rolled inside out and was right next to the body. He noticed a rifle about four feet from the body that looked as though it were placed there, rather than being dropped. The bolt was open and resting on the ground. There were three spent shell casings in a pile near the rifle. He also noticed a blaze orange vest and hat.

Larry recalled that it was exactly ten on the clock in his truck when he saw the man by the Bronco on the cell phone. He also told the deputy what Janice had told him. "She was elk hunting and Bruce was deer hunting. She said that Bruce was looking forward to the hunt and wanted to get a bigger buck than the big twenty-nine inch buck she had once shot. Clearly agitated, the woman talked on and on. She said Bruce insisted that it was love at first sight when they met." Janice had also told Larry that she refused to live with Bruce before they were married because she was old fashioned. She referred to Bruce as her "little honey bunny."

Larry, obviously drained by his own ordeal, continued telling his story to Deputy Patrick. "As we waited for help, Janice straightened out Bruce's glasses and wiped some dirt from his face. She covered him with a down vest that had been lying by the body. She removed her gray sweatshirt and put it over Bruce. After a while, Fred returned with the truck and Janice suggested that they put Bruce into the truck to try to find help." Knowing that nothing could be done, Larry discouraged this idea. Nevertheless, Janice still seemed to feel Bruce was unconscious but not gone. She took a multicolored blanket from the truck and spread it over Bruce's body.

chapter 2

Death Scene

The original 911 call about Bruce's death had gone to a dispatcher in Delta County who spent a considerable amount of time trying to determine which county sheriff's department had jurisdiction. The death occurred on the Uncompahgre Plateau in the Uncompahgre National Forest. Uncompahgre, pronounced "Un-come-pah-gray," is a Ute Indian word meaning "Dirty Water." The place is located at one of the farthest southern reaches of my jurisdiction and just a few miles from the Delta and Montrose County lines. The Uncompahgre River flows from the San Juan Mountains in southwestern Colorado as mineral-laden waters from myriad small streams draining old mining districts and odoriferous, sulfur-rich hot springs water from near the town of Ouray. It is a beautiful, remote location at an elevation of 9,000 feet on the slopes of Snipe Mountain and is in an area with good-sized herds of deer and elk.

To reach the scene from Grand Junction, one travels about forty minutes on paved roads before turning onto a dirt service road that pretty much bisects the plateau, called Divide Road. One then climbs tight switchbacks for several miles before topping out on the plateau, a rolling landscape of mountains, creeks and canyons where ranchers run cattle from spring to fall. It is populated by a wide array of flora, with meadow grass, sagebrush, gambel oak, pinion, juniper and trees like ponderosa pine, aspen and spruce. It is peaceful and bucolic—at least most of the time.

The shooting had occurred just after sunrise on Sunday, the second day of the hunting season. At 12:45 P.M., Investigator Nick Armand, a twenty-year veteran of the Sheriff's Department and an officer with considerable crime scene experience arrived on the scene. Armand is a big red-haired man who carries his considerable excess weight effortlessly. He has a gentle manner which is disarming. He quickly scanned the area to get his bearings and to take note of whom and what was present. The rolling terrain was dotted intermittently with sagebrush, mountain mahogany, serviceberry, and other low shrubbery surrounding patches of gambel oak and larger open grassy meadows. Spruce trees grew in the higher areas and north facing slopes. By this time of the day, the mostly sunny sky had taken the chill out of the air. It was unseasonably warm for mid-October, probably reaching fifty degrees and feeling even warmer in the sunshine. Looking around, Armand noticed a sheriff's department Jeep along with an older Ford Bronco and an even older Volkswagen camper. He also saw several hunters in the area, including a woman. Deputy Patrick, who had arrived first, provided Investigator Armand with what information he had obtained to that point, including the fact that the female hunter was the wife of the victim. He also directed Armand to the location of the body. As he approached the dead man, Investigator Armand continued writing down his observations, which he would later put into report form and detail in several diagrams. One thing which caught his eye was the presence of three fired rifle casings on the ground two and a half feet from the victim's right elbow.

A foot further in the same direction was a bolt-action hunting rifle with the bolt open. Eight inches beyond the rifle was a blaze orange hunting vest. Close to that was a blaze orange baseball-style cap. Colorado law requires all big game hunters to wear five-hundred square inches of blaze orange outer-clothing, including a blaze orange hat, at all times while hunting as a safety measure. The body lay about twenty feet from a barbed wire fence composed of weathered old cedar fence posts and four strands of rusty wire. One post, approximately twenty feet from the body, had what appeared to be a bullet hole a few inches from the top. Special Agent Dan Michaels with the Forest Service discovered this as he was examining the crime scene. What appeared to be the bullet's exit hole faced the body and several fresh wood splinters were blown out in the same direction.

At this point, Investigator Armand was rapidly excluding in his mind the possibility of an accidentally self-inflicted gunshot. An accidental stray shot was still an option. Looking through the hole in the fence post away from the location of the body, Armand could see a patch of oak at the edge of a rise around fifty yards to the northwest.

After he examined, recorded and photographed the scene immediately around the body, Armand "strung" the apparent bullet path. Using a fluorescent orange plastic string, with the help of Special Agent Michaels and other officers who had arrived, Armand ran the string from the location of the body, through the hole in the fence post, and back to an area in the oak brush in line with the probable path of the bullet. It led to a spot just at the peak of the rise. If this wasn't an accident, he thought, it would be a perfect spot for a sniper to remain concealed, while still having a broad view of the trail on which the victim had been walking that morning. Although Armand, Michaels, and Deputy Patrick searched that area for evidence, they found none. Armand took some additional photographs and made measurements that he later used in preparing a crime scene drawing.

By the time he was done with the preliminary processing of

the death scene, it was 3:45 P.M. and it was growing chillier. He went up the hill to the hunting camps and introduced himself to the dead man's wife. "I'm Nick Armand, an investigator with the Mesa County Sheriff's Department," he said. "Please accept my sympathy in the death of your husband."

With a startled look, the woman replied, "No. He's not dead."

Not wanting to further alarm her as she appeared distraught, he didn't argue. Instead, Investigator Armand gently asked her name. She told him, "Janice, pronounced the French way: Janeece." She provided her address in Cedaredge, Colorado. After obtaining this preliminary information, Armand told her, "I really need to ask some questions about your hunting trip, if that would be okay."

She nodded and without waiting for his first question, said, "Bruce and I arrived at our campsite on Friday evening, October 13. I got up around 5:00 A.M. this morning, lit a fire in the stove in the camper and made Bruce some coffee, since he is 'cold blooded' and always needs something hot in the morning. The day before I took him to a spot along the ridge and told him that was where he should sit in the morning." The plan was that she would leave first and that he would leave about half an hour later. This would give Bruce time to get to his spot before first light and Janice would have time to get to the bottom of the draw from where she would drive the deer toward Bruce. Janice had an elk license and Bruce had a deer license. "We did the same thing the morning before. We were supposed to meet back at camp at 9:30 A.M."

Janice continued on, telling the investigator that she arrived back at the camp around 8:30 to get a drink of water. While in camp, she noticed a hunter at a tent just sixty yards from her camp, at the edge of a clump of oak trees. "I went over and talked with him," she said, "and learned that he and I are from the same part of East Texas." According to Janice, she returned to her camp after that and checked the oil in the Bronco. When asked what rifle she carried that morning, Janice spoke almost in a whisper. "It is an Austrian-made .270-caliber Mauser. I unloaded it and put it in the back of the Bronco when I first returned to camp. I haven't fired any rounds this hunting season and Bruce was hunting with a .243-caliber rifle."

"Did you hear any gunfire?"

She shook her head. "No, I didn't hear any shots fired in the area of my camp." She told Armand she changed her clothes upon her return to camp as she had gotten them muddy by stepping into a bog. Turning his head, the investigator could see a pair of overalls with dried mud on the lower portion of the legs hanging from the sideview mirror of the camper.

"When did you miss your husband?" He tried to keep his voice sympathetic so she would not get more agitated.

"I decided to go looking for Bruce as 9:30 approached," Janice said. "Bruce was very punctual and he had never been big game hunting before. I was the experienced hunter of us two." She paused and brushed away a tear. "Today was our third month anniversary." Without commenting, Armand, who was taking notes, wrote down that they had been married three months to the day. Janice was still speaking. She looked lost in memory. "I walked in the direction Bruce would have taken and that is when I saw him lying on the ground. His orange vest was nearby. I yelled at him 'Why did you take your orange off?'" According to Janice, she then picked up his rifle with the intention to fire it to summon help and racked the bolt, ejecting an empty case. "There were no live rounds in the rifle," she explained. After that she pulled his arm, trying to get him up, telling him to get up, all to no avail.

"Did you see anyone else nearby?"

She shook her head, looked off in the distance as if trying to recall the events, then added, "When I was making my drive toward Bruce earlier in the morning I saw a hunter on the ridge, a bit higher than where Bruce was supposed to be, and thinking it may have been Bruce, I waved, but the hunter did not wave back."

Armand excused himself at that point and returned to the crime scene. He finished surveying the area, noting the exact location of the body. Then other officers helped him put the dead man into a body bag. Armand sealed the bag and turned it over to the deputy coroner. He went back up to the campsite. It was 5:25 P.M., nearly twilight; the air was rapidly cooling now and there were a number of people milling about, including Deputy Sheriffs, Division of Wildlife Officers, other hunters and Forest Service personnel. Janice was with Dawn Bray, the Victim Assistance representative from the Sheriff's Department. Armand walked over to Janice. "How are you doing?" he asked.

"Okay," she replied in a flat voice. She asked him how Bruce was doing.

Armand replied, "I am sorry, Ma'am, but he is deceased."

She emphatically said, "No. The paramedics just took him away!"

Armand shook his head. "That was the coroner who took Bruce away. We'll be arranging to take you down the mountain. Can we call anyone for you?" She shook her head. "Janice, will you give me consent to look through your vehicles for any guns and to remove any guns for safekeeping and to examine as a part of my investigation? It will avoid questions that might come up later." She said he could. Seeming frail and unable to walk she shuffled and leaned on Armand as he led her to the back of the Bronco. As the investigator was completing an inventory form for the firearms, Janice collapsed and was carried to the Sheriff's Department Jeep. The captain in charge, Warren Smith, called the Air Life helicopter which soon arrived to take Janice to St. Mary's Hospital in Grand Junction.

When she was safely on the helicopter, the detectives searched her vehicle. The only rifle the detectives found suitable for big game hunting in either vehicle was the .270. There was also a .22-

caliber Ruger brand rifle and a .22-caliber pistol in the Bronco.

Investigator Armand listed the findings at the scene for later study.

- three .243-caliber shell casings
- .243-caliber rifle
- blaze orange hat
- fence post with bullet hole
- wood fragments from fence post
- blaze orange vest

He then collected the two rifles and the pistol from the Bronco.

Armand also made diagrams of the fence, showing the location of the gate and the bullet-holed post; a diagram of the scene with the body and various items of evidence; and another of the fence post showing the location of the bullet hole.

At this point, no one was sure how the man had been shot, so it was important that the preliminary findings on the scene be very carefully noted.

= c h a p t e r 3 =

In Search of Evidence

Back on the Uncompahgre Plateau, investigators were fanning out. The Mesa County Search and Rescue Team and an Explorer Troop joined in the search for evidence at the crime scene by forming lines of searchers walking at arm's length in straight lines, combing the area. Dan Faed, a retired Public Service lineman, had been a volunteer with the Search and Rescue team for the past ten years. He was an experienced game tracker and later worked as a hunting guide for twenty-six years. Chief of Police Rory Clark, from a small town nearby, volunteered to assist with metal detection. Chief Clark is self-taught in the use of metal detectors. A doctor once told him to do a lot of walking to help with a back problem, so he took up metal detection as a hobby. He has operated metal detectors for thousands of hours while searching for coins and other historical artifacts. He also had used them previously for law enforcement purposes. Shortly after beginning his search of the crime scene, Clark's metal detector alerted him to the presence of a metal object in the clump of oak brush pointed out to him by Investigator Armand. Spreading apart some leaves and grass he found a shiny brass rifle casing lying on the ground. Chief Clark is originally from Texas, a quality he brandishes with great aplomb. He is well-known for coming out with a new off-color, redneck colloquialism of some sort each day and that day was no exception. "Well I'll be dipped in shit and rolled in bran flakes."

Dan Faed was examining the muddy boots Janice had left at the camper when he was told about the discovery of the shell casing. He immediately focused on that area. Before long, he located a boot sole impression that appeared to be consistent with Janice's boots about forty feet from the shell casing in a direction away from Bruce's body. Twenty feet from that impression, he found another print that was from a different, larger boot. Using a casting material called Hydrocal, a crime scene investigator with the Sheriff's Department made casts of the two prints and collected them as evidence.

Although careful measurements of the location of the shell casing were taken, no one made measurements of the location of the boot prints. That would later prove to be a huge mistake.

It was at this juncture that I first became aware of the death of John Bruce Dodson. As District Attorney, I am notified whenever a death occurs under suspicious circumstances. In the beginning, all I heard was that a hunter had been found shot to death. Since my jurisdiction encompasses thousands of square miles of federal public lands, including some of the best public hunting areas in the West, and because this could have been an accidental death, I was not overly concerned. There are hunting-related firearms deaths just about every year in Colorado. Nevertheless something about Dodson's death seemed peculiar and I asked my investigator, Bill Booth, to keep an eye on it.

We soon learned that, serendipitously, Brent Branchwater, who had been hunting on the Uncompahgre Plateau the day of John Bruce Dodson's death and reported it, was a fellow law enforcement officer. In fact, he was a captain. Since it was clear that he would be a witness at future court proceedings, should there be any regarding Bruce's death, Police Lieutenant Ron Finley asked Branchwater to write down, in his own words and from the perspective of a police officer, the events of that weekend and bring it to him. He agreed.

LOG OF EVENTS

<u>Thursday, October 12, 1995</u>: *Arrive at campsite about 2:30 P.M. and set up camp. Scout the area until dark.*

<u>Friday, October 13, 1995</u>: *Ryan and I spend the day scouting. Return to camp around dark for dinner. Around 9:00 P.M., two vehicles arrive. One a red and white Bronco, the other a VW Camper. After some trouble getting into the opening from the road, both vehicles park on a rise just above our camp. We have no contact with the people.*

<u>Saturday, October 14, 1995</u>: *Ryan and I get up around 5:00 A.M., eat and head into the canyon by way of the 4 X 4 road over the ridge above camp. Hunt the entire day, having lunch from our packs. Around 3:30 P.M. I shoot a small deer. Ryan and I have to drag the deer from the bottom of the canyon to the truck. We get into camp late. The deer is hung, we take some photos, eat and go to bed.*

<u>Sunday, October 15, 1995</u>: *I plan to stay in camp to quarter my deer because the days are warm. Ryan gets up around 5 A.M. Before he eats and leaves, we make plans to go into town when Ryan comes in for lunch. We need more ice and are going to have a meal. About 7:00 A.M. while I'm still in bed in the tent, a shot goes off awakening me. The first shot is followed by hollering. I cannot tell what words are being hollered. I look at the clock to check the time. I could see 7:0-something showing. In a moment another shot goes off, then another, followed by the thump of a bullet strike. These two shots are clearly com-*

ing from the area in front of the people's camp nearby. Not
wanting to go out while there is shooting nearby, I lay in the
tent until about 7:30 A.M. and then go out and head to the cook
tent for some breakfast. I see a person in coveralls and orange
vest and hat carrying a rifle up the tree line in front of the VW
camper. The person is walking toward the vehicles.

After eating, I start skinning my deer and notice the
same person come to the back of the Bronco. I now can see it is
a female. She is dressed in blue jeans, sweater jacket, orange
vest and sandals with white socks. She steps on the back
bumper of the Bronco and pulls out a gun case. It is a brown
soft case. With her back toward me, she puts the gun in the case
and puts it in the back of the Bronco. She steps down, rolls the
window up then turns and sees me. Neither of us acknowledges
the other. I continue to skin the deer. When I get to quartering
the meat a few minutes later, someone behind me says, "That's
a nice forky you have there." I turn and find the aforemen-
tioned female standing behind me. She has a cup of water and
a toothbrush in her hand. She begins a polite conversation ask-
ing about where we are from, who we are and what we do. I
find she is originally from the same general area Ryan and I
are from. I mention hearing shots and hollering and ask if one
of her group got a deer. She says she has not heard any shoot-
ing or hollering from the area. She says her husband is on the
mountain somewhere. This is his first deer hunt and she is
hunting elk. She asks where my friend is and I tell her he's
hunting over in the canyon and will be down at lunch. We are
going into town for ice and a meal.

She tells me that they haven't brought enough water
and would we mind bringing them some back. I tell her we
would and to just put their containers by our cook tent. She
says they have friends camped on the mountain above and
when her husband comes in they are going there so they can

put him on a deer.

She says he should have been back by now and she is going to circle the area to look for him. She says if he comes to camp while she is gone, ask him to stay. She says his name is Bruce. She introduces herself as what I thought to be "Denise." I tell her my name is Brent. She says again the water jugs will be by her camper. Once more I ask her to put them by our tent. She goes to her vehicles and I return to the deer.

I finish boning the meat and put it into the ice chests and am putting the carcass in a bag for disposal. I have a radio playing and I can hear what I think might be an elk bugling. I turn off the radio to listen. I can now hear the sound clearly. It is a person screaming for help and is coming from the direction of the area in front of the Bronco and the VW. I run up in front of our sleeping tent and look over the rise. The female is standing by someone lying on the ground. She has an orange vest in one hand. When she sees me she starts hollering and beating the vest on the ground. She is saying, "Why didn't you have your orange on?!!" She then picks up a gun lying there and throws it on the ground.

I shout and ask what is wrong. All she says is, "He's hurt." I start to run over and she runs to meet me at the front of their vehicles. When she gets to me she sinks to the ground. I ask if the man has a bad heart. She says, "No, he's hurt. You've got to help him." I run to the man lying there. She gets up and follows me. As I approach the man I can see a hole in the back of his jacket with bloodstains around it. He is lying on his stomach, palms of hands down with his head turned facing a fence to his left. He has on a gray sweater jacket and what I think are faded jeans, some hiking-type boots, an orange cap partially on his head and glasses. He has brown cotton gloves on his hands. The rifle has landed by the man's left hand parallel to the fence. There are two empty casings lying just inside the area between the left hand and his head. There are no other pieces of clothing around except the orange vest she has thrown down at his feet. I ask if this is her husband Bruce. She said it is. I shout at him as I kneel by his right side. There is no response so I lean over to check for a carotid pulse on the neck. I can find none. I notice his face is blue and his eyes are glazed over. I then take the glove off his right hand to check for a pulse on the wrist. I can find none. I can see he is not breathing. As I am doing this, the female picks up the two empty casings and throws them. They hit my leg and glance off the ground in front of me. I tell her I am sorry, but the man is gone. She says, "No, he's trying to talk—see?" His mouth opens and closes in a muscle spasm. I again tell her he is dead. She says, "No, you've got to help him."

Ryan has our truck on the mountain and the key to the four wheeler also. I tell her I have to go for help and ask where the keys to her Bronco are. She says she doesn't know. I ask if they are in the Bronco and she says they may be. I run to the Bronco and find the keys on the dashboard.

I drive the Bronco up the road to look for help. I see two men in a truck and wave them over. They tell me they have a cell phone we could try dialing 9-1-1 on. One dials the phone while the other gives me some water. I can barely speak my mouth is so dry. The man on the phone reaches a 9-1-1 operator and tries to tell her where we are and what has happened. When I have enough water to be able to talk, I take the phone and try to tell her what has happened. I figure I left my camp about 9:30 to go for help. It took ten minutes to find the men and make the call.

After a lengthy talk with the operator trying to find out what county we are in, a maroon Chevy X-Cab comes by with two men inside. They pass by going downhill. In a few minutes the truck is back where I am on the phone. There is *one man in the truck now. He stops and says he needs to use the phone because there is a lady that flagged them down and said her husband has been shot. His brother is with her back at the camp. I tell him I have the sheriff's office on the line and that I am going to meet the deputy on the Divide Road and bring him up. I ask if they will stay with her until I get back with the deputy.*

The female's purse is in the Bronco and I ask the man if he will take it to her, as I don't want to be responsible for it if she has any medications in it she may need. He agrees and I give it to him. I tell the operator the license plate number of the Bronco and its color and where I will meet the deputy. I hang up and go to the intersection of Divide Road and Dominguez Trail.

After about ten to fifteen minutes a forest ranger comes by. He stops and asks if I am the one waiting for the sheriff's officer. I tell him yes and he radios responding officers confirming the location. He says the sheriff's officer is on the way and will be there in about forty-five minutes. The deputy comes along shortly and follows me back to the camp. I park the Bronco next to the camper. Not exactly where it had been before. The two men in the maroon truck had parked next to where the body lay. When I go up with the deputy, Kevin Patrick, I can see the woman sitting on the ground holding the man's head in her lap. The man is now on his back, covered up with a blue quilted cover and a blue plaid cover.

The deputy tries to get her away from the body, but she refuses. Then he asks me to help get her away. She finally goes with me back to where we have a utility trailer parked. I get her a chair and some water and get her to sit down. She wants to know why it has taken me so long to get back. I tell her it was a long way to get help there in the mountains. I try to engage her in conversation to keep her from going back down to the body. She tells me she and her husband were in the medical field. I ask what they do. She tells me Bruce is a lab technician and she is a nurse in the psych ward. She tells me today is their three-month wedding anniversary and they are supposed to have a date tonight. She looks toward where the deputy is working and says, "You did tell them I threw the gun there didn't you?" I tell her yes.

She tells me she is cold so I get out a plaid insulated shirt and give it to her to put on. She then asks me if I have any children. I tell her I have two. She says she has a daughter and a son. She tells me she taught her children to shoot by using a .22 rifle on chipmunks. She also says she reloads all her own ammo for her guns. She says she and her ex-husband had run hunting camps in this area for years. She found out he had a girlfriend where he was working and when she found this out she divorced him.

Vehicles begin arriving. With every one which passes she asks if it is the paramedics or when is the helicopter going to get here. The woman tells me what a great relationship she and Bruce had. That he was so loving and punctual. She talks about his mother and how she often sent money to Bruce, $10,000 usually. Bruce's dad had been an executive with R. J. Reynolds and had bought stock in the company all along. When he died he left it all to Bruce's mom. Also, she tells me that his mother had taken the life insurance and stocks and invested the money and done well with it. She talks about how she and Bruce improved Bruce's home and how it doubled the value. She talks about what guns to hunt with there. She says she broke her back and doctors told her not to be shooting so she has a light rifle; a .270 I think. She tells me she hasn't missed a hunting season and was going to come regardless. Bruce had asked if she was going whether or not he came *along. She told him she was. She says Bruce wanted to use a shotgun, but she had borrowed a rifle for him. She says this was his first time to hunt deer. She says she would get up first and warm the camper and make coffee for him while he lay in bed. She would then leave first to get a head start to go low on the mountain and push the draws up trying to run deer to him. She says she had gotten into a bog and got her clothes muddy and had to come back to change. A little while later the deputy comes over and asks me to give him a statement. The two men who had stayed with her while waiting for the deputy sit with her again. I provide the deputy with I.D. and give an account of events.*

Other law enforcement officers arrive along with the coroner. A female crisis intervention counselor arrives and is brought to the camp to talk to the victim's wife. From this point I sit on the front bumper of one of the sheriff's office vehicles. Every so often one of the men comes and asks me a question then talks to the victim's wife. One investigator asks about the gun she put in the Bronco. They get permission to look and open the tailgate. They remove the brown case and ask if this was the one I saw her put in the vehicle. I tell them it is. He unzips the case and removes a synthetic-stocked, stainless bolt-action rifle. I cannot I.D. the gun as I never saw it clearly until then. They tell the lady they are going to take the gun in for testing and write her a receipt. At this point she begins to faint. One of the officers is an EMT. He produces a medical kit and checks her. The officer decides she is going into shock. A helicopter is called for and she is airlifted out. It is about dark when the helicopter clears. The deputies ask if the woman's vehicles will be okay there as they will be back the next day to investigate further. I tell them I am not going to mess with them and will keep an eye out.

Ryan makes it into camp after being checked on the

ridge by a deputy. He had to wait for the helicopter to take off before he could come down the slope. I tell him what happened and ask why he hadn't come down for lunch. He says he walked a ways and just wanted to stay out. We go ahead and go to town anyway. I need to get away for a while. We drive to Grand Junction and eat at a fast food restaurant. It is about midnight when we got back to camp. We go to bed after caring for the deer meat.

<u>Monday, October 16, 1995</u>: *I stay in camp while Ryan goes hunting. Deputies return around noon and use Search & Rescue team to check the area.*

As soon as Branchwater's report was brought to me, I read it with rising interest, paying special attention to Branchwater's description of Janice's reactions at the death scene. Something in my gut told me there was more to this grieving widow's story than she told.

An Accident, A Suicide or Murder?

Since it was uncertain whether Bruce Dodson's death could be a homicide, the Sheriff's Department assigned two crime scene technicians to respond to the scene to assist with the investigation on the day of Dodson's death. It had been a bit unclear who was in charge of the whole situation with the presence of so many officers.

One of those who became involved was Captain Warren Smith, a tall, dark, handsome, smooth-talking, western-dressing, well-meaning man in his mid-forties who had been the sheriff down in La Plata County a few years back before losing an election by getting crosswise with the NRA crowd. During the last election in Mesa County, Investigator Armand found himself supporting the losing side of an internal battle that had half of the department backing the eventual loser and the other half backing the eventual winner. By the time of the Dodson case, most of those who had supported the loser were gone from the department, voluntarily or otherwise. Armand was still there. Hired as a captain, Warren Smith had been brought into the department to restore order. Technically, Captain Smith now was the incident commander on the Uncompahgre, but the lack of a clear chain of command created some problems.

The two crime scene technicians were Carl Todd and Victor Poste. Carl is a forty-something, pleasant-looking, average-sized man with a peaceful demeanor, close cropped brown hair and above average intelligence. He is the kind of person who can do just about anything that needs to be done, from building a house to applying CPR to save someone's life. Victor is about the same age but taller and also had his blond hair cut military-style. He usually carries a worried look on his face. Carl and Victor arrived at the hunting camp around 4:15 P.M. When they arrived, Deputy Patrick briefed them.

As the investigators proceeded with the case, they sent me reports as to what they found. Todd's descriptions of what he observed that day added to my concern. He wrote:

> The camp is located about 200 yards off Brushy Ridge Trail, about 4 1/4 miles from Divide Road. When we arrived we were met by Deputy Patrick who was there taking the report and doing interviews. I could see that there were two tents to the rear of the vehicles, off in the oak brush. The tents belonged to a Marshall, Texas man and his hunting partner. About 160 feet to the north of these tents were two vehicles. One vehicle was a VW camper van and just to the rear of that was a red and white Ford Bronco. These vehicles belonged to the shooting victim and his wife. I could see that there was a pair of blue denim bib overalls hanging from the passenger side mirror of the van. The bottom twelve inches of the pant legs were muddy. There was a pair of woman's hiking shoes on the ground next to the pants. They were covered with mud. The sliding side door of the van was open and the pop-up roof was up. There was a green Coleman-type camp stove stowed in a recessed area above the cab of the van, held down with bungee

cords. The Ford Bronco was about ten feet behind the van and the tailgate was lowered. There were various items in both vehicles that would normally be found on a hunting/camping trip.

Investigator Armand showed Deputy Poste and me the crime scene, located about 175 yards to the north of the van in a small clearing near a barbed wire fence. There, lying on the ground about 20 feet to the south of the fence, was the body of a man. There were several wires with plastic flags in the ground noting the location of various pieces of evidence. One of the wooden fence posts was flagged and I could see that it had a hole through it that appeared to have been made by a bullet. The south side of the post was blown out, indicating that the bullet was coming from the opposite side of the post from where the body was found. There were several Division of Wildlife officers and Forest Service officers on the scene. Investigator Armand had everyone go on the other side of the fence where we formed a search line and walked through the area where the shot was thought to have come from. We were searching for a cartridge casing that may have been ejected in the area by the shooter. We searched for several minutes, but we didn't find anything.

After finishing with the collection of the evidence that was flagged, we assisted the deputy coroner with the recovery of the body and helped to load it into his vehicle for transport. We then went back to the camp area. Investigator Armand and Deputy Patrick were talking to the victim's wife and Brent Branchwater, the hunter from the adjacent camp. Investigator Armand was examining the rifle in the back of the Bronco and he put that rifle in a case for collection as evidence. The victim's wife, Janice, had been sitting in Mr. Branchwater's camp during our time there. She became very distraught and we felt *she was going into shock. I noticed that she didn't start shaking real bad and acting shocky until Investigator Armand got in the back of the Bronco and started looking at the rifle. Until then she was pretty calm. Captain Smith felt that Janice was going into shock and he asked that I start up my unit and place her in it with the heater going. As we started to switch vehicles, Janice passed out. Captain Smith had Air Life respond to transport her to Saint Mary's Hospital for medical treatment. I drove up to the landing zone and we transferred Janice to the helicopter. After the helicopter left, Deputy Poste and I went to several campsites along Brushy Ridge Trail. We contacted the hunters in those camps and asked for information and checked identifications. We covered about six or seven hunting camps. We drove back to Grand Junction and made plans to return the next day.*

On October 16, 1995 at about 10:20 A.M., we returned to the shooting scene with representatives of the Mesa County Search and Rescue Team, Palisade Police Chief Rory Clark, Division of Wildlife and Forest Service officers, and several Sheriff's Department officers. Chief Clark had come with a metal detector to aid in locating any spent rifle cartridges or other metallic evidence. The Search and Rescue Team members were there to conduct a ground search for footprints, spent cartridges, and any other evidence that might be found in the area. I started to search the vehicles for ammunition that would go with the weapons found in the vehicle and at the shooting scene. I started with the VW Van. When I got to the rear of the van, I found a tan paper bag with a Gibson's Discount Store logo on it. This bag was on the passenger side of the rear storage area. I looked in the bag and found two boxes of Federal brand rifle ammunition. One of the boxes was a box of twenty 7 mm magnum, 165 grain boat tail, soft-point ammo that contained 15 live rounds. The other was a box of twenty-four .243-caliber

100 grain, Hi-Shock soft-point ammo that contained 20 live and one spent cartridges. I collected these boxes of ammo as evidence. I also collected the muddy boots and the overalls from the van.

While I was searching the vehicles, Chief Clark found a shell casing in the area that the shot was thought to have come from. I put on gloves and picked up the casing noting that it was a .308-caliber rifle cartridge casing. I placed it into a small brown paper bag and labeled the bag as evidence. Deputy Poste and I used a tape measure to document the location of the casing in relation to the fence. We also measured the distance from the post with the hole in it to the VW van and the distance from the van to Mr. Branchwater's tents. I talked to Captain Branchwater who told me he remembered a few things he forgot to tell Deputy Patrick. He told me that while he was helping to keep Janice away from her husband's body she started talking about Bruce's dad. She said he had been an executive with R. J. Reynolds Tobacco Company and that he had bought a lot of stock when he worked there. She said that he left a lot of insurance money to Bruce's mother as well as the stock. She said that Bruce's mom would send them as much as $10,000.00 every so often as a gift just to get rid of some of the money. She said that she met Bruce's mom and that Bruce had told her that his mom liked her more than she liked him. She also mentioned that Bruce didn't want to come hunting and that she told him she was going hunting with or without him.

I was told that some footprints had been found and was instructed to make castings for evidence. I took a camera and casting materials to some footprints located about fifty yards from the fence and about one hundred yards northwest of where the body was found. After taking photos of the prints, I then made casts which I collected when dry. Later I made diagrams from my notes and sketches.

Each insight and report about Janice Dodson added to the questions about her. She seemed agitated at one moment, exceptionally poised the next. A loving wife? A devious planner? Which was the real Janice Dodson?

On the afternoon of October 15, the day of Bruce Dodson's death, numerous officers spread out to contact as many hunters in the area as possible. Because hunting camps are so transitory, this had to be done right away. One of the officers involved was Harvey James, a Division of Wildlife officer. Harvey is the strong silent type, right out of an old western movie. He even has a slow, western drawl. He has been the game warden assigned to the Uncompahgre Plateau for the past twenty years and he knows it as well as anyone. During hunting season, he would be checking hunting camps routinely anyway, so this just added a few questions and a higher level of concern. About five miles down Brushy Ridge Trail from the crime scene, Harvey located a camp of Texas hunters. He checked their licenses and asked them the same set of questions he was asking everyone that afternoon, "Where have you been hunting? Have you seen anything unusual or suspicious? Do you know Janice Dodson and Bruce Dodson?" and so on. Well, it turned out that two of the hunters in this camp did know Janice and they knew her quite well. These two hunters were Terence Morgan and his wife Carla. They lived in the town of Pollock in East Texas. Not only did they know Janice, Terence told Harvey, but Janice's ex-husband, Mark Morgan was Terence's brother, was also hunting in the area.

"Can you tell me the location of Mark's camp?"

Terence nodded, "Its about five miles back down Brushy Ridge Trail and on the jeep road about a mile past the intersection where the trail takes a sharp turn to the west after you round Snipe Mountain, down over the hill, and off to the east in a grove of aspen near a stock pond."

Harvey immediately knew the camp from the description. When Harvey returned to the crime scene that evening, he turned all of his contact information over to Captain Smith and made sure to point out this information. He thought it was a bit coincidental.

At the 8:00 A.M. briefing at the Sheriff's Department the next morning, all details known up to that point were discussed, including this new information about Mark Morgan. This was obviously something that needed to be explored. Deputy Victor Poste was going to have a busy couple of days. A few minutes after the briefing, he and Deputy Todd left to return to the scene on the Uncompahgre. After helping Deputy Todd for a while, Victor teamed up with Harvey James to contact Terence Morgan so they could locate Mark Morgan. They arrived at Terence's camp at 12:05 P.M.

Officer James and Deputy Poste got out of the car, slammed the doors and strode over to a man standing outside a tent.

"Are you Terence Morgan?" Poste asked.

At the man's nod, Poste continued, "I'm Deputy Victor Poste and this is Officer Harvey James from the Division of Wildlife. I believe you spoke with him yesterday."

Again, Terence nodded. "That's right."

"We want to speak with you again. You know that your brother Mark Morgan's ex-wife was also hunting in this area and her new husband of three months was killed yesterday by a gunshot wound."

"If it's Mark you're after, I haven't seen him in two days. We were not hunting together nor sharing a campsite. He's been in the area hunting, but not here."

"When did you last see him?"

"On the fourteenth, about one-thirty in the afternoon. I went to his camp to see how he was doing and have a cup of coffee with him."

"Where exactly was Mark camped?" Poste asked.

Terence gave the men a detailed description of how to get to Mark's campsite, but added, "He's not still camped there. He told me he was going to break camp and leave on Sunday evening because he had to be back at work on Monday morning."

"Where does your brother work?"

"He works for a concrete outfit and he said they were doing a job on a military installation. He lives in Layton, Utah."

"Who was Mark hunting with?" Bock asked.

"His boss, Gary Dalton and his girlfriend, Marcy. I understand they got a deer Saturday morning but didn't bring it back to camp."

"Does your brother know Bruce Dodson?"

"I don't believe so."

"What about problems after Janice married Bruce?" Poste asked. "Were there bad feelings between Janice and Mark after her marriage?"

"Not that I know of," Terence responded. "You know, Janice came to Texas in July and I think she wanted to try and get back with Mark. But she learned during her visit that everything was over between them and she left. Wasn't long after that, we heard she married this guy Bruce Dodson."

Terence did not have an address for Mark in Utah, but was able to provide a phone number. After taking Terence's statement, Deputy Poste gave him a business card and told him if he came in contact with his brother to have him get in touch. Deputy Poste and Harvey James then went to the area of Mark Morgan's camp as described by Terence. They found the camp vacant and made note that one had to cross a mud bog to get to it. They did not get out of their vehicles or cross the mud bog because they could see that the camp was empty from where they were. Deputy Poste returned to the crime scene and reported what he learned to Captain Smith. After helping with photographing and evidence collection at the scene, Deputy Poste went back to Mark's camp with Harvey James, Dan Faed and Chief Rory Clark to see if they could find any foot prints, shell casings or other evidence. No evidence was located. Dan

Faed noted that this was the cleanest camp he had ever seen. "There was not so much as a gum wrapper or a cigarette butt," he noted. There were some boot prints, but none that matched the two found back at the crime scene.

That same day, a somewhat disturbing report came into the Sheriff's Department that had to be checked out. I felt from the beginning it had nothing to do with Bruce's death. However, I had concerns that it could be used to confuse a future jury if this was judged a homicide. "All it takes," I told a deputy, "is one confused juror to upset a trial verdict." The incident came to light when someone had called the Montrose County Sheriff's Department complaining of another shooting incident on the Uncompahgre Plateau the same day as Bruce's murder.

October 15, 1995

A deputy was dispatched to the Hanton Motel in reference to the report of a shooting on the Divide Road.

He contacted Clarence Taylor in room number 209. The deputy said Mr. Taylor told him that he and his father were hunting about a quarter mile from the road on the Uncompahgre Plateau near Windy Point. Taylor said he was sitting on a chair next to a tree stump at about 1430 hours, when he saw two hunters walking about twenty yards from where he was. Taylor watched the two hunters walk toward the north, he heard them break off a stick, and then they fired a gunshot into the stump next to the chair he was sitting in. Taylor went on that he could still see the two hunters' orange clothing; he thought they were about thirty yards away. He yelled at them to stop shooting. One of them yelled back in a gruff voice and fired a second shot, hitting the stump. Both shots went clear through the stump. He was about four feet from the stump.

Taylor described the two hunters; one was about 6' 0",

grayish hair, 240 pounds, about forty-five years old wearing blue jeans and brown boots; the second hunter was about 5' 10", 160 pounds, possibly in his teens.

It was obvious to me that if these two would have had anything to do with shooting Bruce to death, they would not have traveled down the road and created a commotion. It appeared to be a case of two idiot hunters, something we see too much of around Colorado.

chapter 5

Simple Questions, Few Answers

Monday, the day after Bruce Dodson's death, a new set of investigators became involved. Investigator Ron Roberts, a young, blond, innocent-looking officer with a stocky build, was newly assigned to investigations. Intelligent, unimposing and well-intended, Roberts was also just a bit green around the edges. This was his first murder investigation. His supervisor, Lieutenant Ron Finley, asked him to go to Saint Mary's hospital to interview Janice to find out any possible information that might help clarify the scene on the plateau. Ron Finley, weathered and tall, western in dress, provincial in attitude, was a regular competitor in shooting matches and known as a fast and accurate shot with a pistol. He had been an investigator for twenty-seven years and not only had a lot of experience, but was extremely confident in his own abilities and insight which tended to make the younger, less experienced officers insecure. When the case was first assigned that morning, it looked like a possible accidental shooting. Still, Ron Roberts, who was eager to do the right thing and not make any mistakes, was nervous. Perhaps because he was young and concerned, Finley thought Janice might open up to Roberts with a large volume of information. So

Finley sent him to talk to her.

Roberts arrived at Saint Mary's Hospital at around 9:50 A.M. and met Janice Dodson in a small waiting room on the third floor of the east wing. Victim advocate Dawn Bray was with Janice along with a friend of hers, a woman introduced to Roberts as Sharon.

After a subdued greeting, Roberts offered his condolences then got down to business. "Mrs. Dodson, we're trying to find out who shot your husband. If you can help us with some information, you'll certainly improve our odds of doing so. Are you able to talk to me about what occurred yesterday on the Uncompahgre Plateau?"

Janice nodded. "I'll try," she said in a whispery voice.

To Investigator Roberts, the widow appeared to be both physically and emotionally drained. Her voice was weak and hard to understand and he felt that she was about to break into sobs at any moment.

"Why don't you just start at the beginning and tell me what happened," he said in a gentle, encouraging tone.

She nodded again, but then sat there staring at him as if unable to speak.

He tried again. "Tell me a bit more about yourself, Mrs. Dodson, and about your husband. What is your full name?"

"Janice Morgan Dodson," she said in a low monotone.

"And where do you work?" Roberts hoped answering simple questions would get the woman talking. To him, she appeared somewhat dazed, as if she were still in shock.

"At Memorial Hospital," she said. "I'm a registered nurse. I've been there about six years...in the Psychcare Dependency Center."

Janice rose and walked to a nearby table where there was a box of tissues. She grabbed a handful and returned to her chair next to Roberts. He noticed that she appeared to be very stiff and sore and it seemed as though it was difficult for her to move. She stared into space as if he wasn't there.

"Mrs. Dodson, have you taken any medications while you've been here at the hospital?"

She blew her nose and nodded. "Two Ativans last night to help me sleep. I've taken nothing today, though."

Roberts began again. "And your husband, what did he do for a living?"

"Medical technician," she said. "At County Hospital...for a little over five years." She paused, staring intently down at the floor. After a minute of silence, she looked up at Roberts with a small, forlorn smile. "We only got married last July, on the fifteenth. We dated for four years, but we're married only three months."

Roberts nodded sympathetically. "I understand you were married before, Mrs. Dodson. Is that correct?"

"Yes, to Mark Gordon Morgan. We're divorced." She shook her head and looked at Roberts with a wry expression. "He ran off with our daughter's best friend, Marcy. That girl used to call me Mom, that's how close we were. I kind of lost it after that. Tried to kill myself and ended up in the hospital for eleven days."

"Were there problems in your marriage to Morgan, Mrs. Dodson? I mean before he ran off?"

"Well, one time I had to pull a gun on him during an argument, but he took it away from me."

"When did you last speak to Mark?" Roberts asked.

"About a week ago, I guess. I called to tell him about our children. We have a son and a daughter who are grown."

"When did you last see your former husband?"

"My father died earlier this year and I had to go to Texas to make arrangements for his funeral. Mark came by my aunt's house in Chirito, where I was staying. He offered his sympathy and we talked over coffee. That's when I told him I was going to marry Bruce Dodson."

"How did Mark respond to your news?" asked Roberts.

Janice shrugged. "He wished me the best of luck." She leaned back in the chair and blew her nose again. "I had a long talk with Mark at that time and realized he was not the kind of guy I wanted to be married to. That's when I decided marrying Bruce would be the best thing for me to do."

Ron Roberts leaned toward her. "Tell me more about Bruce, Mrs. Dodson. How old was he?"

"Forty-eight."

"Was Bruce married previously?"

"No."

"Did he have any enemies that you know of?"

She shook her head and wiped the tears that had begun rolling down her cheeks. "He didn't. He was a good man, not involved in drugs, no debts and he was very self-sufficient."

"What kind of financial condition was Bruce in, Mrs. Dodson?"

"Well, he had an investment portfolio, but I don't know the value of it. Bruce tried to explain his investments to me every so often, but I just never paid much attention, because I really don't understand that stuff and figured that was his responsibility. He had a rental home in Leadville and we just bought a hot tub, so I figured things were going well financially." She stopped to wipe her eyes and dab at her nose. "My mother-in-law is a wealthy woman. And in extremely good health," she added a moment later.

Investigator Roberts pondered her response for a moment, but decided he didn't want to get sidetracked by probing the issue further. There were more questions he had to ask about her husband's death. "Have you hunted before in the area where the accident occurred, Mrs. Dodson?"

She nodded. "Yes, just three or four weeks earlier. I was by myself, grouse-hunting. I bagged one grouse. I'm an experienced hunter; I've been hunting since I was about six years old."

"Prior to your recent grouse hunt, when was the last time you hunted on the Uncompahgre?"

"Oh, a while ago. Before my divorce from Mark."

Janice told Roberts that she did not want to go up there after the divorce, because she knew all of them— Mark, his brother, Terence, and her former sister-in-law, Carla, would be hunting in that area and, at that time, she didn't want to risk seeing any of them.

"I understand Bruce was not an experienced hunter. Is that true, Mrs. Dodson?"

"Yes, but he was very excited about going hunting," Janice said.

"Was this the first time Bruce had hunted with you in the four years you had dated?"

She began to weep quietly. "Bruce didn't want to go, because he never liked the cold and there always seemed to be work schedule conflicts. This time I told him I was going whether he went or not, so he decided to go."

"Tell me about the hunting trip, Mrs. Dodson," Roberts said. "You hunted on Saturday, I believe."

Janice nodded. "Yes. On Saturday morning we decided that I would go below where Bruce was sitting and make a drive toward him. You know, try to push some deer up to where he was so he could get a shot. He took a shot at a buck at around eight o'clock, but missed. I met up with him at his spot and we walked back to camp together, arriving in camp at nine-fifteen or nine-thirty. We agreed that on Sunday morning I would make the drive in the same way and he would be the stationary hunter in the same spot."

Inspector Roberts shifted slightly in his chair. "And what did you do on Saturday afternoon?"

"Bruce went out and hunted alone. I stayed in camp and only went out to hunt when Bruce came back around four o'clock."

She dabbed at her eyes with the tissue and gave a small laugh. "He made it plain I had to be back by six-thirty for dinner. Bruce always cooked dinner and was very punctual about it."

He knew where he was heading now. "Tell me about the day of the shooting, Mrs. Dodson," Roberts requested in a gentle voice.

Janice told Roberts that her husband had planned to take a stationary position Sunday morning on a hillside while she made a drive just like they had done on Saturday. She was going to walk down through a draw and try to push some deer up his way so he could get a shot. She was going after elk and he was hunting deer. Bruce was carrying a .243-caliber rifle and she was carrying a .270-caliber rifle. She left their campsite before he did on Sunday morning at about 6:00 A.M., telling him that he had to be on the hillside at six-forty-five. She estimated his hunting position to be a half mile from their campsite. She went down and circled the pond then zigzagged the ridge, making the drive through the draw. On her way up the hill back to camp, she stepped into a bog. The bog was large, but she just didn't see it. "I was afraid I was going to lose my boot in it. I got my shoes and pants muddy and the first thing I did when I got back to camp was to change out of my soiled clothes."

Roberts interrupted. "How is it you didn't meet up with Bruce after your drive and walk back to camp with him, like you did on Saturday morning?"

"It was out of the way, I suppose," Janice said. "I wanted to get back to camp and have everything ready—breakfast and coffee—to surprise Bruce. That way, we quickly could go back out to hunt."

"I see. Go on, please."

"Like I said, I was a muddy mess, so when I got back to the campsite I changed my clothes right away. Then I put the ice chest in the Bronco, picked up the trash, put water in the Bronco, unloaded my gun and put it in the Bronco and got out some eggs and oatmeal for breakfast. I brushed my teeth and went over and talked to the hunter at the next campsite for a while. He had game that he was skinning and I wanted to talk to him about it. He was a Texas peace officer, I found out."

"Your muddy boots were off at this time. What were you wearing on your feet?"

"Rubber sandals. You know, the kind you wear in the shower."

"Okay. Then what?"

Once again Janice's eyes began to well up with tears. "Around nine-thirty I started to worry about Bruce. He was very punctual. So I went out to look for him. As I started to walk down the hill I saw an orange vest on the ground. I called his name and ran over to him. He was lying on the ground. I picked up his rifle and tried to shoot, to get help, but it was empty. His orange vest and hat were lying on the ground beside him. I just…I just started screaming for help."

She was sobbing now and Roberts gave her a few minutes to pull herself together before asking, "Did you see anything suspicious on either Saturday or Sunday prior to the accident?"

Sniffling and dabbing at her eyes, Janice said that on Saturday evening she had seen a guy wearing full camouflage clothing and no orange safety gear. She was off the trail in some oak brush and he did not see her when he passed. He was walking at a fast pace, unlike someone who was hunting and he did not have a weapon with him. Thinking it was odd, she talked to Bruce about it when she returned to camp. She told him how dangerous it was for someone to be out in the woods without any orange. On the way back to camp on Sunday morning, she had seen another man about 200 yards higher than where Bruce was supposed to be. At first, she had thought it was Bruce and waved at him, but he did not wave back.

"What time did you see this man?"

"Early—before the sun came up."

Roberts nodded and wrote a few lines in his notebook. Then he said, "I just have a few more questions, Mrs. Dodson, then I'll leave you to get some rest." He smiled encouragingly at her. "Now when you went out looking for Bruce, you didn't have your weapon with you. You had stowed it in the Bronco. Is that correct?"

"Yes."

"Why was that, Mrs. Dodson?"

"I was done hunting for the morning and I figured if Bruce was in trouble and had an animal down, I would need both hands to help him."

Roberts was inexperienced but sharp. He realized immediately she had contradicted her earlier words. "Oh, I thought you planned on going out again with Bruce after breakfast," he said quietly, not wanting her to think he was being argumentative.

"Yes, well, I wasn't sure. Maybe I was going to go out again. And then I thought maybe I would go up higher on the hill and meet some friends who were hunting in the area, so I wanted the gun put away safely and..."

"What friends were these, Mrs. Dodson?" Roberts interrupted.

"My ex-brother-in-law and his wife, Terence and Carla Morgan. We've remained friends even though Mark and I divorced."

"I thought you hadn't hunted in that area because you didn't want to run into them after the divorce."

"That's true, but years have gone by and I've gotten over feeling that way."

"Was your ex-husband also going to be there?" Roberts asked

She shook her head, growing a bit more distracted. "I wasn't sure. I knew he had been up there two weeks earlier to help his brother set up his camp, but I didn't know if he was going to be there this hunting season."

"What vehicle would Mark have been driving if he was there?" Roberts asked.

"Either a blue and white Chevy pickup or a Suburban, both

with Texas plates."

Roberts nodded and jotted something in his note pad. "Tell me, Mrs. Dodson, how did you expect to be able to find Mark's brother and his wife up there? It's a big area."

"They've hunted up there for years and I know their camping sites. I talked on the phone with Carla last week—just to see how her children were doing and all. We talked briefly about hunting and she told me that she and Terence would be on the Uncompahgre, arriving on October seventh or eighth."

It was the moment to try to pin down the facts. "What kind of weapons does your ex-husband generally use?" Roberts asked.

"Oh, he's used all types, at one time or another, I suppose. I used to hunt with Mark all the time."

"On the Uncompahgre?"

"Not in the exact spot where Bruce and I camped, but closer to where Terence and Carla camp on the other side of Snipe Mountain." Janice looked out the window, a far away expression on her face. "As a matter of fact, I used to work with Mark as an outfitter. He would do guides and drop camps. I would cook in the camp. Sometimes Mark would make videos and show them to Texans to get their hunting trip business. But that was a long time ago," she said with a heavy sigh.

Roberts realized the interview had been lengthy. He told Janice he appreciated her time, shook hands with her and the other women present and returned to his office to report to Lieutenant Finley. There, Roberts awaited the results of the autopsy.

= chapter 6 =

Blood Red River

The color of the Colorado River can change from indigo blue to blood red hour to hour or minute to minute, depending upon the nature of upstream runoff. It was blood red that Monday when the autopsy was conducted at the hospital in Montrose. Oddly, both Bruce and Janice knew the pathologist who performed the autopsy. Dr. Tom Canfield is a medical doctor and an experienced forensic pathologist with many years of practice under his belt. Having been a prominent, successful medical doctor in a small western Colorado town for many years has left him with a substantial amount of self-assurance some might mistake for conceit. He keeps a sailing vessel on Blue Mesa Reservoir and on warm summer evenings can be found yachting in a blue blazer while sipping martinis. Dr. Canfield has had significant experience with gunshot wounds. He was Chief of Legal Medicine at the Armed Services Institute of Pathology at Walter Reed Army Medical Center in Washington, D.C. and retired from the Army Reserves as a Colonel. Janice worked as a psychiatric nurse at Memorial Hospital and Bruce was a laboratory technician at the hospital in Delta, a small town twenty minutes from Montrose. Bruce actually worked under Dr. Canfield in his capacity of laboratory director for both hospitals.

Also present at the autopsy were investigators Bill Booth and Nick Armand. To criminal investigators and certainly to an experienced pathologist like Tom Canfield, autopsies are routine matters and they sometimes joke or make remarks that seem unfeeling to outsiders, but this allows those to whom death is an everyday occurrence to break the tension. Dr. Canfield identified the body by the tag on the body bag as well as by the fact that he personally knew Bruce. "I also know Bruce's wife, Janice," he said with a wry smile. "I saw her having a good old time at a hospital party just last spring. She is flighty and prone to mood swings," he said offering his opinion. Once the body bag was unsealed and unzipped, the clothing was carefully removed, described and examined. Dr. Canfield recorded all details.

Investigator Booth pointed out, "There's a small copper-colored metal fragment, consistent with a small portion of the jacket of a high-powered rifle bullet, in the clothing on the man's chest near a large entry wound." This was just right of midline, nipple high, near the sternum. The bullet traveled across the ribs, fracturing several, and exited under Bruce's arm. Canfield shook his head. "That wound would not have been immediately fatal. With this wound alone, Bruce could have survived for hours and would have lived had he made it to a hospital within a reasonable amount of time." When the body was turned over, Canfield saw another entry wound in the lower right back. "This one was nearly immediately fatal," he noted. Dr. Canfield removed a small lead bullet core from the left lung. There was no exit wound associated with the shot to the back. Because of the three spent shell casings found next to Bruce, there had been some speculation that he may have been wounded by a stray bullet and then fired three shots as a distress signal. Dr. Canfield summarily dispatched such a scenario, "Bruce would not have been able to fire his rifle after his spine was severed by the shot to the back," he concluded.

Any thoughts that this may have been an accidental shooting or suicide had now evaporated. You are not *accidentally* shot twice by a high-powered rifle, and you cannot, without great difficulty, shoot yourself in the back with one. Dr. Canfield took photographs of the body. The bullet fragments and clothing were marked, sealed, and forwarded to the Montrose office of the Colorado Bureau of Investigation.

The Autopsy Report made plain the fact that this was murder.

GENERAL EXTERNAL EXAMINATION:
The body is received in a blue pristine body pouch which is zipped shut. Across the zippers of the body pouch are multiple red evidence seals. The seals are intact. There are initials, "NA, 10-15-95." The intact seals are ruptured and the body pouch opened revealing the body as described below.

IDENTIFICATION:
On the handle of the body bag is identifying tag in the name "John Bruce Dotson" [sic]. There is accompanying paperwork from the Mesa County Coroner's Office. Additionally, the body is that of an individual personally known to the undersigned.

JEWELRY:
1) On the left wrist is a "Timex Iron Man, 8 Lap" brand triathlon watch showing the correct day and date and essentially the correct time.

2) On the 4th finger of the left hand is a gold-colored metal ring which has the logos of mountains and a single mounted dark crystalline stone therein.

3) A pair of bifocal prescription lenses is present on the face in the appropriate position labeled in part "Acutech 108 with Flexons 4018140."

CLOTHING:
The body is partially covered with two items of clothing in the body bag.

1) The first is a blue and red, reversible, down-filled vest showing several defects in the outer fabric from which feathers flow.

2) The second item over the body is a multicolored, plaid, hooded, long-sleeved shirt which contains in the left breast pocket a Montrose Sporting Goods license envelope in which is a hunter safety card in the name of Janice K. Morgan as well as a 1995 resident antlered elk license and antlered elk carcass tag in the name of Janice K. Morgan.

The body is further wrapped in a multicolored, plaid, green-red-blue-purple-yellow, lightweight blanket.

The body is clad in multiple layers.

1) The feet are shod in a pair of grayish-brown, 5 D-loop, 2 speed lace, hiking boots, size 11, "Merrell" brand, showing moderate wear.

2) On the upper torso is a gray, hooded sweatshirt-type jacket, size extra-large, "Lee Midway cotton and poly-ester" zipped-front jacket. The zipper shows a traumatic defect with disruption of both tracks of the zipper and the cloth about it several inches from the top of the front portion of the neck. Additionally there is a traumatic defect in the right lateral aspect of the jacket on approximately the anterior axillary line and a traumatic defect to the right of midline in the back. There is massive blood staining of the jacket. The next layer is a gray in color, "Windridge Mervyn's" brand, 100% cotton, large size, long sleeve sweat-shirt which shows a traumatic defect in the anterior right lateral portion, the anterior lateral and approximately the anterior axillary line and the posterior right portion with massive blood staining over the entire garment. The next

layer is a pair of blue, polyester and cotton, "Big Mac" brand bib overalls. In the front chest pocket is a license envelope from Leisure Time Sports in Cedaredge, Colorado, which contains a Colorado hunting license in the name of John B. Dodson with a resident antlered deer license dated 10-13-95. Also present in the pocket is a "Kershaw" brand knife which has one 4-inch, drop point blade in a lock blade configuration in the closed folding knife. The blade appears clean. There is an apparent acute traumatic defect in the chest just to the right of midline and in the right side of the back of the straps. There is marked blood staining of the overalls. The under shorts are a pair of "Hanes," size 36, 100% cotton. There is marked blood staining of the under shorts which are brief style. The hands are covered in a pair of brown, cloth gloves. There is a moderate amount of vegetable material on the clothing and grass stains on the knees of the bib overalls.

Found on the anterior chest beneath the clothing is an irregular, over folded and disrupted, 7 x 5 x 2 mm portion of copper colored metal consistent with the metal jacket of a hunting bullet.

EXTERNAL EVIDENCE OF TRAUMA:
There are three traumatic lesions on the body consistent with gunshot wounds:

1) In the right anterior chest 51 ½ inches from the base of the right *os calcaneus* to the right of midline, 1 ¼ inch from the center is an irregular, 35 x 28 mm defect. There is a 5-8 mm irregular rim of contusion about the wound medially greater than laterally and there is a gray-black, 2-3 mm apparent margination at the site of the central defect which is 5 x 6 mm. There is no evidence of powder burning, heat damage, tattooing or stippling about the wound.

2) In the right flank, 49 inches from the base of the right *os calcaneus* in the anterior axillary line, 6 ¾ inches to the right of midline is an ovoid, 45 x 32 mm acute traumatic defect which has an irregular subcutaneous hemorrhage about the defect, up to 40 x 40 mm medially with an additional, up to 65 x 50 mm medial area of multiple petechial and ecchymotic hemorrhages. There is a drying artifact at the margins of the wound. There is some tearing at the margin of the wound as well. There is avulsion, disruption and hemorrhage on the underlying tissues. There is no evidence of powder burning, heat damage, tattooing or stippling about the wound.

3) In the right back 49 ½ from the base of the right *os calcaneus* and centered 2 ¾ inches to the right of midline is an ovoid defect which is irregular, rectanguloid with some tissue bridging measuring 20 x 12 mm. There is a definitive 4-5 mm area of margination surrounding the wound. There is no identifiable stippling, smoke, burn or tattooing about the wound. There is some irregular fraying of the margins of the epithelium. There is an irregular, 130 x 60 mm area of subcutaneous apparent bruising and hemorrhage about the wound, laterally and superiorly.

4) Additionally over the back of the right shoulder and lateral to the scapula is a 9 mm, double tapering to 2 mm superficial abrasion-contusion.

INTERNAL EXAMINATION:
The body is entered by way of the standard Y-shaped, thoracic-abdominal incision revealing 2 cm of yellow subcutaneous adipose tissue and thick red-brown musculature. There is acute traumatic injury from the defect #1 described above which transverses from medial to lateral through the subcutaneous tissues with avulsion, disruption and hemorrhage.

Ribs 8, 9 and 10 show multiple fractures with avulsion, disruption and hemorrhage. Wound #2 on the right flank is in continuity with the above-described track. A laceration on the dome of the liver is directly under this area. Wound #3 described above the right back perforates the subcutaneous tissues with avulsion, disruption and hemorrhage and perforates the paravertebral muscles of the right back with avulsion, disruption and hemorrhage with disruption of vertebral body L1 and avulsion of the spinal cord. It exits on the left lateral aspect of the vertebral body perforating the diaphragm and penetrating the lower lobe of the left lung. A bullet lead core is recovered from the lower lobe of the left lung with lodging from the missile track on the posterior, to the midportion of the lower lobe of left lung with avulsion, disruption and hemorrhage.

LUNGS: The right lung weighs 325 grams; the left lung weighs 375 grams. Cut sections show collapse of the lung on the right and some congestion of the lung on the left. The above-described traumatic injury is present in the lower lobe of the left lung with a bullet track causing avulsion, disruption and hemorrhage and a recovered bullet in the lower lobe of the left lung. The bullet portion is apparent lead and is marked at its base "TMC 105" and shows significant disruption of the anterior portion of the bullet. There is no jacket portion present at this location. The missile is consistent with a high-powered rifle hunting bullet core.

DIGESTIVE SYSTEM: The stomach contains approximately 500 cc of fluid with minimal digested foodstuff.

MUSCULO-SKELETAL SYSTEM: There are fractures of ribs 8, 9 and 10 on the right and L1 due to the passage of missile with avulsion, disruption and hemorrhage.

Dr. Canfield concluded that each gunshot wound was consistent with having been fired from a large-caliber rifle at a distant range. The lack of any evidence of powder burning, heat damage, tattooing or stippling about the wound ruled out a close-range shot, as did the nature of the wounds themselves. Under cause of death, he wrote, "This forty-eight-year-old Caucasian male died as the direct result of a gunshot wound of his back. Additionally he suffered a gunshot wound to his chest."

= chapter 7 =

Family Ties

It was time to contact Bruce's relatives to see if we could learn more from them. John Bruce Dodson had no family in Colorado. He had moved to Colorado from Maryland as a young man and made Colorado his home. Most of his family lived back East.

Bruce Dodson's brother Michael lived in Maryland with his wife. The authorities who informed Michael about his brother's death had told him that some unusual circumstances surrounded the event. I felt certain that Michael wanted to talk to someone about what had really happened in his brother's death and would be appreciative of our call.

Michael told us that when his sister learned that her brother had been killed in a hunting accident, she said, "that bitch." According to Michael, after her marriage to Bruce, Janice had made dozens of calls to his mother, asking her to convince Bruce to put Janice's name on the titles to his property. "She called about money matters and the will at least a dozen times," Michael revealed. Bruce's brother thought Janice was strange. He had met her twice. The first time, about a year and a half earlier, she told him she was from a rich family and had a great childhood; the following year she told him she grew up poor and was abused as a child.

A week later Michael Dodson and his sister, Martha, flew in for the memorial service in Delta County and made arrangements to meet with us before returning home to Maryland. We asked them to be open and speak about whatever came to mind about their brother, Bruce, and his wife, Janice Morgan Dodson. Martha said that Bruce told them he would send a video and photographs of the wedding since they were not able to attend. She said she finally received them on the day before Bruce's death, Saturday, October 14, along with a note from Janice.

Michael Dodson told us that Bruce did well in high school and went on to the University of Maryland. After college, he enlisted in the Navy. Bruce had always wanted to live in Colorado, ever since their family made a trip out here when they were kids. Michael went on to say that his brother was a "retired hippie" who joined the Navy. In the service, Bruce worked in the laundry and as a clerk. After his discharge, Bruce moved to Colorado where he lived for about twenty years. He worked as a laboratory technician in hospitals. Investigator Roberts asked if Bruce had any relationships before Janice. They said that Bruce lived with another woman and was very serious about her and that she died from cancer. As others would, Martha commented that Bruce was a lonely man. After Janice came into the picture, Bruce appeared to be infatuated with her. When Bruce's siblings were together with Bruce and Janice, Bruce acted as if no one else but Janice was around. The siblings felt it was a strange relationship. They said he sat by her constantly and held and stroked her hand and pampered her to the point it made them all nauseated. One time, Janice fell asleep in front of the television and instead of waking her, Bruce picked her up and carried her to bed. His siblings said Bruce told them that his relationship with Janice was non-sexual even though they had been living together for some time. They were all suspicious of that. They said that they had heard from

Bruce's friends at the memorial service that Bruce had been happy during the last three months of his life, that he seemed to be taking better care of himself and dressing nicer.

Martha contradicted that, however, telling us, "I spoke with Bruce just after Christmas last year and he told me he and Janice were having problems." The next time he called her was near the end of June and he asked her what she was doing on July 15. He told her he and Janice were getting married. This was three weeks before the wedding. "My mother made it clear to Bruce that she was not happy about this marriage and would not attend." Martha said Bruce told his mother that Janice had revealed to him her many problems, including having been abused by her father. Bruce felt badly for her and all he wanted was his mother's blessing and to be happy. Martha was surprised to hear this because when Janice had visited her in Maryland months earlier, she told Martha she came from a rich family and had a wonderful life growing up on a big ranch in Texas. Janice bragged that she hunted all her life and was a pilot. "Janice once told my mother that she could make anybody believe anything she wanted them to."

The next day, Investigator Roberts spoke with Mrs. Ruth Dodson by phone at her son's home in Maryland. He asked her to tell him about her son and Janice Morgan. Though Mrs. Dodson was shocked and saddened by her son's sudden death, she wanted to talk about his new wife—new widow—and her thoughts on the marriage. She started by indicating that her son, Bruce, had called her and said he had met someone named Janice or "Ja-niece" as the woman called herself. "I was happy for Bruce, because I knew he was alone. I was glad he had found someone." Roberts asked her if Janice ever talked about her background. She indicated that Janice said she was wealthy and had grown up on a large cattle ranch in Texas. According to Ruth, Janice had told her that caviar and pate every day for lunch was common for her. Yet she noticed that Janice was always asking for money for different things. "During my phone conversations with Bruce before the wedding, I would always hear Janice in the background trying to get Bruce to ask for money for a wedding gift." Ruth said her whole family was of the opinion that Janice was a flake, "a psycho case." Ruth confessed she had doubts about Janice upon first meeting her and always thought the young woman was a "kook" and a con artist. "I felt that way from the beginning. It's a mother's intuition," she confessed. During the time her son and Janice had been together, Janice had called numerous times wanting Ruth to convince Bruce that he needed to change over the title to his property so in case anything happened to him Janice would still have a place to live. Ruth knew Janice was making out their wills at the time she and Bruce were planning their wedding. "How many brides are worried about wills at the time of their wedding?" she asked incredulously. According to Bruce's mother, Janice would also call her all the time and say, "I just called to tell you I love you," and hang up. She said that her other son and daughter used to joke about Bruce needing to check his brakes.

Mrs. Dodson went on to say that Bruce had purchased a diamond ring for Janice. Janice commented to Ruth that the diamond looked like a mere chip to her eyes, which upset Ruth because she knew Bruce was very proud of the ring. That sealed the deal for Ruth; she definitely had no intention of going to the wedding, "I didn't want to go, because I thought Janice was a mental case."

Bruce's mother said finally that the thing that bothered her most was that Janice was always calling her and asking about finances, saying, "What if something happens to Bruce?" Ruth indicated that she had sent Bruce $13,000.00 at the time of the wedding so that he could pay off the mortgage on the home he owned in Leadville. Bruce told her he wanted to cut his expenditures since Janice had bills they needed to pay off. Before hanging up, Ruth made a final comment about her son. "You know, I thought it was strange that Bruce was going hunting, because he was such an animal lover. Bruce told me he was going because Janice wanted him to."

One of Bruce's friends, Ann Patton, sent a letter to the police department about the dead man. Reading the letter gave me my first real glimpse of the gentle character of John Bruce Dodson. Dry police reports and photographs of Bruce lying dead on the Uncompahgre gave me no personal perspective on the man. The letter was written in neat and precise handwriting. Included were photographs of Ann Patton's wall depicting framed prints of several exceptionally nice landscape photographs taken by Bruce.

Estes Park

I finally have some time off. Hope you can read my handwriting. Notes about Bruce Dodson: smart, talented, capable, dogmatic, intolerant, funny, irritable, caring, independent, versatile, self-disciplined, moody, frugal, prickly, careful, sometimes lonely, seldom bored, painfully principled, thoroughly responsible, a closet romantic, an interesting human being.

As a friend, he was sometimes puzzling, sometimes painful (seemed to sabotage himself socially), sometimes amazingly supportive. We sort of adopted each other. Bruce joined the lab staff in 1988, just a few months after I did. We had many conversations. Bruce's search for a mate was sporadic and cautious. There were two serious past relationships that occasionally entered our conversations. His first love died of cancer. He mentioned taking her on perfect backpacking trips. There was another relationship later, with a lady pharmacist, which lasted several years and left him embittered.

And then came Janice. Bruce fell head over heels. I recall when he escorted her to the lab Christmas party; he looked so proud. Janice is quite beautiful when she gets gussied up. Prior to Janice, Bruce made a couple of honest, but hesitant attempts to connect with women through dating services aimed at outdoorsy people. Now and then he would borrow my car to take one of his contacts to a concert or play in Grand Junction. (He thought his VW Camper was too suggestive.) That VW van was an important acquisition as it offered great freedom. We used it camping a few times. Most of our talking took place en route somewhere. He drove very carefully. He did everything carefully. We talked about many things—people, places, paintings, plans, ideas. He didn't talk about his family much, but his fondness for his sister and his nieces and nephews was apparent. It is sad that none of Bruce's family came to see him in his element—the West, which he loved.

Bruce's maverick sense of humor sort of poked out between his many serious characteristics. So did his creative nature, expressing itself through his photographs. Bruce biked, hiked, skied, and rode horses. One summer he climbed Mt. Sneffles—alone. Bruce's impressive frugality grew out of his determination to retire early, independently and comfortably. I moved to Estes Park in the spring of 1993 and saw little of Bruce after that. My quilting pals at the Delta lab said Bruce and Janice were still an item, but sometimes stormy—nothing specific.

When he called me at work to ask if I could come to his wedding, I was surprised and delighted for him. That spring was particularly wet, turning the slopes of Grand Mesa into a garden. So one of his hopes had come true—to own a home in his favorite country, a place where he could keep his horse and share it with a wife.

It's really hard to believe someone would intentionally kill this gentle man. How dare they? I don't really know Janice very well. Lauren and Gail probably know her best. Bonnie says there may be two Janices—apparently she was a quiet, mousey, colorless person when she first came to work in Delta. Janice always seemed kind of spooky—like she was on stage all the time—and vulnerable and confused. I don't want to think she killed Bruce. I don't want to think he had to watch his wife shoot him.

All of us who care about Bruce are pulling for you to figure this out. Frank said to me, "Who would kill this harmless man? I want to sit in the courtroom and look into the face of this person who has no conscience."

What was in his will? I hear that Janice urged him to change his will shortly after the wedding. Did he? It seems like odd newlywed behavior; newlyweds think they're immortal.

Good luck,

Ann Patton

Later I spoke again with Bruce's sister, who was obviously grieving. Martha was fifteen years younger than Bruce and looked up to him as an almost heroic figure. When she was in grade school, Bruce was in college and later went off to serve in the Navy. I also had a number of other conversations with Bruce's brother, Michael. He was angry about what happened to Bruce, but did not convey the intense feelings of sadness and loss I felt from Martha. After speaking with her, my need to bring justice to this situation intensified.

= chapter 8 =

More Questions for Janice

In this judicial district, the preliminary work on an investigation is ordinarily conducted by the law enforcement agency with jurisdiction—here that was the Mesa County Sheriff's Department. In most situations, the District Attorney's office has little involvement until the investigator brings the case to us for prosecution. This case was different. I was involved right from the start as was my investigator, Bill Booth. Bill and Nick Armand were partners when they worked narcotics together at the sheriff's department, so it was natural for Nick to include Bill in on the case from the start. Bill kept me updated on a daily basis. From day one, we both kept current with the progress of the investigation and were involved in many discussions on future courses of action. As one by one the investigators in the sheriff's department made career or lifestyle changes and left the department, the entire investigation gradually shifted over to my office, to the point where the sheriff's department assumed the minor role.

Murder cases always take top priority in a District Attorney's office, but there was something particularly intriguing about this case from the beginning when we still were unsure whether Bruce

Dodson's death was an accident or homicide. As each new report came across my desk, it became more and more clear that this was going to be a bizarre case to unravel. Never had I seen such a cast of characters or such a complex and intertwined set of facts. Beyond the barrage of strange witnesses and circumstances, part of the allure was the interesting developments in forensic evidence. It seemed that each set of tests, rather than answering questions, brought a new set of possibilities. Soon, thoughts of this case came to occupy a large portion of my consciousness, day in and day out. Even in my so-called off time while hiking or climbing with my friends, I chewed their ears off examining possibilities, using them as sounding boards to discuss issues and to gain their perspectives as outside observers.

Over the years, I had handled many homicide cases. Sometimes I made a connection with the victim and the victim's family and sometimes I did not. Now I was more than connected, I was becoming obsessed. Two factors made this investigation a personal mission for me. One arose from my conversations with Bruce's sister, Martha. The pain of her loss was so palpable it touched me. She was hurt and confused as to why someone would do this to her brother. She clearly needed justice if she was ever going to gain closure and I wanted to help her get it. The other thing drawing me close came more slowly. This was my personal connection with the victim, Bruce. I developed a sense of a lonely and sensitive man, interested in the environment and animals. He loved his horse and his dog and appreciated the beauty of nature and its solitude, as I did. As a photographer, I connected with his photographs of nature's glory.

At the same time I was developing this compassion for Bruce, my questions about Janice were growing. Was she a cold-hearted woman? Had she married Bruce just so she could murder this gentle man in order to steal his money, plus whatever insurance proceeds she could add onto the pile? If so, Bruce deserved better. Was it her or someone else? Usually in a murder case there is some obvious, understandable, if not reasonable, reason why it happens—rage, jealousy, intoxication. I felt we had to find which motive had brought Bruce Dodson to his sudden death.

On Tuesday morning, close to noon, the two Rons, Finley and Roberts, drove back to Saint Mary's Hospital. They had more questions for Janice and hopes that she would accompany them to the Uncompahgre Plateau. When they got to Janice's room she was dressed and ready to check out. Janice is a good looking woman, about five foot eight and trim, with ample curves and a nice smile. When freshly showered, made up and dressed in the latest fashion, as she usually was, she cut a fairly flamboyant figure. On this day, she appeared to be in the same generally despondent condition as she had on the day of the murder, replete with blank stares and tears.

Roberts tried to explain their purpose. "We are having a hard time fitting your story with the crime scene and it would be a great help if you would accompany us up on the mountain and point out where you and your husband traveled that day." He added, "It will help the investigators working the scene to have this information so that they can narrow the scope of the search. Time is of the essence, as we are contending with weather changes, hunters leaving the area and other changing circumstances." He told her all these things would make it less likely that they would be able to determine what had happened.

Janice shook her head. "I don't know if I can handle going back up there so soon, in light of what occurred."

Roberts tried to convey a sympathetic tone. "I understand how difficult this must be and I would not ask if time were not such an important factor. I know it will be tough, but I hope you want to help to find the person who shot Bruce." She looked confused, so Finley added in a firm voice, "We've determined that it was not an accident."

She appeared surprised and said, "You mean someone shot Bruce on purpose?"

Roberts replied, "It appears that way."

She appeared concerned. "What is it that makes you believe that?"

Investigator Roberts was cagey. "In most hunting accidents where someone shot a person, the shooter normally comes forward within a couple of days." While Ron Roberts was running this line by Janice, Ron Finley stood by nodding with a look of sincere caring and agreement, while all he really wanted to do was to get outside and light up a cigarette and figure out what they had. Roberts went on, "We figure there are two possibilities: it was either a random act of violence, meaning that someone shot Bruce Dodson just for the thrill of doing it or an accidental shooting and the person who did it is worried that he will be in trouble." Both Rons' hearts began to pound in their chests when Janice asked if someone would be in trouble for an accidental shooting like this. Roberts replied, perhaps a bit too quickly, "No, whoever did it would not be in trouble. Accidents are accidents."

While Janice stood there, Lieutenant Finley pulled out a form he had previously prepared for Janice to give written consent to search her vehicles. He explained, "It's just a routine matter," and reminded her, "You already gave consent at the scene." She nodded and fumbled her signature onto the form. They also got Janice's permission to pick up whatever clothing and other items she had when she checked in to the hospital. As they walked, Roberts told Janice, "I'm interested in seeing whether you had on your orange vest when you left camp and discovered your husband's body." She told Ron that she did, but wondered if they found her orange hat and sunglasses. "I'll go downstairs and pick up your belongings and let you know if those things are there." When Ron went to pick up Janice's belongings, he learned that hospital security officers had discovered five rounds of ammunition and a knife in her clothing. At the hospital storage locker, Ron took possession of Janice's blue jeans, green camouflage T-shirt, sandals, blaze orange vest, bra, panties, plain shirt, socks, jacket, and sunglasses. There was no hat.

Investigator Roberts went back to the hospital room where he gave Janice her sunglasses and told her, "Your vest is there, but no hat." Both Rons traveled down several floors and through hallways of labyrinthine, too-bright, fluorescently lighted corridors, to the hospital security department to retrieve the knife and ammunition. The security officer on duty was Jason Palafox, looking a pasty green in the artificial light.

The men collected the knife and ammunition from Palofax. The ammunition was five live rounds of Federal Brand 7 mm magnum. It had been in Janice's pocket when she arrived at the hospital.

In the car, Janice appeared to sleep for most of the trip. By the time they arrived at the crime scene it was 3:40 P.M. The afternoon was overcast and there was a breezy chill in the air. Ron Roberts asked Janice to walk over to the VW Van so that she could point out and describe the routes she traveled Saturday and Sunday.

After taking a moment to look around the area and gather herself with a deep breath, Janice said, "On Sunday morning it was about 8:45 A.M. when I came up from the bottom of the draw." She pointed across the way to a fence that was due north and said, "It was there that I crossed the fence in order to make my drive. I left Bruce in camp and told him to be in place on the hillside at 6:45." She expected him to be in the same general vicinity he had been in Saturday morning, perhaps a little higher. When she left camp he was still in bed and she gave him a cup of coffee. She pointed out the route and where she had crossed the fence. She said she could not get the gate open, so she went through the strands of barbed wire. She said she dropped over the ridge and went around the pond looking for game. According to Janice she paused on the hill before dropping off the edge as the sun was coming up to see if she could spot any game. She said she ate a banana at that point. Her story was that after she circled the pond, she went down through the bottom of the draw and made a drive, zigzagging back and forth across the bottom and coming back up the draw. She said when she came up the draw she hit the mud bog which is about 100 to 200 yards from camp. She said she came up the draw and went through another couple of clumps of oak brush and came around behind the back of the van. Ron Roberts noted that the place where Bruce's body was found was visible from where they were standing at the front of the van. Lieutenant Finley had been down where the body was found during most of their conversation and could clearly be seen. When he returned Roberts asked Janice if she would explain again to him. At that point she began to feel weak so the two officers took her back to the jeep and gave her a seat in front. When she felt a little better, they then drove the jeep up to the front of the VW van where they had been standing so she could go through it again with Lieutenant Finley. Roberts was in the back seat while Janice and Finley conversed up front.

Once again she repeated her story. It was about 8:45 when she came up from the bottom of the draw. She pointed out where she came up. She said it was about 9:00 when she was back in camp. She repeated that she came around to the back of the van to change clothes and didn't happen to look in the direction of the draw.

"When I got to the far point of my drive, I saw a hunter who was up on the point of the hill where Bruce was supposed to be," Janice said. Lieutenant Finley asked her when she first started hearing shots. She said she heard shots even before she got to the pond and made note of the fact that they were occurring early as the sun was not yet up. She heard shots all the rest of the morning. She took note of the fact that she thought she heard a 300 H&H Magnum to the northwest and thought to herself that these guys were bringing out the big guns. She said she even heard shots when she was talking to the guy who was camped next to her. Lieutenant Finley asked her to tell him what she did when she returned to camp. "I came through the oak brush and walked around behind the van. I was thinking that Bruce might already be back in camp. I thought he might be playing games with me because we used to do things like that. So I looked in the van and the Bronco to see if Bruce was hiding from me. He wasn't." Figuring Bruce was still out hunting, Janice changed her muddy clothes, secured her gun in the gun case and put it in the Bronco. Then she got a drink of water, started to brush her teeth, and went to visit the guy camped nearby who had an animal hanging from a tree. "About 9:30 I decided to go look for Bruce. I was getting worried about him."

Trying to be nonchalant Lieutenant Finley quietly asked, "Where was the ammo for your rifle?"

"I had one round in the magazine and three or four in my pocket when I unloaded my gun. I left them all in my pocket." She explained that she normally did that—she'd have one in the magazine and three or four others in case she needed an extra shot, because she didn't get the animal down. She said when she got to Bruce his vest and hat were lying on the ground next to him. "I picked up his rifle to fire rounds to summon help, but when I pulled the trigger it just made a clicking sound." She opened the chamber and an empty cartridge ejected. As the two officers watched her closely she added, "I picked up the empty shell and put it with the other two that were laying there." Lieutenant Finley asked her if she touched the other two and Janice shook hear head, "I don't know. I got up and ran screaming for help." According to Janice, she was going to run back to the van to honk its horn and get her rifle and fire three shots in the air. On the way back she saw the hunter from the other camp and ran to him for help.

Lieutenant Roberts cocked his head. "Did you fire your rifle at all on this trip?"

She said she had not shot the .270 at all. "I had it bore sighted, but have not fired it for two years or more." Janice went on to say that she had the rifle sighted at Freedom Gun Shop in Eckert just before the season started. "Bruce used the .243 with open sights and had never shot it before that I know of."

A moment of silence fell.

Above Janice's head the eyes of Roberts and Finley met and locked for a long moment. Then, not wanting Janice to clam up, they both looked away and Finley began asking some less pointed questions before they ended the session.

= c h a p t e r 9 =

Finding Pieces of the Puzzle

At 9:00 A.M. on October 18, 1995, a briefing was held at the Mesa County Sheriff's Department. At this meeting it was determined that investigators needed to return to the scene of Bruce Dodson's death, and to share all of their information on a timely basis. We had to be sure we hadn't missed a thing.

Deputy Poste was sitting in on the meeting when he received a phone call. It was Mark Morgan, Janice's ex, calling from Utah. Morgan said, "Mr. Poste, my brother called and told me that you want to talk to me." Poste was flustered; all he could do was to take a phone number and tell Mark that an investigator would get back to him.

Another investigator called Mark's brother Terence and reported back to Poste. "He asked me if Mark had contacted the sheriff's department and I told him he had. I asked him when he had last seen his brother on the Uncompahgre. Terence said that he and his wife went over to Mark's camp Saturday morning on their ATV and estimated arriving there at 10:30 A.M. He said his brother had been hunting, but he didn't know what type of rifle he was using, and said that he thought there were two people in the camp. Terence also volunteered information about Janice. He said when she first married

Mark she was sixteen. Terence also told the investigator he planned to stay through the second season of the hunt and if they needed him they could call him on his cell phone.

At the briefing, the investigators went over all their notes and interviews together. One investigator spoke of revisiting Captain Branchwater's camp. He had told Branchwater he was sorry to bother him again and asked him if he minded going over some information that there still were questions concerning. "Do you remember when Bruce and Janice arrived?" he asked the Texas lawman.

Branchwater thought hard for a moment. "It was late Friday night. It was dark and they had a hard time getting the Volkswagen van into the camp road from the main trail." He remembered seeing Bruce pull up in the Bronco and then get out to guide Janice in the van.

The investigator told his colleagues he then asked Branchwater if he had seen Bruce or Janice on Saturday and he said he had not. Branchwater said both he and his camp mate had gotten up early and left camp around five o'clock in the morning to go to the canyon they hunted in.

Dispatch records show that the first call to 911 was made at 9:40 A.M. By the time Deputy Patrick met up with Captain Branchwater it was 12:10 P.M. It was 12:25 by the time they got back to the crime scene.

While he was speaking with Captain Branchwater, Lieutenant Finley and Investigator Roberts arrived on scene along with Janice. The two men talked with her to try to find out where she had gotten full of mud and to see if she could point out how she had come into camp without seeing her husband's body, which was in plain view from camp.

After the two Rons and Janice left and Investigator Armand finished processing the scene, they all left. They had driven the

Bronco and the VW Van to the sheriff's department and parked them in a garage for safekeeping.

The briefing ended and Deputy Poste headed to his desk, hoping to put his work of the past several days into report form, and Captain Gardner came into his office. "I want you to search the two Dodson vehicles." Victor Poste felt frustrated, but he kept it to himself. It bothered him not to have his reports done. Deputy Paul Kardos was assigned to the vehicle search as well. They were to go through both vehicles, take photographs and seize any items relating to firearms or that appeared to show evidence of blood or mud. Deputy Poste, as usual, was very thorough. His report began:

"The search of the 1981 Ford Bronco, red and white in color, having Colorado license plate number EGV082, was started at 1:15 P.M. The VIN number could not be read from the dash. A VIN number of 1FMDU15F5BLA24543 was found on an insurance card. A registration card that was located inside the glove box on the passenger side of the vehicle showed that the vehicle was registered to John Bruce Dodson with an address of 2089 Highway 65, Cedaredge, Colorado, with an expiration date of 02/96. Also in the glove box was a Ford Bronco owner's guide for 1981 vehicles. There was also an orange in color inhaler; brand Proventil inhalation aerosol with a control number of 2-BBS-322 with an expiration date of 09/94."

Since these vehicles contained myriad items, his report went on for seven pages. There were hunting items, clothing, foodstuffs, cooking utensils, tools, oil, papers and whatever. There were compartments in the VW Van that appeared not to have been cleaned out for years and Deputy Poste recorded every item in great detail. At the trial, what would be important to me was not what these deputies found, but what they did not find. There were no more weapons and no additional ammunition or spent cartridges other than what had already been recovered by Investigator Armand and Deputy Todd up on the Uncompahgre.

The investigators quickly became interested in Janice's ex-husband, Mark Morgan, and his possible involvement. Was it too much of a coincidence for Janice's ex-husband to be hunting a mile away from the murder? It was not as if he lived nearby. He lived a seven-hour drive away. They found out that on the day of the murder, the second day of the hunting season, he left the area without shooting his quota.

At the meeting that morning, it had been agreed that the two Rons would drive to Mark's apartment in Layton, Utah to interview him later in the afternoon. On Wednesday, October 18, 1995, they arrived at Mark Morgan's home, but found he wasn't there. Parking in front of his apartment, they waited several hours until 8:30 P.M. when they finally saw a man emerge from a Chevy pickup truck and head toward the apartment door. He was about five foot ten, well-built, handsome in a rugged way, with close-cropped blond hair and piercing blue eyes. "That's our guy," Roberts said. Finley nodded. They introduced themselves to Morgan and Roberts told him, "We're investigating a homicide that occurred Sunday in Mesa County, Colorado." Mark looked as though he had been working construction, as indeed he had. His clothes were soiled and he seemed worn out. Mark invited the two investigators in and asked them to wait a few minutes while he cleaned up from his day's work.

When the interview finally began, the investigators found Mark guarded in conversation. He came across as something of a redneck, but was clearly intelligent. Some would call him "street smart," but that is not quite it. "Street smart" implies a city-grown mentality, and while Mark has been around the block a time or two (he worked on the Alaska Pipeline and did construction work in Saudi Arabia), mostly he evolved by having been reared in the piney woods of East Texas. "It's a 'piney woods smarts,'" I said later to some of the investigators, "that has resulted from many intertwined and overlapping generations that survived fighting Indians, Mexican armies, bands of Confederate renegades and marauders, government revenuers, various other outsiders and wild animals, while feeding families by trapping and hunting for food."

Roberts and Finley first asked Mark about his marriage to Janice Morgan. He told them, "We've been divorced for approximately five years." When questioned about any mental problems that Janice Morgan had, Mark answered, "After we divorced, I heard that she had been committed to an institution, possibly because of the divorce." He didn't seem to know much more about her emotional problems except that he had heard she had a hard time dealing with her father's death.

Finley asked Mark, "Were you in Texas earlier this year?"

He nodded. "I was."

Finley asked if Mark had seen Janice there and he said he did. "It was in April or May." Then Finley asked if Janice talked to Mark about a possible reconciliation of their marriage.

Mark sighed. "Yeah, she did so on that occasion and she also had talked to me about three or four times in the year or so prior to that meeting. Each time I told her no, I did not want to get back together with her." According to Mark, it was during their conversation in Texas that Janice told him she had a friend named Bruce back in Colorado who wanted to marry her. "I told her, 'Do whatever you want to.' She said she was going to go back to Colorado to marry Bruce." Mark went on, "The next time I saw her was in Colorado around the fourth of July." Again, she asked about getting back together and again he declined.

Finley questioned Mark further. "Can you give us a little background information about Janice, how you two met and what you did during your marriage?"

Mark described them marrying young, when Janice was sixteen and he was eighteen. "I worked construction and was away a lot on jobs. Janice got into the nursing field and worked in psych wards and with alcoholics." When Finley asked about their financial situation, Mark replied that they were always able to pay their bills, but like most young married couples with kids, money was hard to keep. Then Finley turned his questions to the death scene, and asked, "Were you up on Uncompahgre Plateau last week?"

Mark said he was, telling the officer he had hunted in the same area for most of the past twenty years. When Finley asked if Mark had seen his brother, Terence, up there, Mark said they did not hunt together this year, mostly because they each have their own area they like to hunt, but also because Terence's wife is religious and does not approve of Mark living "in sin" with his girlfriend, Marcy.

Finley probed further. "Did you know that Janice and Bruce were going to be hunting on the Uncompahgre last weekend?"

"I knew they were going to be hunting somewhere, but did not know it would be on the Uncompahgre." Mark explained that he did not find out they were camped close to him until he returned home to Utah on Monday night, October 16. The reason he knew that Janice was going to hunt this year was because she had called him several times within the past month and mentioned it to him. According to Mark, Janice called him and said she was going to borrow a gun and wanted to know what bullet weights she should purchase for a 7 mm magnum. "When I asked her what the rifle was going to be used for, she said elk, so I told her to buy 160 grain bullets for elk. Then she asked about deer also and I told her to get 100 grain bullets for deer." He said that within a week of that call she called again and told him that she had found two rifles at an acquaintance's house that she had previously reported stolen. One was a Mauser .243 and one was a Mauser .270. He was quite familiar with those weapons as they had been his and were given to Janice in the divorce. She said she had forgotten she had stored them at the friend's home.

Then Finley told Mark about the 7 mm magnum ammunition Janice was carrying for use in her .270. He asked Mark if he could explain that to him. Mark said, "I can't explain that; that combination won't work." Then Mark said, "Janice was a good, accurate shot with a rifle, but her technical knowledge about calibers and ammunition was not good."

During the time Investigators Roberts and Finley were in the apartment, they noticed a yellow legal tablet on the table. On it they were able to make out some names along with a list of items. Finley pointed to the pad and asked Mark what the list was about. Mark informed them that a theft had occurred in his hunting camp. "I believe it happened on Saturday, October 14 in the afternoon." He went on, "When we left camp in the afternoon, we left the tent secured with snaps, as is my habit. Upon arriving back after sundown, I noticed the flap was unsecured. I asked my boss and my girlfriend if either of them had come back to the tent and opened it after leaving that afternoon. They both said they had not. I looked around the tent, but did not notice anything missing. In fact, I did not notice anything missing until I arrived home in Utah on Monday and began to unload my gear." According to Mark, at that point he looked for his knives so that he could butcher the deer his girlfriend shot and could not find them. He also realized he was missing a rifle, a Remington Model 700, .308-caliber, heavy barreled, which was loaded with five Federal Premium hunting bullets. Knowing there would be more questions later, Finley took down Mark's next words as he spoke. "I fired the rifle on Friday, the day before the season opened and there were four empty cartridges in the box along with eleven live rounds and they were missing as well. I was also missing a brown, blanket-lined, Carhartt brand coat." He said he was preparing a list to report to the proper authorities. Finley asked Mark if Janice would know where he was camped. He said he did not think she knew exactly where his camp was, but she would know he was in the general vicinity of Snipe Mountain.

Mark described the setup in his hunting camp that year. On October 8, one week before the start of the season, he helped his brother, Terence, with his camp, and then set up his own camp on October 9. He told Finley he'd been hunting the opening weekend of the season, which was October 14 and 15, and then left Monday, October 16. When asked if he saw his ex-wife Janice on the trip, Mark claimed he had not seen her since July. "On Saturday, me and my boss took his truck and went north out of camp to Red Creek. We all split up and met back at camp later that morning." That afternoon, Mark told the officers, his two hunting partners took the truck back over to Red Creek and he left on foot from camp in the direction of his favorite hunting spot, which was north out of their camp. "On Sunday morning, Gary, my boss, and Marcy again left in the truck over to go over to Red Creek and I left on foot toward a spot where I had seen a nice buck the day before. It was light enough to see when we all left that morning."

Roberts asked, "How did you find out about the shooting?"

Mark explained that his daughter called him and told him about it. He then described driving an older Chevy pickup truck to the Uncompahgre, "The same one I was driving this evening." Finley asked him if he left the truck in camp to which Mark replied vehemently, "It was in camp all weekend." Then Finley asked if Janice was familiar with that truck. "Yes, she was," Mark insisted.

Finley asked, "Did Janice receive a 7 mm magnum rifle as part of the divorce settlement?"

"We owned a 7 mm magnum," Mark answered, "but I still have it and, in fact, my girlfriend was hunting with it during this hunting trip. That was the rifle she used to shoot her deer on Saturday."

Finley pressed on. "Would you voluntarily submit to giving us a set of fingerprints?"

Mark said he would gladly and Roberts opened up his kit and readied the equipment The officers noted that Morgan was very cooperative in providing a full set of prints. These prints were placed into evidence at the Mesa County Sheriff's Department.

After a long and grueling interview, the two Rons left Mark's apartment and checked into a room at a nearby motel. They discussed what they learned and their general feelings about Mark Morgan over dinner. They found him to be likeable and thought he was being forthright, but still had concerns. As they discussed the interview and some other facts of the case, they decided they needed to talk to Mark once more before returning to Colorado. The next morning they reached him on his cell phone and arranged a meeting back at his apartment over his lunch break.

Shortly before noon the next day, Roberts and Finley drove to re-interview Mark Morgan at his apartment.

"There are a few things we still need to clarify with you," Finley said when Mark opened the door and let them in.

"No problem," Mark said. "Ask me whatever you need to."

"Mark, would you be willing to take a polygraph examination regarding the shooting on the Uncompahgre Plateau?" Roberts asked point blank.

Mark answered immediately. "Any time. I'll take a polygraph to clear myself."

"Good," said Finley. "When did you decide to leave the hunting camp?"

"On Sunday afternoon, my boss, Gary Dalton, and I hunted while Marcy loaded our personal property from the tent. She wasn't feeling good and she wanted to leave, so while I hunted, she loaded the truck and we left the mountain that night. We drove to El Rancho Motel and spent the night and I left in the morning for Utah. Marcy had her own car down in Grand Junction. She had left it in the parking lot of the City Market grocery store. She left in the morning to return to Fort Morgan, where she's been living." Mark sat down at the kitchen table and motioned for the officers to join him. Scratching his head, he said, "When I noticed the gun was missing, I called Marcy and asked her if she had my knives and the rifle. She said she didn't. So I tried to call Gary on his cell phone but couldn't get through to him. When I saw him on Tuesday morning at the job site I asked him about it. Gary didn't know where the gun and knives were either."

"What guns did you have in camp, Mark?" Finley asked, pulling out a notebook and pen from his pocket. He wanted to take a few direct quotes down while they were fresh in his mind.

"I was using my .300 Weatherby. Marcy used a 7 mm magnum. But I also had a 30-06 in camp as well as the .308 that turned up missing. Tell you the truth, I'm not sure what caliber rifle Gary had."

Roberts changed the subject. "How did your divorce from Janice come about?"

"Well, I guess our problem was past cheating. I suspected her of cheating several times during our marriage." He gave a small chuckle. "Look, when we lived in Montrose I did some cheating of my own."

"Mark, let me ask you one last question," Finley began. "Do you think Janice could have shot her husband, Bruce, if there was a large sum of insurance money on the line?"

Mark responded, "While I was married to her, I don't believe she could have done something like that for money, but there's been a lot of water under the bridge since then, and now I don't know if she's capable of that or not."

The two detectives said nothing, but each of their minds was clicking off the possibilities.

What Is True? What Is False?

The two Rons discussed Mark Morgan with me, with each other and with the other investigators working the case and we decided there were still too many loose ends. Since Mark apparently was willing to take a polygraph, we decided to follow up. A polygraph is one of many tools available to an investigator. Sometimes polygraphs are used to exclude possible suspects based on whether they pass or not, but the more common goal is to obtain a good statement. An experienced polygrapher can often question a suspect into a corner. Over the years, I've come to feel there's something about being hooked up to a bunch of wires you believe are revealing your innermost secrets to the examiner that helps one to unload pent-up guilt. However, there have been both inaccurate conclusions and valuable statements obtained during polygraph examinations, statements that are inculpatory or at least lock the suspect into one version of events or exclude him or her from suspicion.

Ron Roberts called Mark in Utah. "We plan to be back in your area tomorrow. Would you be willing to take the polygraph then?"

Mark's answer was an emphatic no. It seemed that, he'd had a change of heart. He said he would be willing to do another interview, but he would not take a polygraph, alleging he had heard too many horror stories about them. Mark also told Ron, "I think that the sheriff's investigators are ganging up on my family. I found out they have been talking to my girlfriend and my daughter. You guys came to Utah and ganged up on me and I am hearing all sorts of stories about accusations that are being made."

Ron assured Mark that the investigators were just trying to clear his name so that they could move onto other areas.

Mark replied, "I understand that, but I still don't want to take a polygraph test." This, of course, made the two Rons more suspicious about Mark, whereas they had previously found him to be believable.

The following day the Rons traveled back to Utah and met Mark at his apartment at 12:30 P.M. They had both decided they needed to know more about Mark's story and they felt that asking him again about the items he'd reported missing would give them the opportunity. The Rons brought along their polygrapher, Lieutenant John Hakes, and arranged to use a polygraph machine at the Sheriff's Department in Layton, Utah, just in case they were able to talk Mark into changing his mind.

Roberts began the questioning. "Could you be specific as to where the theft of your property was committed?"

Mark indicated that his campsite was at the head of the Red Creek off the Divide Road and off Brushy Basin Trail in the Uncompahgre National Forest. He said that sometime between the hours of 3:00 P.M. and 7:30 P.M. on October 14, 1995, someone entered his unsecured wall tent and removed a Remington Model 700 Varmint, .308-caliber rifle, along with three knives, a coat and ammunition for the rifle. The total loss was estimated at $1,005.00. Mark reiterated that his girlfriend and his boss were hunting with him and were camped in the same camp. "They left camp after lunch, around 3:00 P.M., and returned after dark. I asked them if they had returned ear-

lier and they said they had not." Mark added that when he went in
the tent he felt something was out of place, but he didn't realize that
anything was missing as it was dark and he had only a lantern to see
by. According to Mark the .308 rifle was stored between two foam
mattresses. He told the investigators he had kept that rifle locked in
his truck, but had brought it into the tent the night before because
he had heard a bear. Mark noted that the ammunition was with the
rifle and it was equipped with a Leupold 3 x 9 variable scope and a
sling. He said two Uncle Henry 3 ½-inch blade knives and a custom
fixed-blade knife were also missing. He said they hunted the following day and that his girlfriend stayed behind on Sunday afternoon
to break down the campsite while he and his boss continued to
hunt. "When we returned, the camp was already broken down and
we drove off the mountain to Grand Junction." His boss stayed
behind to spend one more night at the Rio Rancho motel in Grand
Junction while Mark headed home. "My girlfriend drove her car to
Fort Morgan, Colorado, and I drove my truck to Layton, Utah. It
wasn't until the evening of October 16 that I realized the items were
missing. I called Marcy in Fort Morgan to see if she had them and
she told me that she did not have any of the missing items. The following morning at the work site, I asked my boss if he had the missing stuff and he also said he had none of those items."

After this third interview of Mark Morgan was completed,
Roberts and Finley returned to Colorado and turned in a report
with the details of what was said. There was no doubt that the case
was becoming more and more complex. I kept asking myself as each
new angle surfaced and my own questions grew if my original gut
feelings were going to be proved out.

The search of the crime scene was complete. The one .308
shell casing was the only evidence of a thirty-caliber weapon possibly having been involved. The fact that Mark Morgan claimed to

have had a .308-caliber rifle loaded with this brand of ammunition was of thought provoking. Further discussion of how the various pieces of firearms evidence might fit together would have to wait until the Colorado Bureau of Investigation analysts completed their work. We were especially interested to discover what caliber of bullets had struck and killed Bruce Dodson. A further question was whether that ammunition was consistent with either of the two rifles recovered at the crime scene.

The Sheriff's Department assigned a female investigator to interview Mark Morgan's girlfriend. Christie Blake, a tall, attractive, blond-haired woman with bright blue saucer eyes and a quiet contemplative speech pattern, had been a deputy sheriff for fifteen years. To unknowing outsiders, her insistence on feminine-style dresses instead of uniforms might seem to indicate an emphasis on appearance over professionalism. Even I thought she might be somewhat ditzy, until I took one of her cases to trial. It was a rape/kidnapping trial. She had taken a nine-page statement from the defendant. When it came time for her to testify about it, I expected she would need to refer repeatedly to her written report to refresh her recollection, like most other investigators. I stood at the lectern, half-stunned, as she recited verbatim the entire nine-page statement. I was impressed. The two Rons had spoken with Christie and outlined various areas for her to discuss with Marcy.

Marcy Cleary is a big-boned, good-looking country girl. She comes across as sweet, hard working and honest. We already knew from Janice that Marcy met the Morgan family through their daughter, with whom she was friendly when they all lived close to each other just outside Montrose, Colorado. She is seventeen years younger than Mark Morgan. Janice had told us she was tremendously upset when she learned that her husband was having an affair with her daughter's friend. She hadn't told us, however, what Marcy revealed to Christie Blake. According to Marcy, back before Mark left Janice, but at a time when Janice was beginning to suspect what was going on, Janice and Marcy were out on a horseback ride when Janice told her if she found out anything was going on between her and Mark she'd kill her. Marcy said she was afraid of Janice.

Christie asked Marcy to tell her about the preparation for her and Mark's hunting trip this year. Marcy said, "In January or February 1995, I put in an application for a cow elk license which I received in June. I hunt every year, as does Mark." Marcy commented that it is an important source of meat for them. Marcy and Mark have hunted in the same area on the Uncompahgre Plateau every year since 1992. She described Mark as her common-law husband. "Mark's boss also went hunting with us this year," she told Blake. The weekend of October 7, while Marcy was at her parents' home, she spoke with Mark by phone to arrange some details of the trip. Mark's boss had said he would only be able to hunt Saturday and Sunday and that he would have to return home on Monday. Marcy told Mark she would meet him in Grand Junction on October 11.

Blake gently prodded Marcy. "Tell me what happened after you arrived in Grand Junction."

Marcy nodded. "On October 11, Mark and I spent the night at the Peachtree Inn." She was not sure when Mark had left Utah. He had been on the Uncompahgre Plateau with his brother prior to Marcy's arrival in Grand Junction. On October 12, Marcy and Mark went to Gene Taylor's Sporting Goods where they bought film, deer licenses, ammunition and a gun case. Then they purchased groceries.

Blake leaned toward Marcy. "Could you tell me about the guns you had with you?"

Marcy said they numerous guns. The rifle Marcy was to hunt with was a 7 mm magnum. "I don't know the make or serial number for this gun. To me, a rifle is a rifle." She went on to explain that they also had the .300 Weatherby that Mark usually hunts with.

Marcy believed Mark brought the other rifles because he was afraid of losing the guns if someone broke into his residence during his absence. Marcy also had a .45 Colt revolver with her.

"Marcy, do you know anything about a gun being stolen?"

Marcy nodded. "The night I arrived home, I had messages on my machine from Mark's two brothers and his daughter. They were all looking for Mark." Marcy called his daughter back and she told her Bruce had been shot while hunting on the Uncompahgre and people were trying to find her father. Shortly after she hung up the phone, it rang. It was Mark. He called to ask Marcy if she had his knives. He also asked what rifles she had and they discovered that the .308 was missing. Marcy knew this rifle had been in their tent against a wall. They discussed when it was last seen. She told him the last time she noticed it was October 14 between 1:00 and 2:00 P.M. She told Blake, "When Gary and I returned to camp after dark, Mark asked us if either of us had returned earlier, but we told him we didn't. Gary asked why he was asking and Mark said it was because when he returned to camp he had found the tent flap was open." Marcy went on to explain that she wanted to return to town because she had not been feeling well. Mark brought her back to town the night of October 15. Marcy felt it was possible Mark had not missed the rifle because Marcy had been putting things into the truck and it was not where he'd left it.

Blake then maneuvered the questioning to the subject of Mark's ex-wife. "Did you see Janice at any time during your hunting trip?"

Marcy shook her head. "No, I didn't."

In her soft tone, Blake then asked a more provocative question. "Do you know if Mark saw Janice?"

Marcy said she didn't know for sure, but felt that he did not. "Mark would not have remained in the area if he had seen Janice."

Blake made no comment. After a pause, she asked Marcy to tell her what happened on Saturday, October 14.

According to Marcy, they had gotten up very early, well before sunrise. "Mark woke his boss and me and we all had coffee and I had a granola bar. I told Mark and Gary I would cook eggs when we returned from our morning hunt." Gary dropped Mark and Marcy off. Marcy sat down on a tree stump and relaxed until it was light enough to see. She and Mark hunted for some time, and then headed towards camp. On the way back they caught up with Mark's boss. The three returned to camp together and Marcy fixed them an egg breakfast as promised. "The guys helped me with the dishes and we all stayed around camp for a while. Mark and I went over to his brother and sister-in-law's camp in the late morning." Early in the afternoon Mark and Marcy returned to their camp and grabbed some snacks. Then the three of them each went off hunting in different directions. Mark walked from camp and Marcy and Gary, left in Gary's truck. When she and Gary returned it was after dark and Mark was already back. Because they were so late, Mark asked them if they had gotten an elk. They said no, neither had gotten anything. Then Mark asked them if they had returned to camp earlier and told them about the tent flap. He told Marcy he felt that some things had been moved around. Unable to tell if anything was missing, they decided not to worry too much about it. Then they all sat down and had a dinner of coffee and sandwiches. As they ate, they shared their hunting stories from that afternoon. Mark told them about a big buck he had seen but had not been able to get a shot at because it had been in the brush. "After that, we cleaned up and went to sleep."

"Okay," Blake said quietly. "Can you tell me about your activities on Sunday, October 15, 1995?"

In a stream of consciousness discourse, Marcy rattled on about what she remembered. Mark had a hard time waking her that day, because she did not feel well. Once he roused her, Mark went to wake his boss in his tent and then returned and asked Marcy if she was going to hunt. She said she would. They left camp later that morning than the previous day. Mark was still in camp when Marcy left. By the time Marcy got to where she wanted to be there was enough daylight so that she could see clearly through her scope. She shot a deer and then went back to the truck to wait for Gary, who returned before long. It was still fairly early in the morning. They went back to camp and had eggs and coffee. Marcy was doing dishes and waiting around camp for Mark's brother and sister-in-law, Terence and Carla, to help them get her deer, which she had shot in a low area. "I cut up some vegetables because we planned on making a stew of the fresh deer meat. When everyone arrived at the camp, they decided to take Mark's truck to get the deer, but it had to be unloaded so that everyone could ride in it. Mark's brother followed on his ATV."

Blake thought she seemed nervous and awkward as the rest of the story tumbled out.

Marcy took a deep breath and hurried on. "They went to the spot where I shot the deer and loaded the animal onto Mark's brother's four-wheeler. I was back at camp alone. It was becoming dusky when I saw a white helicopter with a blue stripe fly overhead." A while later, Marcy thought she saw the same helicopter flying back over in the opposite direction. After dark, Marcy saw a strange vehicle pull into their camp. She had not been able to see anything of this vehicle but its lights, but she remembered it came to a halt and backed up in a hurry, spinning its tires as it did so. Marcy felt this hasty retreat may have been made after the car's occupants saw her. A while later, Gary and Mark returned to camp together alone, as the others had returned to their campsites. Marcy had not taken the wooden beds out to the truck yet.

Blake interrupted. "Did you know of anything hidden between the foam mattresses?"

"There was nothing to my knowledge, however I didn't check." Marcy explained to Blake that she did not think it was possible for anything to be hidden there, because she would have felt it poking her when she slept. She continued with her story. "Gary volunteered to take the tent down so Mark could take me to town. We drove to the El Rancho motel. We picked up a couple of sandwiches and brought them to the motel." They turned on the television and watched the news as they sat and ate. There was a story of a hunter being shot, but Marcy didn't pay much attention. On the news the next morning, they both perked up and listened more carefully when they heard that Flight for Life had to fly in to bring the shot hunter's wife out. They became concerned as they discussed the possibility of someone from Terence and Carla Morgan's camp having been shot. They quickly dismissed their fears after deciding that if something had happened they would have been contacted. After they checked out, Marcy and Mark each left for their own homes.

"Did you notice anything you felt was unusual in relation to the hunting trip?" Marcy shook her head and said she noticed nothing out of the ordinary. "Did you notice Mark acting strangely?"

"No, I didn't."

Blake pushed further. "What about the relationship between Mark and Janice?"

"They were friends," Marcy said bluntly.

Blake asked if there had been bad feelings between Mark and Janice.

Marcy shrugged. "It's normal for there to be some bad feelings at the end of a relationship. However, I feel if Janice still had bad feelings, they were toward me."

Blake asked Marcy about the phone call in which Mark's daughter told her of Bruce's death. "His daughter sounded very shook up. She asked, 'Is my daddy there? I really need to talk to him.'" To Marcy, it sounded as if the phone call was an emergency, which scared her. After she was told about the shooting, Marcy asked Mark's daughter where it happened. "She responded, 'On the western slope.'

Then I asked if it had been on the Uncompahgre. His daughter said it had." Remembering the newscast she had heard, Marcy asked if Janice had to be taken to the hospital by the Flight for Life helicopter. Mark's daughter confirmed that Janice had been flown out of the campsite and was currently in the hospital in a suicidal state.

Blake thanked Marcy for answering all her questions. She wrote up a report and turned it in. Investigator Bill Booth made inquiries to verify the information received from Marcy Cleary and found her statements to be credible.

Since nothing conclusive had come from the crime scene investigation and the interviews, we knew the inquiry had to move out along several fronts. While the Colorado Bureau of Investigation was processing the evidence collected to date, I told our detectives to find out all they could about Janice and Bruce...and Mark Morgan. During the next few weeks, a daunting list of necessary follow-ups accrued. We followed every possible lead. Since we knew where Bruce and Janice worked, we sought out information and listened to the gossip about the couple's habits and friends from co-workers.

The first coworker encountered, Lauren Winters, was a close friend of Janice's. Janice and Lauren had lived together before Janice married Bruce. A red-haired, athletically built woman with the sun-tanned look of an outdoorswoman, Lauren has the air of someone who could ride herd over a trail drive and get the job done right. She worked at County Hospital in Delta as a radiology technician. The two Rons interviewed her there.

Roberts asked Lauren about her relationship with the victim, Bruce Dodson. "I have known Bruce for quite a long time. In fact, I knew him longer than Janice had. I introduced the two of them." For a moment Lauren looked off in the distance and then went on. "We were good friends. Bruce was a very nice man."

Roberts nodded sympathetically. "Everyone seems to have that opinion of him. What about the relationship between Dodson and Janice Dodson's ex-husband Mark Morgan?" She told him that Bruce did not trust Mark and was suspicious of him and did not like having him in Janice's house.

Roberts wanted to delve further. "Why didn't Bruce trust Mark? Why was he suspicious of him?" The investigator inquired. According to Lauren, Bruce thought that Mark wasn't honest, based on things Janice had told him about her ex-husband.

Roberts asked Lauren if Janice had gone to Texas to try to get back together with Mark. Lauren looked off in the distance for a moment then nodded. "To a certain degree she did. She said that they had been married for twenty-five years and she wanted to see if there was still a shot." According to Lauren, Janice had told her Bruce did not know that this is what Janice went to Texas to do. Upon her return from Texas, Janice told Lauren she was able to find out some things about Mark that she never really knew before and that was when she decided to forget about Mark and marry Bruce.

Roberts and Finley thanked Lauren Winters for her time. When they returned to my office, I scanned their report and determined that we not only needed to fill in the gaps in Lauren's story, but we needed to revisit her and ask about several areas not yet covered. "Let's send someone new who can get other perspectives." The next day another investigator, James Lange, went to see her. Sometimes getting a new slant helps.

Lange met with Lauren Winters at County Hospital in the X-ray room. At first they went over old turf, the beginning of her relationship with Bruce. As the interview went on, Lauren talked in more depth of the past. Lauren described how she met Bruce in 1990 while working at the hospital. She said Bruce had a lot of women friends at the hospital. Approximately three years before, Janice worked at County Hospital. Lauren said Janice and Bruce dated for approximately six months and then they started living together. Lauren went on, "Approximately two years ago Janice left

Bruce. Bruce was real upset about the situation and about two months later they got back together." Lauren said during the two months Janice and Bruce were apart, Janice went to New Mexico to see an older gentleman. Lauren did not know his name.

Then Lauren spoke of Bruce and Janice after they got married. "Bruce took out a mortgage on a rental house he owned up in Leadville to pay off all of Janice's debts." Lauren had heard that Janice had in excess of $10,000 in credit card debt.

As Lauren continued reminiscing, she seemed more comfortable and let the words flow. "Janice was very adamant she was not going to marry Bruce before she went to a family reunion in Texas to see Mark's side of the family on June nineteenth. When Janice came back from this trip, she told me she wanted to marry Bruce." Lauren also told Lange that after Janice returned from Texas, Mark showed up and spent a night at their house. He slept on the couch. Lauren's face paled as she told the investigator that Janice and Bruce got married approximately three weeks after she returned from Texas. Bruce had wanted a winter wedding but Janice didn't want to wait. Janice claimed there were too many dates already slated within her own family for birthdays and stuff like that in the winter and she wanted to be married as quickly as possible anyway. Lauren told Janice that she thought Bruce might have a drinking problem and suggested that Janice postpone the wedding to find out for sure and to decide if she really wanted to get involved with someone who had such problems. Again, Janice insisted she did not want to wait.

Lauren's voice faltered as she went on and she looked upset. "After the wedding, Janice purchased a half million-dollar insurance policy on Bruce. Janice was quite adamant about getting the will together and getting everything transferred into both their names. She told me she was concerned if anything happened to her, she was worried her children would try to get things from Bruce so this was the reason she had the will changed." Lauren also stated Bruce wanted a prenuptial agreement before they got married. "When Bruce approached Janice about this, she was very upset and told him if he really loved her, he wouldn't want a prenuptial agreement." A wistful look crossed Lauren's face before she continued. "Bruce really did love her and would probably do anything for her."

Lange tried to delve further. "And after the wedding?"

Lauren paused then said, "After the wedding Bruce and Janice sent away for information about burial plots and funeral arrangements. Lauren said they received this information in the mail and had it partly filled out before they went hunting."

According to Lauren, on the Wednesday before Janice and Bruce were to go hunting, Janice went to Grand Junction and bought a hunting knife as a present for Bruce. This would be a three-month anniversary present.

Lange probed further. "What about now? Have you seen Janice?"

"Well, Janice has been staying with me since she got out of the hospital in Grand Junction."

Lange studied his notes then asked, "Has Janice made any long distance phone calls while staying at your home?"

Lauren nodded and said she had. "But she has a long distance calling card and charges calls on that." Then Lauren disclosed a strange conversation in which Janice told her Colorado had a death penalty so maybe she should confess so she could be closer to Bruce.

"Was she depressed?" Lange asked.

Lauren nodded. "Janice was suicidal right after the shooting, and she's definitely depressed now."

Lange ended the interview and turned in his report. The new light Lauren shed on Janice made Ron Finley want to see Lauren again.

At their next meeting, Finley immediately asked Lauren if Bruce Dodson had a drinking problem. Lauren said he did, but never at work. "Only at home did he drink any alcoholic beverages." Finley asked what Bruce drank. "He liked beer, good wines and good scotch." She stated approximately a year before, when things started falling apart between Bruce and Janice, Bruce started drinking heavily. "Then, last February 1995, the two split up for the second time and Janice told me that she was never going to get back together with Bruce." However, Lauren noted that on June 19 Janice went to Texas for a family reunion. Janice came back and got married. She said after she returned from Texas she approached Bruce about his problem and Bruce promised her he would stop drinking, so the two were married.

Lauren said she had spoken to Janice about this since the wedding. Janice told her Bruce was doing much better with keeping his drinking under control and was now starting to look much better. Finley followed up by asking Lauren what she thought about the marriage taking place so soon after Janice stated unequivocally that she was never going to get back together with Bruce.

Lauren told him, "Gail Warner and I were close friends with Janice, and both of us thought that neither of the two was ready for marriage."

This new information caught Finley's attention. He immediately asked her why. She said one reason was that Janice dated many guys after she had broken up with Bruce in February.

"What guys are you referring to?" Finley asked.

"There was an older gentleman by the name of Ted," Lauren said, explaining that she didn't know the man's last name. She did know that he was from Albuquerque, New Mexico. She said that when Janice left Bruce in February she went to Albuquerque and stayed with this Ted for several weeks. According to Lauren, when Janice came back, she said that Ted was very nice, had lots of money and bought her some expensive clothing. Lauren said that three days before the wedding, Ted was in Montrose and called Janice. Janice drove to Montrose to have dinner with Ted and wound up spending the night with him. Lauren said that the next day Ted called her house looking for Janice. In the course of her conversation with him, he told her that he couldn't understand how Janice could marry someone when she had just slept with him last night. When Janice returned, Lauren confronted her about spending the night with a man three days before her wedding with Bruce. Janice replied that they were just talking cordially and it was late, so she spent the night on Ted's sofa.

Finley raised an eyebrow but continued his questions. "Were there other reasons why you didn't think Janice was ready to marry Bruce?"

Frowning, Lauren said Janice had a lot of boyfriends. "She was flirty and suggestive with men when she danced." Then she added that Janice had strange ideas about inviting other men to the wedding and had even asked her ex-boyfriend, Skip Kay, to be in the wedding. Lauren said Bruce did not like this, but didn't say anything to Janice about it. "Even after the wedding, Janice kept a framed photo of Skip Kay in her and Bruce's home."

Finley noted her revealing remarks and changed the subject. "What do you know about the financial affairs of Janice and Bruce Dodson?"

"I know that Bruce owned a rental home that was free and clear." She said that after the wedding, Bruce took out a $15,000 mortgage on that home to pay off Janice's credit card debt. Janice was supposed to pay off that note, which was a $300.00 monthly payment. "Bruce also owned the home in Cedaredge where they lived," Lauren explained. Finley leaned toward her to encourage her to go on and she did. "Well, Bruce and Janice planned to take out mortgage insurance on that home. The paperwork only arrived on October 23, so they obviously never got the chance to complete it." She commented that Bruce was tight with his money and had some money in CDs. She also reported that an attorney in Cedaredge prepared a will for them.

"Is there any other information you can give me?" Finley asked. Coloring, Lauren said there was one thing in particular that really bothered her.

"Janice lived with me from February until she got married in July. I like to get up early to jog or ride horses. When Janice went along with me, I always had to drag her out of bed. I heard Janice say that on the morning of the shooting she got up early, fixed coffee for Bruce and left to go hunting while Bruce was still in bed asleep. That would be very uncharacteristic of Janice." She bit her lip pensively.

"Have you reached any opinion on Bruce's death?" Finley asked softly.

Lauren's nervousness visibly increased, but she seemed to want to get her feelings out. "I think Janice did it or was involved in it with Mark Morgan."

Finley said nothing to confirm or deny her suspicions and commented, "I would like to speak with Janice about this case. What mental and physical state is she in now that the funeral is over?"

"Janice had to be helped into the funeral home, escorted by two people, because she was so weak and in shock, but after the funeral she walked out by herself without any problems."

When Finley turned in his telling report, we spoke about Lauren Winters' revelations. I knew the investigation needed to shift into high gear. However, that same day an acquaintance of Lauren Winters' called with a different view of the case. After her call, Finley wrote yet another report, one that raised further questions about who was telling the truth.

"Babs Roland called today giving me information concerning the Dodson homicide case. Roland said she is a long-time acquaintance of Lauren Winters, Lauren Winters' ex-husband, Judd, and Janice and Bruce Dodson. She said she heard several things from the media coverage of Bruce's murder that caused her concern and she felt she must call me and share those concerns. She stated that Lauren Winters has had some mental problems, uses medication heavily and was accused by Judd Winters of having a lesbian relationship with Janice Morgan Dodson. She told me Lauren had been spending Judd's money after they split and said she would be locked up in jail for two years if she didn't get the money back before the divorce was final. She indicated the divorce date finalization was drawing near. Roland told me that Lauren called Judd Winters three days ago and said that she would have the money for him when he got back from his hunting trip in Alaska. She said it was thousands of dollars and there was no way Lauren could get that much money.

"I asked Babs Roland what she knew about Janice and Bruce Dodson. She said she knows Janice has a reputation of having men around a lot. She told me that two weeks ago Janice called a friend of hers and told him she wanted to sell a horse, because things were not working out between her and Bruce. She told me that this friend was at the wedding reception for Janice and Bruce and saw a man walk up to Janice while she was still in her wedding dress and place his hand on her butt. Roland stated her friend told her Janice slid his hand away and looked around to see if anyone saw what happened. I asked if there was any other information she had. She said Judd Winters told her that Janice, who was supposed to have been heavily sedated, had immediately called Lauren from the hospital after she was airlifted on the day of the murder. He *also told her that when Janice moved in with Lauren they slept in the same bed."*

The case was becoming even more bizarre. Next we sent Christie Blake to see Lauren in order to sift out more of the real facts and because getting a woman's view of these prospective character witnesses would be very helpful.

When she sat down to interview Lauren, Christie immediately brought up the fact that Lauren and her husband separated shortly before Janice moved in with Lauren and that Lauren's ex-husband was telling people that Lauren left him for Janice.

Lauren responded, "When Judd, my ex-husband, is angry he can tell despicable lies." Lauren denied that she left Judd for Janice. Lauren admitted that she has a friend in Denver who is gay. "I've been to gay bars with this friend, but I am not gay."

Lauren also told Blake about a time in September when she, another friend and Janice had plans to go horseback riding. "Janice canceled this engagement saying that she needed some time to herself and was going to go grouse hunting. I felt it was uncharacteristic for Janice to go off by herself like that."

Blake asked, "Did Janice discuss her trip to Texas during the summer of 1995 with you?"

Lauren told Blake that Janice never mentioned seeing Mark down there, but Lauren assumed she had some contact with him, because it was just a couple of weeks later that she came home and found Mark sleeping on her sofa. Lauren continued, "Janice had frequent phone contact with Mark in the past. When I brought Janice home from the hospital on October 17, Mark called my home. I asked if he wanted to speak with Janice. He said he did not and that I should just tell Janice he was sending his condolences." Lauren felt this was odd, because Mark had always spoken directly to Janice when he called. Mark said he also called because he wanted to hear Lauren's voice and he hoped that when her head got clear, he and

Lauren could get together.

Christie locked eyes with Lauren. "Did Janice mention Mark's girlfriend?"

Lauren shook her head. "Janice only mentioned that the girlfriend had been Mark and Janice's neighbor and Mark had an affair and ran off with her and left Janice with a lot of debt."

Blake asked Lauren to elaborate on what she knew about Janice's friend Ted from Albuquerque. Lauren said, "According to Janice, Ted is very wealthy and Janice has gone places with him as his escort. Ted's a good deal older and owns his own airplane. I don't know what Ted does for a living, but I believe he owns a very successful business or is high up in some big corporation."

"What else can you tell me about Janice's relationship with Ted?"

"Janice said that Ted took her to 'major' parties. Ted bought Janice a lot of new clothes and allowed her to drive fancy cars. She also stayed at Ted's large estate." Lauren told Blake that when Janice is dressed up she is very attractive. "She is also well educated and would have been someone Ted would have been proud to have as his escort."

Blake watched her carefully as Lauren disclosed all this. Then Blake asked, "Do you know why Janice left Ted?"

Lauren replied, "Janice led me to believe that Ted was becoming serious. But I think that Janice didn't want to be seriously involved with Ted due to his age."

It was time to get to the bottom of the comments Ruth Dodson had voiced with regards to Janice's mental state, and see if Lauren felt similarly. Blake chose to pose these queries without letting Lauren know who revealed the information to the police. Blake asked, "Do you know about Janice having previous psychological problems?"

Lauren nodded. "Janice told me she had multiple personalities but that when she was hospitalized in Denver in 1994 the doctors were able to reintegrate Janice's personalities so that now she only has one." Lauren said that after breaking up with Mark, Janice had been in a catatonic state and received psychological treatment in Montrose.

Blake then asked Lauren if she had anything to gain by Bruce's death. Lauren sucked in her breath in shock, tears forming in the corners of her eyes. She shook her head vigorously saying, "The only thing I experienced was the loss of a good friend." Then she became choked up, trying hard to hold back her emotions.

Blake gave the distraught woman some time to compose herself and when she still seemed very upset, Blake decided it was time to end the interview.

= c h a p t e r 1 1 =

A Woman's Perspective

Gail Warner is a beautiful woman. She turns heads now and, without question, turned many more when she was younger. At five-foot seven, with medium length red hair and bright deep green eyes, she is thin and shapely, with a bubbly personality and a lovely, rosy complexion. Janice, Lauren and Gail had been close friends for some time, and when I finally met all of them, I could tell that they probably broke a few hearts along the way. This attractive threesome could take over most venues in rural western Colorado. I felt Bruce, the rather plain man who'd been described to us, did not really fit in with this good-looking, savvy bunch, but we needed to further assess their interactions and feelings.

Once again I felt Investigator Christie Blake could give us some good insight. Blake spoke with Gail in private at her workplace. Blake asked Gail to tell her about Janice and with little prodding, Gail opened right up. Surprisingly, Gail quickly volunteered that she felt Janice might have killed Bruce and the motive was money. "I felt it was unusual that although Janice and Bruce had only been married for three months, Janice had really pushed for financial arrangements to be made. Janice pushed for her and Bruce to have wills prior to taking a trip in September 1995." Gail said that

Janice has a tendency to exaggerate things so she wasn't sure whether to believe it when Janice claimed to have a half million dollar insurance policy on Bruce. Gail's husband, Frank, who worked with Bruce, told her that Bruce joked at work about how he was worth more dead than alive. Unfortunately, the joke became a serious fact.

Blake then asked Gail what she could tell her about Janice's past. "I became acquainted with Bruce through Frank. I met Janice when Janice and Bruce started dating." Since Janice and Gail shared a love of horses, they quickly became friends. She confirmed what we'd heard before, that prior to getting married, Janice and Bruce had lived together. "Janice left Bruce several times. Bruce seemed very depressed whenever Janice left." She also discussed how Janice broke her back in a horse riding accident. This caused them some financial problems. Bruce was tight with money and in Gail's view, this was one of the reasons Janice left him.

"What do you know of Mark's girlfriend, Marcy?" Blake asked.

"Janice had told me that Marcy had often been in Janice's home and that Janice treated her like a younger sister."

Blake then went on to pose another question that lingered in all our minds. "Do you know how Bruce and Mark got along?" Gail did not know.

Gail also said that sometime before the hunting season Janice was missing some rifles and reported them stolen. After Janice reported the rifles stolen, she called her friend Skip Kay to see if she could borrow two rifles for hunting season. Skip asked her why she would want to borrow rifles when she had several nice hunting rifles that were stored at his house. Janice claims she did not remember leaving them at his house, which is why she filed a police report saying they were stolen. Janice had already received an insurance payment for the rifles. Poor Bruce was stuck with explaining this to the insurance agent.

Blake questioned Gail in more detail about Bruce's personality. Gail said he could be sweet and very caring. "I have ridden horses in the past with Bruce but the last time we rode together, he yelled at me the whole time so I quit riding with him." No one had talked about a change in Bruce's usually even temperament before this so Blake made a note to this to bring up this information with the sheriff's department later.

Since she had mentioned Bruce having a temper, Blake asked Gail if she was aware of any domestic violence between Bruce and Janice. "Janice told me that one night prior to her going to live with Lauren, Bruce was intoxicated and came to Janice's bed with a gun and threatened to kill her. Janice asked me what she should do. I asked her if she feared for her life. Janice said at times she did."

Here was an unusually juicy tidbit; Blake bit her lip and went on to another subject we were wondering about. "Has Janice talked about what her life was like when she lived in Texas?"

Gail nodded. "Janice talked a lot about this. She made it sound like she was from a wealthy family and had everything she wanted. Shortly after Janice returned from her trip to Texas in June, she informed me she was going to marry Bruce. I asked Janice why she had suddenly changed her mind, because before she was quite adamant about being through with Bruce. Janice said she had talked with Mark and realized she was no longer in love with him."

"Do you know if Janice tried to reconcile with Mark in Texas?"

Gail shrugged her shoulders uncertainly. "All Janice told me was that she asked Mark why he didn't marry his current girlfriend and Mark told her because he was still in love with Janice."

Blake was still interested in recent changes in the Dodson marriage or any suspicious events. "Have you seen any recent changes in Janice?"

Gail took a deep breath, "Well, after Janice and Bruce were

engaged, Janice acted as if she was very much in love with him." Then, as if an aside, Gail noted that Janice and Bruce had received a brochure for funeral arrangements and they had filled it out prior to the hunting trip. When Janice was staying at Lauren's after being released from the hospital, Janice called Gail and asked her if she would get the brochure from her house and bring it to her. "I went to Bruce and Janice's house and the funeral planner was on the kitchen table. I brought it to Lauren's house and gave it to Janice."

When Blake revealed the content of her last meeting with Gail Warner, I found it very interesting. Gail's negative view of her old friend and her reasons for marrying Bruce Dodson added to my questions about Janice. Though Blake added much to think about, I wanted to be sure we had the right perspective on what Gail had seen and felt and what really occurred. Ron Finley went out to gather information to put the finishing touches on our investigative insights of Janice's friend. This time we also sent Bill Booth, investigator for the Mesa County District Attorney's Office.

Finley now asked Gail if she remembered Janice moving out of Bruce's house before the two were married and before Janice went on a trip to Texas for a family reunion. Gail confirmed that Janice did move out of Bruce's house and that Janice went to Texas for her ex-husband's family reunion. Gail said she and her sister were also going to Texas on their own family visit and they saw Janice at the airport in Grand Junction. Gail said when she spoke to Janice at the airport, Janice said that Bruce had driven her there from Delta. Gail thought this was strange because the two had broken up and Janice had moved out of Bruce's house. When Gail questioned Janice about why Bruce had taken her to the airport seeing as how they had broken up, Janice said, "He's got to be good for something."

As if sensing Gail's confusion over her relationship with Bruce, Janice confided that she moved out because Bruce wanted Janice to pay $250.00 a month to help with expenses. Janice refused to pay the money, because she thought her cleaning the house, cooking for Bruce and washing his clothes were worth that. "If you knew Janice," Gail added wryly, "you knew that she didn't clean, wash or cook." She commented that after Janice moved out she stated that Bruce drank too much. Janice also told her she was going to sue Bruce for palimony, because Bruce had lots of money and Janice had put a lot of work into his place. Gail said that Janice made this comment at around the same time she reported the theft of her guns and told the Delta County Sheriff's Department that Bruce had taken them.

Finley decided to switch gears for a moment. "When did you first meet Bruce?"

"I first met Bruce Dodson and Janice Morgan in 1992 or 1993. My husband worked with Bruce and there was a work-related social function that Bruce attended with Janice. Janice had apparently rented a motel room for Bruce and her to use for the evening. Janice bragged to me that she had brought along a pair of crotchless panties and was excited about the prospect of Bruce undressing her and finding them." Gail said that a year or so after this, Janice made a comment to her about never having had sex with Bruce. "Janice is a good actress and has multiple personalities; she must have forgotten about telling me the crotchless panty story."

Finley asked, "Have you ever had a conversation with Janice about the shooting?"

She replied nonchalantly, "Many times. Janice told me the shooting was a big mistake and the person who shot Bruce will come forward." Janice told Gail that she hired a private investigator to find out who shot Bruce.

It seemed the more Finley and other investigators found out about Janice, the stranger the case became. Next, he asked Gail a question that had run through his mind on several occasions. "Do you think Janice was using Bruce?"

Without hesitation, she nodded and softly said, "Yes." She went on. "Janice is used to having lots of money and wanted Bruce's."

Finley pressed Gail. "Do you know of any insurance companies that have paid off or do you know how Janice is supporting herself? I'm aware that Janice has not worked since the time of the murder."

Gail replied, "When Bruce was killed he had fourteen thousand dollars in his bank account. I know that Janice has sold Bruce's home in Leadville for sixty thousand dollars and she cashed out his retirement account for something like twenty or thirty thousand dollars."

Finley wrote down the figures then asked Gail if Janice ever told her anything about Bruce wanting a prenuptial agreement. "Janice told me that prior to the marriage Bruce wanted her to sign one. She was mad at Bruce for making that suggestion and she told Bruce that she would not marry him if that was the way he felt about her." Janice told Gail she believed that marriage is for a lifetime.

"I had no idea," Gail said, almost in a whisper, "that a lifetime for Bruce would be ninety days of marriage to Janice."

In an effort to follow up and confirm some of Gail's comments, an investigator contacted Gail Warner's sister. She corroborated what Gail had said about the encounter with Janice at the airport in June. She even recalled seeing Bruce drop Janice off and saying "hi" to him. She also said that Gail and Janice sat together on the flight and she remembered the statement Janice made about Bruce: "He's got to be good for something."

chapter 12

Murder We Said

Because we now had a homicide case on our hands, we knew every element of Bruce Dodson's last moments was important. We wanted to learn as much as we could by retracing the paths of Bruce and Janice leading to the Uncompahgre Plateau. Janice had told the investigators that she had been to Freedom Gun Shop in Eckert on the way up to the plateau in order to have some work done on her rifles. She also told them that she and Bruce bought their ammunition at Gibson's, a department store in Montrose. Investigators found the receipt for the ammunition in a brown paper bag in one of the Dodson's vehicles at the hunting camp. As I worked on this case, it became increasingly clear to me how crucial it was to establish the fact that Bruce and Janice brought no additional large caliber ammunition with them, besides the two brand new boxes of ammunition they bought on their way to the campsite.

We asked Ron Roberts to talk to Kyle Koel at his business, Freedom Gun Shop, in Eckert, Colorado. Kyle Koel is tall and thin with a salt and pepper beard. He looks somewhat Lincolnesque. As Ron spoke with him, he came across as an intelligent and honest person, basically a nice man. Kyle has a bachelor's degree and a master's degree in education and was a teacher for twenty years.

Ron Roberts asked him if a woman had come into his shop any time recently to have bore sighting done. He indicated that a woman had indeed come in on Friday, October 13, 1995. He explained that one of them came in around 2:00 P.M. on Friday with a Ruger, model 70, bolt-action .270-caliber rifle with a wood grain stock. He said she told him she was a nurse from Montrose and that her mom lived in Delta County. "She asked me to clean and bore sight the rifle and she wanted some ammunition. I ran a patch and a brush through the rifle, bore sighted it and sold her a box of 150-grain .270-caliber ammunition." A second woman, according to Koel, came in with a man, though they were driving two different vehicles. He said the man came into the store for a moment, then left to go buy some ice and water. "I don't know if this was the husband or boyfriend of the woman. She indicated he would be using a .243 rifle due to the fact that the man had never been big game hunting before. She said it probably didn't matter what rifle he used because he would probably get 'buck fever' and miss." She said they were headed up on the Uncompahgre.

"Did she buy anything?" Roberts asked.

"She had a Ruger, bolt action, model 77, .22-caliber rifle with a variable scope." Koel said she requested him to remove the scope from the .22 and put it onto a military-action Mauser .270-caliber rifle. The woman did not buy ammunition and by the way she talked, she seemed to be an experienced hunter. He also sold her a set of scope rings so that he could change over the scope and he bore sighted the rifle at her request. The rifle described by Koel matched the rifle Janice Dodson was carrying on the Uncompahgre Plateau.

He explained that this woman had paid by check, and said, "You should be able to get copies of the checks from the bank. It's Western Community Bank in Cedaredge."

After speaking with Kyle Koel, Roberts headed straight to

the Western Community Bank in Cedaredge and spoke with the bank manager. He arranged to obtain copies of the checks in the last deposit for Freedom Gun Shop. Later, he faxed me copies of the four checks from this deposit. The bank manager was able to determine from the checks that Janice K. Morgan had written Kyle Koel a check on October 13, 1995 for $35.30. The check was signed "Janice K. Morgan-Dodson."

We also needed to find out more about Janice's ex-husband, Mark, and his girlfriend, Marcy, who, they said coincidently, were hunting on the plateau the same day Bruce died.

Acquaintances of Mark's girlfriend, Marcy Cleary, had previously told Christie Blake that Marcy's closest friend was Bobbi Delray. Christie jumped in her car and drove to Bobbi Delray's home to learn more about Marcy Cleary.

Bobbi described Marcy as being hard working and full of energy. Bobbi said Marcy was protective of herself and those she loves. She said she had never seen Marcy as being a violent person.

Blake then asked Bobbi about Mark. Bobbi described Mark as quiet and mild mannered. "I met him when he was still married to Janice. Marcy has told me that even though they are divorced, Mark still treats Janice very nicely." According to Bobbi, when Marcy started seeing Mark, Marcy had just left her husband and Mark was still with Janice. "Janice is the only one of the three that I have known to be violent. After Janice found out about the affair, she called and threatened Marcy."

Blake leaned forward in her chair. "Do you know why Marcy and Mark would have been hunting in the same immediate area as Janice and her new husband, Bruce?"

"Marcy and Mark always hunted in that area," she replied casually. Then she lowered her voice. "If Marcy had known Janice was in the same area, she would not have gone there."

Bobbi went on to say that Marcy called Bobbi at work on

October 16 to tell her there had been an emergency. "She told me Mark's daughter, Dana, called her and told her about Bruce's death. This seemed to floor Marcy. Marcy actually called me to get a phone number for one of Janice's friends to ask that friend to call Janice on her behalf," Bobbi stopped and smiled. "Marcy is a caring person and wanted to help Janice when Janice needed the help," Bobbi confided.

"Do you know," Blake asked, "if Marcy knew why anyone would want to harm Bruce?"

Bobbi slowly shook her head. "No. Mark and Marcy were happy for Janice when she married Bruce." Blake wrote some final notes on yet another interview that seemed to raise as many questions as it answered.

The conflicting views of Bruce Dodson's wife and my own distrust of her prompted me to get back to the source herself, Janice. We asked her to come in and she complied.

Janice was driven to the sheriff's department by Gail Warner, who stayed with her as we talked to Janice. We hoped from this to get a feel for the background with regard to time factors and the firearms. During it, we listened carefully and watched her body language when Janice insisted, "The only hunting rifles I own are the .270 and the .243 we had with us on the hunting trip, as well as the .22-caliber Ruger rifle that was in the Bronco." When asked about owning a 7 mm rifle, she stated she did not have one. "I did have a 7 mm rifle but it was stolen from my car in Montrose along with a .300 H&H custom rifle and a Thompson Contender."

We questioned Janice about not finding any .270-caliber ammunition in the searches we did of the scene and the vehicles. She stated that there was no .270-caliber ammunition, only 7 mm magnum. According to Janice her husband Bruce told her she could shoot 7 mm magnum ammunition in her .270 rifle to get more power. She went on to say she was out of ammunition prior to this trip so she and Bruce went to Gibson's in Montrose just before the hunting season and bought a box of 7 mm magnums and a box of .243-caliber ammunition. When asked if the 7 mm magnum ammunition was the same that Ron Finley recovered from the hospital after it had been removed from her pockets, she said it was. "Did you use that ammunition in the .270 rifle you were carrying while hunting?"

"Yes," she replied quietly. Then Finley, who had been studying the scene closely, asked Janice how she loaded the rifle prior to entering the field to hunt. Janice explained she loaded the rifle with only one round, stating she inserted it into the magazine, compressed it down, and closed the bolt over the round on an empty chamber. "I only carry one bullet in my rifle magazine. I only fire one round to get my game."

Finley pressed on. "Was this how you hunted Saturday morning, the opening day of the hunting season?"

"Yes."

"Was this how you hunted Saturday afternoon?"

Her voice grew softer. "Yes."

"Was this the way you loaded your rifle for the morning hunt on Sunday?"

Once again she said barely audibly, "Yes."

Finley asked how she unloaded the rifle. She said that she was very safety conscious, always unloading the weapon before entering camp.

Finley prompted her, saying, "Would you explain how you unloaded your rifle?"

Janice sighed then said, "The same way I loaded it, in reverse." Then she added, "I would open the bolt from the closed position, reach into the magazine and remove the live round."

"Had you shot that weapon with this ammunition on this trip or prior to this trip?" She stated she had not. Since we knew she had not hunted in the 1994 season, we prodded her. "Weren't you concerned about the accuracy of a rifle you hadn't shot in several years?"

She nodded, saying she was concerned about accuracy. "So I took both rifles to Freedom Gun Shop in Eckert on the last day before the start of the season." She explained that she had the gunsmith remove a 2 x 7 variable Leupold scope from her .22-caliber Ruger rifle and mount the scope on her .270. At that time she had to purchase a set of rings and mounts to have this task accomplished. She also had the gunsmith bore sight the .270.

"Who accompanied you to the gun shop?"

She assured us that Bruce came with her. "He stayed a short time in the store and then left to have the propane tanks filled. I stayed at the gun shop until the work was completed." According to Janice, she had been on the Uncompahgre "just three or four weeks ago. I was grouse hunting up there." When asked where she went, she answered, "To the same campsite I was at with Bruce." She told us that she was there by herself because she needed some time alone. "It was September 16 or 17. I was just up there one day. I did not spend the night."

Finley wanted to go over the rifle issue again. He asked Janice how she loaded the .270-caliber rifle with the 7 mm magnum round. She explained it the same way she did previously. Then he asked Janice if she knew the 7 mm magnum round would not fire in her .270 weapon, and, not only would it not fire, it would not fit into the chamber. She looked startled. "Yes, it does fit," she insisted.

Finley shook his head. "If the largest bull elk on the mountain had walked in front of you, you could not have shot it. All you had was a pocket full of bullets to throw at it."

At this statement Janice smiled and said, "Bruce told me to carry them." We wondered, since Bruce was not an experienced hunter, why she would take his advice. "I did not question his judgment," she said.

I was sure if there was one thing Ron Finley knew well,

above all else, it was firearms. He had been a life-long hunter, a career law enforcement officer and a competitive sharpshooter. He knew that any hunter worth his or her salt would know you cannot use a 7 mm magnum cartridge in a .270 rifle and later, when he mentioned this to me, I agreed. Although not as experienced as he was, I had a pretty good idea of where he was coming from. A cartridge is the complete shell casing and bullet, loaded with gunpowder, assembled and ready to use. The shell casing or cartridge casing is the brass portion of a cartridge that holds the powder and the primer and into which the bullet is seated. The bullet is the part that goes whizzing out the barrel of the firearm and flies through the air at tremendous speeds. A hunting bullet is composed of a lead core within a copper jacket. The size of the bullet is measured in caliber, which is the diameter measured in the decimal portion of an inch. All modern firearms are clearly marked with the caliber on the barrel. A .50-caliber bullet is half an inch in diameter. The .22-caliber, or twenty-two one hundredths of an inch, is the smallest. A .243 is not much larger, but the shell casing is significantly larger, giving it enough power to fell a deer at hundreds of yards. A .243 is not generally considered powerful enough for elk hunting, as elk are a lot bigger than deer. Mule deer can be over 200 pounds; an elk can be over 600 pounds. Some firearms are measured in millimeters. These calibers originated in Europe.

I began reminiscing, remembering how my Dad brought an 8 mm German Mauser back with him from World War II. I used it as a hunting rifle when I was a teen. A common hunting caliber and equivalent in size to .270-caliber is 7 mm. The bullets may be the same diameter, but the shell casing is not. A magnum round [cartridge] has a larger shell casing and holds more gunpowder. The term "rifle" refers to a long gun with twisted grooves in the barrel, called rifling, that spin the bullet as the force of the exploded gunpowder forces it through the barrel. These grooves leave markings on the bullet that can be used by a forensic firearms expert to determine the type of rifle from which the bullet was fired and sometimes can be detailed enough to identify the exact rifle used, assuming a suspect rifle is available with which to make the comparison.

A forensic expert can also examine a shell casing to determine if it was fired through a specific firearm. This is because the breech face, where the bolt sits against the end of the cartridge, and the firing pin have minute machining striations that can be transferred to the shell casing and to the primer, leaving an individual signature, not unlike a fingerprint. The term "gun" is most properly used to refer to a shotgun or a handgun, but many people call rifles guns. The term "weapon" refers to a firearm designed to kill people, such as a military weapon, although many people use the term "weapon" for all firearms, including those strictly designed for hunting or target shooting. Many rifles use 30-caliber bullets, including the .308 and the .300. There are many more. It is a common hunting caliber with a great variety of different sized shell casings. Thirty-caliber bullets actually measure .308 inches in diameter. A magnum is a cartridge that is larger, because it holds more gunpowder. The chamber of a rifle is the end of the barrel into which one inserts the cartridge to make it ready to fire. The chamber is precisely the size and shape to fit the cartridge. The brass of a cartridge is subjected to tremendous forces when the trigger is pulled, releasing the firing pin into the primer, igniting the gunpowder which explodes, propelling the bullet through the barrel. A larger cartridge, such as a magnum, is simply too big to fit into a smaller chamber. Bore sighting is a procedure where a calibrated device is inserted into the barrel of a rifle. Attached to this device is an extension, to which a small target is attached. The target is viewed through the sights, usually a scope, so that the sights can be adjusted to line up the barrel with the target. A scope is a sighting mechanism with a series of optical glass lenses that enlarges the object viewed and places a cross hair where you want the bullet to hit. It can make something far away look very close.

It is common knowledge among hunters that bore sighting is just enough to get you "on the paper" of a target at 100 yards, a standard distance for sighting-in. Bore sighting is done when a new scope is mounted on a rifle and is no substitute for actually shooting a rifle at a target. A properly sighted-in rifle is accurate enough at two hundred yards to hit something the size of a quarter. With bore sighting alone, there is no guarantee that you would hit a refrigerator at two hundred yards. Two hundred yards is close to the average distance at which one can expect to get a shot at a deer or an elk. It is not uncommon to take a shot at three hundred yards or more. And even a fairly inexperienced hunter would know that you could not use a 7 mm magnum cartridge in a .270 rifle.

"I know Janice is lying about this," Finley said when we were conferring alone. I had to agree with his assessment.

= chapter 13 =

Sleuthing

Over time, several potential areas for follow-up flowed from our intense interviews of Janice's friends and associates. The business of the missing rifles was certainly an important one we wanted to learn more about, the negative remarks about Janice's motivations for marrying Bruce were another and the insurance that had been paid to the widow was possibly the most interesting of all. So we turned to the insurance issue next.

Investigators were able to locate the small agency in Delta where Bruce Dodson bought insurance. The proprietors were a charming older couple named Faith and Alan Kellog. We sent Christie Blake to see them to gain information that might shed more light on the death of Bruce Dodson.

At their meeting, Mr. Kellog told Blake that according to his information, Janice Dodson lived with Bruce for a while prior to their being married. Blake also found out Janice had insured numerous guns with Mr. Kellog through Bruce's homeowner's policy on July 26, 1993. She gave him a list of guns, but he never checked them or the serial numbers to ensure they were accurate. He said, frowning, "I took her word for it."

We had already learned that three days after she insured the guns, Janice reported to the Montrose Police Department that her car, containing three of the guns, was stolen. The stolen guns she reported at that time were a Remington FBR Model XP-100, a Remington Model 700 .300 Weatherby and a Deutsche Waffen-und-Berlin, model 1908 in 7 mm. Each had a scope and a case. She also reported as stolen, besides the car, a variety of contents, such as a screwdriver set, leather-lined gloves and a pair of wool socks.

On March 7, 1995, Janice reported that other guns had been stolen. She reported these as a .357 magnum Smith & Wesson revolver, a Cougar Voere Austria .243-caliber rifle, a FABNAT D'Armés de Guerre Herstal Belgique .270-caliber rifle, as well as two scopes and three gun cases.

On September 17, 1995, after Bruce and Janice were married, Mrs. Kellog received a message on her answering machine from Bruce Dodson. Bruce was requesting that the Kellogs return his call, which Mrs. Kellog did. Mrs. Kellog told Blake, "Bruce seemed to be extremely upset; his voice was trembling and he seemed nervous." Bruce told Mrs. Kellog that the guns Janice had reported stolen on March 7, 1995 had been located. He seemed to be afraid of getting in trouble, because these guns were reported as stolen when they actually were not. He asked Mrs. Kellog what could be done to clear up the matter.

When the Kellogs told Blake that Bruce had been their neighbor for two to three years prior to Bruce and Janice getting a house in Cedaredge, she asked, "What kind of neighbor was he?"

"Bruce tended to spend most of his time indoors and was not extremely sociable, but was never a bother to any of the neighbors," Mr. Kellog replied. Then he returned to the matter of the guns. "On September 19, 1995, we wrote a letter to the Dodsons requesting an updated list of the guns they still owned by October 15, 1995. We received no response," Mr. Kellog said. They felt this was out of character for Bruce, who had previously been so conscientious about their business dealings.

Mrs. Kellog soberly added an aside about the widow. "I wondered how many personalities Janice had."

"Personalities? I'm sorry, ma'am, I don't understand. What do you mean?" Blake asked.

Mrs. Kellog elaborated. "She is one way the first time and another way the next time. One time she would be as nice as could be and the next time she was totally different."

Blake thanked the Kellogs for their time and returned to the office to update me and other investigators on what she'd learned. We got some investigators working on looking into the reported theft of Janice's car in Montrose. They quickly learned she reported a brand-new Chevrolet Lumina stolen from the parking lot of the hospital while she was at work. Her car insurance paid nearly twenty thousand dollars. Later the burned-out hulk of the car was found on the Uncompahgre Plateau. There was no evidence of any guns in the vehicle.

The Delta County Sheriff's Department provided reports from Janice's March 1995 claim. The able Sheriff, Bill Blair, has been around for a long time and knew just about everybody in the county and everything that was going on. He and his department were of great assistance in our investigation.

The first report had been taken during a brief phone call received from Janice on March 8, 1995. In it the officer had noted the descriptions of the firearms, the location and the names of the parties.

Delta County Sheriff's Department
Crime Report ID# 500244.A08
Report date 03-08-95
Offense Description: Theft, class 4 felony

Janice Morgan told me that she put the guns up when she moved into the house in August and she noticed they were missing on 03/07/95. She said that her boyfriend, Bruce Dodson, said he noticed they were gone on 02/24/95. She said she was housesitting for a friend and he thought she took them with her. Janice said the only persons who might have keys were a realtor in Cedaredge and the previous owners. Janice said the two rifles had hard cases and both had Leupold scopes. She said the .357 was in a case.

Another deputy had called Janice back the next day to get additional information. His report added to our perspective on the widow.

Delta County Sheriff's Department
Crime Report ID# 500244.A08
Report date 03-08-95
Offense Description: Theft, class 4 felony

On 03-09-95 I called Janice Morgan. She told me:
a. She works as a Charge Nurse at Memorial Hospital.
b. Lauren Winters works in Radiology at Memorial Hospital.
c. Bruce Dodson works in the lab at County Hospital. Bruce has his degree and is a Medical Technician.
d. She divorced Mark Morgan in early 1992 and moved in with Bruce Dodson 12/95. She had begun dating Bruce in April 1993.
e. She guesses she and Bruce are common law spouses. They have presented themselves as Mr. and Mrs. Dodson.

f. She pays Lauren Winters $200.00 a month for rent. She and Bruce are having problems and are currently separated.

g. She broke her back last summer in an accident while riding her horse.

h. She believes Bruce has her guns.

i. Bruce is having problems with the consumption of alcohol. She has seen him messing around with guns and believes that he may harm himself or her. Bruce has never been married.

j. She looked in Bruce's VW and Ford Bronco for the guns.

k. She did not sell the guns that she reported missing. If she was to sell them she would sell them to Mark Morgan. He has offered to buy them.

I went to the Dodson home and visited with Bruce Dodson. Bruce was cooperative and showed me through the house. He opened closets for me and I did not find the weapons. Bruce told me:

a. He believes Janice has the guns or has left them somewhere and forgot where.

b. He does not have the guns. He has enough of his own.

c. Mark has been to the home. Maybe he has them.

d. Janice has problems remembering some of the things she does. She purchased items on her credit card in Denver and didn't remember doing it. She sometimes forgets.

When I left Bruce's home the dispatcher told me that Mark Morgan was waiting at the office for me.

Mark Morgan told me that he had talked to Janice and Janice told him that I wanted to speak to him. I told Mark I thought he was in Texas and Janice thought he was in Texas. He told me he didn't tell people everything about his activities. Mark verified that Janice owns the guns she reported stolen. Mark gave me permission to search his vehicle, which I declined. He gave me a phone number where I can reach him.

On 03-10-95 I returned to the Dodson home and had contact with Bruce Dodson. Bruce provided written consent to search and let me search the home, outbuildings, vehicles, curtilege and fields. I did not find the missing weapons. Bruce said he guessed he would take a polygraph examination if needed but questioned whether it would work on Janice since she showed a loss of memory.

That was the end of the theft investigation at that time. However, the sheriff later learned that the two rifles that were reported stolen had purportedly been carried by Bruce and Janice Dodson at the time of Bruce's murder, so he had the deputy who'd been involved earlier reopen the investigation as a False Reporting case.

Delta County Sheriff's Department
Crime Report ID# 500244.A08 Follow-up
Report date 02-29-96
Offense Description: Theft, class 4 felony unfounded

On 02-29-96 Janice Morgan Dodson came to the Sheriff's Office to keep an appointment that I had made for 03-01-96. Janice told me she was in the area and she had the insurance papers in her purse so she stopped by. I made copies of the papers and gave her the originals back. During my interview she alleges:

a. When she made the report of the stolen guns in March of 1995 she really believed the guns were stolen. She claims the .357 revolver is still stolen.

b. She does not remember leaving the guns at Skip Kay's house.

c. She dated Skip Kay and knew they were not meant for each other. She has house sat for him.

d. She found out in September that the guns were at Skip's house.

e. Bruce Dodson immediately called the sheriff's office and reported the guns were found.

f. She paid the insurance company back, in two payments, for the insurance claim.

I talked with Janice about her memory loss that Bruce says she has. She told me: "It is not really a memory loss. What it is I can be doing something and not know I am doing it, so I don't remember doing it." She explained this as the situation that existed when she used her credit card in Denver and ran her balance up. She did not know she was doing it while she was doing it.

I told Janice I am looking at this as a false report because: 1) The guns were not stolen; 2) She took the guns and left them at Skip Kay's house; 3) She got the guns back from Skip Kay; 4) She did not report getting the guns back from Skip Kay to the sheriff's office.

Janice was visibly angry with me and told me: 1) I don't take life; 2) I don't give life; 3) I am not a criminal; 4) I know why I was called down here; 5) I am not an idiot.

As part of his investigation into the false reporting, the deputy spoke with Janice's friend, Skip, and had him submit a handwritten statement.

*Janice called me and left a message on my answering machine,
asking to use one of my guns to go hunting. I later called her
back and asked her why she did not want to use one of her own
guns. She told me she did not know the guns were there. She
told me she had reported them stolen to the sheriff's office. I
told her to call them and tell them that I have them and they
could come and get them if they wanted to. She said she had
already got the money from the insurance company. I told her
she could call the insurance company and make arrangements
to pay it back. She told me she would do all that and get back
to me. She called me about one week later. She told me everything was taken care of. She wanted the guns and was going to
come over and get them. I told her I was leaving and would
drop them off at County Hospital where she and Bruce were
having dinner. I did so at about 6:00 that evening. I never saw
the guns again. The guns in question are a .270, custom-made,
no scope, no sights, custom black stock and a .243, Austrian-
made, wood stock, open sights and no scope.*

When the young deputy went to Janice's house to serve her
the summons for False Reporting to an Officer, a misdemeanor in
Colorado, she took her copy, ran into the house and slammed the
door. In fact, she slammed it so hard you could hear items falling off
the walls.

chapter 14

Grave Suspicions

Nothing I had learned through the recent interviews or police reports eased my first impression of the new widow. My suspicions about Janice were gaining momentum. It was time for me to gather more in-depth information from some of the other players. I was surprised when I first met Skip Kay, who Janice had briefly dated. Janice had described him as being handsome. She didn't say he was nearly a decade younger than her. My first impression was that he was extremely nervous. I only spoke to him for a short while and, once again, I thought it was advisable to delve deeper. We sent Christie Blake to speak to Skip at work. She also thought him to be extremely nervous, though she reported later that as the interview progressed he became more relaxed.

Blake asked Skip what he could tell her about Janice. He said that Janice was "different," but he could not explain why. He said she seemed to like him and carried his picture with her. He met Janice about five years before they dated. "She was going through a divorce at the time. I like to provide a shoulder for people to lean on." He helped Janice move and let her store some of her things at his house. Janice stored numerous guns, reloading items, ammunition and furniture at his house. She allowed Skip to use these items until she sold them off bit by bit.

Blake continued questioning Skip. "Do you know anything of Janice having lost some guns?"

Skip told her, "A while ago, Janice left a message on my answering machine that she wanted to borrow a gun to go hunting. I assumed she wanted to pick up one of the guns she had stored at my house." Skip asked her which gun she wanted. He reminded her that he had her .270 and her .243. Janice sounded surprised and said she didn't recall giving these rifles to Skip. Seeming embarrassed, she confessed to him that she had reported them as stolen. She asked what she should do. "I told her she needed to call the sheriff's department and the insurance company to clear up the mistake." Without replying, Janice asked if he also had ammunition for the rifles. He told her she had picked up the ammunition, reloading equipment and returned it to Mark. Janice did not seem to recall doing this either. "I had trouble perceiving Janice didn't know she still had guns at my house," Skip confided to Blake. He went on to explain how he told Janice the .243 had open sights and the .270 had no sights. Janice told Skip that Bruce could not hunt with open sights so she would have to use the .243. Bruce could use the .270, which she could put a scope on.

Blake interrupted. "Does Janice have a 7 mm rifle?"

"Yes, she does," Skip answered.

Blake then asked, "Would Janice know what ammunition to use in which gun?"

Skip nodded in affirmation. "Janice is very knowledgeable about guns."

To see how he would respond, Blake told him that she had heard that Janice had possibly lived with him. "No, that's not true," Skip said firmly. "We had, at times, spent the night together at one of our homes." He added, "Janice seemed to like me a lot and hinted that she wanted our relationship to be more serious. But I didn't."

"Did Janice ever talk of reconciling with Mark Morgan?"

Skip sighed. "Janice claimed Mark wanted to reconcile their marriage, but she told him no."

Blake said quietly, "Well, Janice and Mark recently appeared to be friends."

Skip seemed annoyed and said that when Janice was picking up her rifles, she told him that even though Mark sent her $500 that he owed her from the divorce, it only a small portion of what he owed her.

Blake could not suppress her own smile. "I heard you were in Janice and Bruce's wedding." He reddened, "I was a groomsman. Janice called and asked if I would give her away. I told her I would not. Eventually I agreed to be a groomsman, but only after talking to Bruce about it."

Blake asked Skip about his impression of Bruce.

He said that Bruce seemed to be "different," but Skip never knew Bruce well. "Bruce seemed to be a loner but very nice. I helped Janice move from Bostwick Park to Bruce's home about five years ago." It was at this time that some of Janice's belongings were stored at Skip's residence. Janice told Skip that Bruce had been persistent about being with her and finally convinced her to marry him. "When Janice called me and told me she and Bruce were to be married, I was very surprised. Janice had previously told me she did not want to marry Bruce. Janice told me that Bruce had gone out of his way to make the changes she wanted. I asked Janice if she was in love with Bruce. She replied, 'Yes. I think I always was. I just never opened my eyes before.' I thought this was a lot of hooey because if I am in love, I know it. I wondered if this was just going to be a marriage of convenience."

Blake brought the interview to a close and thanked Skip for his time.

The next morning, Skip left Blake a message relating additional information. She spoke with him by phone a few hours later. Skip said he remembered Janice called him concerning the fateful hunting trip. Skip did not recall Janice having seemed to be so interested in hunting in the past. Blake asked if Skip felt that Bruce wanted to go hunting. Skip said it was his opinion that hunting was strictly Janice's idea. Then he added, "Janice left a message on my answering machine last night stating she wanted to speak with me. I have not yet returned her call." Janice's message was that she could not believe Skip had not called her and complained, "My heart is broken." He said Janice's voice on this message seemed to be okay at the beginning but by the end of this short message, she was sobbing. Skip seemed quite sincere and concerned.

Then we got a surprise. Hank Rogers, a policeman who also was an acquaintance of Skip Kay, reported that he had once been approached by Skip, who seemed to have a weight on his shoulders. At the time, Skip asked Hank to explain the elements of conspiracy. Slightly taken back, Hank said, "You'll have to be more specific as to the charge." Skip continued by telling Hank he had some guns belonging to his girlfriend and he wanted to sell them ASAP. Hank asked if the guns were stolen and Skip replied that they were not stolen; they were from a divorce and his girlfriend needed some money and wanted to sell them fast.

Unaware of the Dodson investigation but uncomfortable at the conversation, Hank relayed it to Ron Finley, who decided to track down Skip Kay and confront him with it. They went to his workplace and asked if he would mind coming with them to the sheriff's department to answer some more questions.

Skip complied, arriving at the sheriff's department offices late that afternoon. Investigators Bill Booth and Ron Finley were waiting. I had hired Bill Booth as an investigator the previous February. The announcement of the opening for an investigator position in the District Attorney's Office drew a lot of interest, including twenty or thirty well-qualified applicants. I already knew Bill when he was a deputy sheriff with the Mesa County Sheriff's Department. He worked for several years as a narcotics officer and I had handled several cases for prosecution where he was one of the main officers involved. I knew Bill to be a smart cop with keen street smarts. He is a fourth generation law enforcement officer. His great-grandfather, George C. Booth, became a police officer in Elizabeth, New Jersey in 1862. Bill's grandfather, Isaac W. Booth, and father, William C. Booth, Sr., were also police officers. All together, the Booths worked more than 120 years in law enforcement. Hiring Bill as an investigator was a decision I have not regretted. He has a powerful interest in seeing that justice is done. We also seem to work well together. We think alike and although I am constantly all over him trying to get him to quit smoking, we have become good friends. Originally from New Jersey, Bill was in the Army during Viet Nam and when he got out, he went to work as a roofer in New Jersey before he, his wife and two children moved out to western Colorado. Bill has seen a lot. With his salt and pepper hair and beard and disarming Irish smile, he looks good in a suit and makes a good witness that juries trust. Juries know when someone is trying to fool them and they know when someone is telling the truth. Bill speaks the truth. He sees through falsehoods and can shed light on the way it really is. I am fortunate that Bill was involved in this investigation. He reported to me on an almost daily basis and we spent many hours discussing the case.

Finley began by asking Skip how he met Janice. Skip recalled that he first met Janice in 1991 or 1992. He said that he and his sister were at a country western bar in Delta, as they both like to dance. Skip danced with Janice that night and that is how they met. He said the two dated for some time, never one on one, but with groups of people. He said they were close friends, not lovers. "Janice once stayed with me for two to four weeks. She had her own bedroom and I had mine."

Finley asked Skip what type of person he thought Janice was. Skip said he had a lot of respect for Janice. He felt she had very high morals. He has never heard her say anything bad about another person and had never seen her lie, cheat or steal. He continued by saying that even though he and she lived together, he never had sex with her. Skip said they had kissed and cuddled and even slept in the same bed, but he never had sex with her. Bill asked him if that was a true statement and he said yes. He said again that she had high morals and that on one occasion he and she were kissing and they both had all their clothes off, but she said she needed more of a commitment from him to continue. Skip said he was not going to make that commitment, so he put his clothes on and went to a softball game. He said he would have had sex with her, but he didn't want the relationship to go further than that.

Finley asked Skip again about the .243 and .270-caliber rifles that were found at the scene of the homicide. "The two rifles were left at my house from the time I helped Janice move five years ago."

"Is the hunting good around Janice and Bruce's house?"

Skip replied, "Yes."

Finley pressed on. "If the hunting was good in their area, why did they go to the Uncompahgre Plateau to hunt?"

Skip shrugged his shoulders indicating he did not know. "Janice wanted to take Bruce hunting and she talked him into going with her."

Booth weighed in. "Skip, do you remember anything Janice may have told you about her background in Texas?"

Skip reiterated one of the stories many others had. "Janice told me both her parents abused her. Janice also mentioned her father had lots of money."

Finley asked Skip what Janice thought of him.

Skip replied, "She liked me a lot. There is a photo of me in her purse and also one in her house." Bill asked Skip if it was true he attended Janice and Bruce's wedding. He said yes.

"Did you grab Janice by the butt at the reception?" Bill asked pointedly.

Skip smiled. "I don't remember grabbing her by the butt, but I did kiss her."

"Did you see anyone grab her?" Bill asked.

"No."

Finley shifted the questions to a new topic. "Do you know a person by the name of Hank Rogers?" Skip nodded and answered yes. "Do you recall speaking with Hank Rogers about the Dodson homicide?" He said he did not. "Well, we spoke with Hank earlier today and he told us of a conversation you two had."

Skip reddened and asked, "What conversation?"

Finley proceeded to tell Skip what Hank had said.

Skip got incensed and his voice rose. "That's a lie. I never had that conversation with Hank Rogers and I don't know why he would say such a thing."

After the interview was completed, Bill and I shared a long laugh when we reviewed the notes and came to the part of Skip's story in which he claimed to have been naked in bed with Janice without having sex. The part about getting up and going to a softball game put him over the top.

The accusations of lies and truths flew back and forth. When the interviews and reports were finalized later, I was sure of only one thing: it was our job to find out which was which.

Other Players

Working diligently to separate truth from lies, we continued to talk to as many friends and foes of Janice and Bruce Dodson as we could. One, Frank Warner, seemed a friendly person. He's tall and nice looking with a good sense of humor and remnants of a Rhode Island accent. He worked with Bruce for over five years. Frank's wife, Gail, is a good friend of Janice. We'd already talked several times to her. However, this was the first chance we'd had to spend any time with Frank. We were interested in finding out his perceptions of Bruce Dodson and Janice.

We sent Christie Blake to speak with him and she found him very willing to share his impressions. "Bruce was a nice man on a personal basis," he began. Frank and Bruce were good friends for the first couple of years they worked together and socialized some outside work. They developed professional differences over the past year to fourteen months and their working relationship suffered. Due to this, Frank broke off their social relationship. Gail maintained a friendly relationship with both Bruce and Janice. Frank said Bruce was preoccupied with money and took advantage of people at work. Bruce would ignore obvious responsibilities at his job and leave things he should have done for others to do. "It wore on me and I had enough. However, there were times when Bruce would reach out and be kind." According to Frank, Bruce seemed to be a different person away from work. Bruce seemed to treat other employees at the hospital better than he treated the laboratory employees.

Frank said that his wife, Gail, is a gregarious type of person. Gail was a matron of honor at Bruce and Janice's wedding. "I chose not to attend, but my wife is still friends with Janice."

Blake asked Frank to tell her about Janice. "I first met Janice when she was a nurse at County Hospital. Janice left County because of an allergic reaction she had to some medicine. Bruce and Janice started dating after Janice quit working there." Then Frank lowered his voice a bit and told Blake he felt Janice had some psychological problems.

Frank also commented, "It was probable that Bruce felt the marriage to Janice was his only chance to be married. Bruce was still single at the age of forty-eight and he was a loner most of his life." He acknowledged that Bruce did seem happier around Janice. Then Frank added that he felt they had an odd relationship because Bruce was so tight with money and Janice had lots of bills. Janice blamed the bills on her divorce. He shook his head. "I felt she had a spending problem. She saw it; she wanted it; she bought it," Frank said. "Bruce was the opposite." Apparently, Bruce took Janice in and was helping her resolve her financial problems. Frank felt Janice "talked a better game than she played."

"What do you mean by that? Can you give me an example?" Blake asked.

"Well," Frank began, "Janice wanted a horse so Bruce bought one for her. The horse bucked her off. They got rid of that horse and got another. She couldn't ride that horse either. Janice claimed she had been brought up riding horses and was an experienced horsewoman." What Frank saw did not substantiate this. He felt Janice seemed to need to feel accepted and accomplished.

Blake asked about Bruce's relationships with women. Frank said that a long time ago Bruce was very close to a woman who died of cancer. "My wife could tell you more about the last six months of Bruce's and Janice's relationship than I could." As of late, Frank had distanced himself from Bruce in order to avoid the bad feelings he had towards him.

"Do you know anyone who would want to harm Bruce?" Blake probed.

"No," Frank said, shaking his head. "Bruce was not a guy who would cause anyone to want to kill him." Frank went on to say that he was suspicious Janice had something to do with Bruce's death but admitted, "I have no facts to substantiate this." He personally knew of no reason anyone would want to harm Bruce.

Blake asked, "How did you learn of Bruce's death?"

"Lauren Winters came to tell me and Gail on October 15 at approximately 10:00 P.M. Lauren was visibly upset at the time."

Blake tried to put the next question gently. "Do you know of any domestic violence in Bruce and Janice's relationship?"

Frank thought for a moment. Then he said, "I do not think Bruce would harm Janice." He went on to explain his reasoning. "Bruce appeared to me to be a very meek person." Then he paused for a moment and appeared to reconsider his earlier words. "I also doubt Janice would harm Bruce. Bruce and Janice were in the hospital during the week of October 8 and were like a couple of kids holding hands."

However, when Blake asked Frank what he knew about Janice's experiences with guns, he said, "Janice told me she was a good shot and had been in shooting competitions."

After thanking Frank, Blake left a few minutes later. She got in her car and drove to County Hospital, Bruce's place of last employment, to interview one of Bruce's co-workers. Dressed in her hospital uniform, petite, raven-haired Sylvia Simmons sat down at a table in the hospital cafeteria across from Christie Blake.

Blake asked her about her relationship with Bruce.

"I have known Bruce since he started working at County Hospital. Bruce did not talk much about his personal life. He seemed to like to keep his personal life separate from his work." Sylvia said that Bruce appeared to be a caring person, who loved his dogs and his horses. "He seemed lonely when he first came to the hospital."

Then Blake asked Sylvia about Janice. Sylvia admitted she did not know Janice well and had not seen much of her since Janice quit working at County Hospital. Sylvia said that during Janice's first marriage, Janice seemed to be a rather serious person. After divorcing her first husband, Sylvia noticed that Janice changed. She started dressing in classy clothing and became more of a socialite. Sylvia also noticed that Janice sometimes did not seem to be a stable person.

Blake changed the subject. "Did you know of any problems that Bruce was having?"

Sylvia said she did not. To Sylvia, Bruce seemed to be on top of his finances. She knew he owned a house in Leadville that he was renting out and he seemed to have savings. Sylvia commented that the last day she saw Bruce at work, which was October 11, Bruce had a big bouquet of balloons with a note attached that said, "I love you." Sylvia assumed Janice had sent them to him.

"Do you know anything about Bruce and Janice's hunting trip?" Blake asked.

She said that on the same day he was showing off the balloons, Bruce told her, "You know, we're going out to get a deer this weekend."

"Bruce seemed to be excited about it, although I never knew him to go hunting before."

Blake thanked Sylvia for meeting with her and left. She spent the next two days in the office filing reports until we sent her out to meet with two other workers at the hospital. Susan Keith and her husband, Brent, added another dimension to our knowledge of the dead man and his wife. Blake's first impression was that Susan seemed a religious, meek and quiet person before beginning her questions.

"Tell me how you know Janice Dodson."

Susan said, "I first met Janice when she started working at County Hospital approximately seven years before. I only knew her as a co-worker at first. Janice left and started working at Memorial Hospital, but then she started dating Bruce, who I did not know before that. I began to see more of Janice after she started coming to the hospital to see Bruce." Susan explained that she would occasionally see both Bruce and Janice socially, but spent more time with Janice and rode horses with her. She felt Janice was "full of energy, bubbly, fun and compassionate."

She was only getting to know Bruce, but had started to like him. Bruce had seemed quiet at work. Susan said once she got to know him, she found he had a sense of humor.

Blake asked if either Bruce or Janice had done anything to indicate they had a premonition something bad was going to happen. Susan thought for quite a while and then said, "Bruce and Janice had their wills made out recently and, on October 13, Janice asked me, 'Will you sing at our funerals?'"

Susan fell silent again. Blake tried to draw her out. Finally, Susan spoke haltingly in a way that made Blake think she was very introverted and found it hard to speak. "Janice made this request in a lighthearted way, but it nevertheless it made me very uneasy. I sang at Bruce and Janice's wedding. On the morning of October nineteenth, Janice called me and asked if I would sing at Bruce's funeral," Susan said sadly.

My impression upon meeting Susan Keith was somewhat

different from the one Christie Blake had formed. I found Ms. Keith to be an attractive woman who was outspoken and assertive in addition to being religious. Perhaps she was meek and quiet with Christie because she felt strange talking to police, but having broken the barrier she was determined that her real convictions be known. Her husband proved to be equally candid when Bill Booth later spoke with him. He told Bill that if Janice did kill Bruce it was not really Janice that did it—it was her other personality. A provocative theory…

Another person we sought out had an entirely different view of the many sides of Janice Dodson. Bill Booth met with Carol Jonas, a nurse at County Hospital, who knew Janice when she was a nurse at the same hospital. She stated she understood that after Janice divorced her first husband, he pretty much "emptied the bank account. Janice said her husband ran off with a neighbor's wife and left her without a penny." Since Janice had no place to stay, Carol offered to let her stay at her house until Janice could get back on her feet. Janice stayed there for six months or so. Carol said Janice's moving in with her was a cover, because she never stayed there.

Booth asked, "Can you explain what you mean by 'a cover'?"

Carol nodded and said, "I'm a respected person in this community and as long as Janice could say she was staying at my house, she was respected. Janice came and went. She stayed with Skip Kay and she stayed with Bruce and others."

Upon further questioning, Carol recalled a time when Janice left Bruce and went to live with a man in Albuquerque, New Mexico. According to Janice this was an older man who was well off and bought Janice several thousand dollars worth of clothing. Carol said she wanted to dress like a model, but most of these new clothes made Janice look like a prostitute. "I believe his first name was Ted. When that situation bottomed out, Janice moved back to Colorado and got back together with Bruce." When Janice came back from

New Mexico, Carol revealed, she was driving a brand new Chevrolet with a turbo charger. "She always had to have the best. She was always over her head in spending."

Carol sighed. "Janice once told me that she was being treated for a multiple personality disorder."

"Do you believe that she really suffered from the disorder?" Booth asked.

Carol replied, "I believe that Janice is an excellent actress who knows enough about psychological disorders from working as a psychiatric nurse to know what to do and to say. She is cunning and calculating and she will lie to get what she wants."

However, yet another co-worker of Janice's saw Janice differently. Merrill Carlin told Christie Blake that she felt Janice did have a personality disorder. "Janice is the most unstable person I have worked with." Merrill went on to say, "My opinion of Janice is that she is highly intelligent but has a borderline disassociative personality disorder."

"Can you give me examples of things about Janice that give you this concern?" Blake asked.

Merrill nodded. "Janice changed the pronunciation of her name so that it would rhyme with Denise, although this is not the way it is spelled." She went on to describe how Janice often became upset when someone did not pronounce her name the way she wanted. Merrill even witnessed Janice telling patients that the traditional pronunciation of "Janice" is what her mother called her when she abused her.

Merrill was concerned that, because Janice was so intelligent, she would be able to come up with a scheme so good that she would get away with the murder. Prior to leaving on the hunting trip, Janice was making such a big deal over going hunting with Bruce that Merrill wondered if Bruce would come back alive. And he hadn't.

Grieving wife, cunning and calculating predator, emotionally disturbed woman—which was the real Janice Dodson? I asked myself.

= chapter 16 =

Friends or Foes?

Just as some people were highly critical of Janice, others were equally supportive.

Since we had heard that Robin and George Strickland were long-time friends of Janice, we wondered what they thought of her.

Christie Blake spoke with Robin Strickland at Robin's home in Nacogdoches, Texas regarding any information she might have that would give us clues as to how Bruce Dodson died. Robin said that to her knowledge, neither she nor her husband George had any contact with Janice since mid-August of 1995. "George is at our hunting cabin on the Uncompahgre Plateau which has no phone, so I can't ask him right now." Robin went on to explain that she and George had had a major falling out with Mark Morgan. "We have not spoken with him since he was unfaithful to Janice." They did not trust Mark. Robin said that as soon as she heard that Bruce had been killed, she suspected Mark. This was due, in part, to what she knew of Mark's history. She was from the same part of East Texas and knew Mark in his younger years. Not only had Mark been in some trouble as a teenager, but he and Janice had four houses and several cars that burned. Although there was suspicion these fires were due to arson, there was never enough proof to charge anyone.

Robin told Blake that during the summer of 1993, she received a long letter from Janice. Janice wrote that Mark apologized to her and wanted to remarry her. Although Janice considered this possibility, she decided it would not work out. Later in the letter, Janice wrote that her car had recently been stolen and burned. In June, Janice spoke to Robin, telling her that when she went to Texas earlier that month, Mark visited her every day and wanted to get back together with her. However, according to Robin, Janice had decided that for the first time she could see Mark for the man he had become and realized she did not want to be with him.

Blake asked, "What is your general opinion of Janice?"

Robin said she felt that Janice was thoughtful and considerate. Then she paused, seeming to reconsider her answer, and said, "I am a strong Christian and Janice would not have wanted to show any bad side around me."

We felt Blake should speak to Robin's husband as well, so she went out to his cabin on the Uncompahgre Plateau to talk about any background information he had on Mark and Janice and any revelations he might have concerning the death of Bruce Dodson.

George opened the cabin door and asked Blake to sit down. She came right to the point of her visit.

"What can you tell me about Janice Dodson?"

George sat down across from Blake and said, "I met her when I built her parents' home. Janice was approximately fourteen years old." He explained that at that point Janice's mother and father lived in Chireno, Texas. They were divorced, but lived in the same home up until Janice's father died. According to George, Janice's dad had worked in a steel yard, loading and unloading, and her parents were not wealthy as Janice always claimed. "The house I built for them was on an FHA loan (meaning they had little money) and was about 1250 square feet. It cost them $10,000 when I built it and is now worth about $50,000."

Bruce and Janice Dodson on their wedding day, July 15, 1995, only ninety days before the murder.

One of the first photographs taken at the scene, showing the fence post with a bullet hole and the covered body of John Bruce Dodson.

The crime scene. Flags in the fore-ground mark the location of evidence..

Sighting through the bullet hole in the fencepost indicated a likely position for the sniper in the oak bush.

All photos courtesy of Mesa County Sheriff's Department

There, hidden in the leaves, was a shiny new .308-caliber shell casing.

Investigator Bill Booth standing in the position where Bruce Dodson was estimated to be at the time the first shot was fired. The string runs along his back reconstructing the approximate trajectory of the bullet.

Pictured right, the Nosler Partition bullet.

Pictured left, a First Federal Bank Insurance credit life insurance form dated less than two months before the murder.

Photo by Frank J. Daniels

All photos, except as noted, courtesy of Mesa County Sheriff's Department

The search for the murder weapon led investigators to a pond near Mark Morgan's hunting camp. Here, a CBI agent helps Investigator Bill Booth out of the mud.

The author with *ABC News Primetime*'s Chris Cuomo.

From left, Investigators Dave Martinez and Bill Booth, the author, and Chris Cuomo.

"So," Blake asked, "the story of Janice's father owning an airplane is untrue?"

George chuckled. "Her father never had an airplane; he drove a Chevy pickup."

Blake could tell George was a straight shooter who didn't mince words. When Blake asked George about Mark Morgan, she expected to hear some interesting opinions as well.

"Mark is not a man to be trusted," George said firmly. George further stated that he felt it was possible Mark could be capable of killing someone. But then, to Blake's surprise, George also disclosed that he felt Janice could also be capable of killing someone. According to George, Janice was a person who knew how to avoid responsibility. "She can be very convincing to others. She will shun responsibility by acting as if she is unable to accept it. I have known both Janice and Mark for a long time and feel they are both strange." George certainly didn't mince words. He added that he did not feel Mark would ever admit to having been involved in Bruce's death and he believed Janice knew Bruce was going to be shot before it happened.

George recalled that Janice and Mark lived in various places in Texas including San Augustine, Chireno, Lufkin and Redland. Furthermore, he remembered they always had a lot of trouble with fire. Almost every residence in which they lived had burned.

In his opinion, Mark and Janice were still close. George made it clear he had no animosity toward either Mark or Janice and that neither had ever treated him badly. He just felt he had to tell the police what he really thought. "This is just my honest opinion."

It was an opinion we took seriously.

On the other hand, we also learned that Janice's friend, Alicia, considered Janice a good friend and a fine person.

At first, when Christie Blake tried to contact her, Alicia had refused to return her phone calls. When Blake did finally talk to her,

Alicia confided that she had not wanted to speak with the detective because Janice was her friend. Finally, however, she reluctantly agreed.

Alicia told Blake, "I've known Janice since we worked together at County Hospital." Alicia went on to say she did not feel Janice would have shot Bruce. In her opinion, Janice had seemed to love Bruce and had a good job so she would not have needed financial gain from Bruce's death. Alicia had always felt Janice was kind and considerate, although she admitted that Janice could use people.

Janice's plans to marry Bruce came as a surprise to Alicia, she said, despite the fact that Janice lived with Alicia in May of 1995. At the time, Janice was separated from Bruce and was considering suing him for common-law property. However, Janice claimed to Alicia that her relationship with Bruce had never been intimate. Alicia had a lot of reservations about the relationship, but said her concerns about Janice marrying Bruce were laid to rest when she visited with Janice and Bruce shortly after their honeymoon. When Alicia saw them together, Janice and Bruce seemed very happy.

"What do you know of the hunting trip that Janice and Bruce took recently?" Blake asked.

"Janice had just returned from a grouse hunting trip. Bruce had commented afterward that he was not a hunter, that Janice was the one who hunted." Alicia felt that Bruce was going hunting with Janice just because this was something Janice wanted him to do.

When Blake asked about Mark Morgan, Alicia frowned. She said she knew and did not like Mark. In fact, Alicia though it was strange that Janice never hated Mark even though he had stripped her of her dignity when he left her for Marcy.

"Are Janice and Mark still close?" Blake asked.

"I don't know how close they've remained. As recently as late May, Janice talked about getting back together with him," Alicia replied, shaking her head.

Blake and Alicia discussed motives and why anyone would want to kill Bruce. Alicia told Blake that Janice would not need the money since she was from a wealthy family. On the other hand, Alicia felt Mark was capable of killing someone and felt it was unusual that Mark was hunting so close to Janice and Bruce. Alicia confessed that she had never found Bruce to be a likeable person, but knew of no enemies he may have had.

When Blake asked if Alicia could think of anything else important, Alicia thought for a moment then brought up the subject of Janice's emotional instability. "I don't believe, however, that Janice has multiple personalities," she added definitively.

And so more reports were added to our bulging files. We read and reread them as we tried to factor in all the diverse opinions of the charismatic woman who had been with Bruce Dodson on the day he died. And each time we thought we'd sorted out the real truth from opinion, another view or question came to light that we had to investigate.

On October 24, one of Bruce's former co-workers, Terri Connors, called to share her thoughts on the dead man, saying she had known Bruce for almost seven years.

I wanted to learn more so I took the phone call. Terri told me she and Bruce were good friends at work. Terri related that about one month after Bruce married Janice, Terri went outside for a cigarette break and Bruce joined her. Bruce did not smoke; he was just keeping her company. Terri noted that Bruce was usually a private person who only talked about himself if he was very happy or upset. On this day, Bruce initiated a conversation with Terri about Janice's ex-husband, Mark, being back in the picture. Janice apparently owned a motorcycle that was worth in the area of $5,000. She had a buyer in Grand Junction for it and Mark offered to deliver it for her. When she took him up on the offer, Mark just took the motorcycle and did not deliver it to anyone. Bruce told Terri that Janice did not seem too upset over the situation and did nothing about it. Seeming irritated, Bruce then added that Janice treated Mark like a long lost friend. She always seemed to be glad to see him.

"Did you have any other conversations like this one with Bruce?" I asked.

Terri recalled a conversation with Bruce where the subject of hunting came up. Bruce told her he did not care to hunt and if he shot anything, it was with a camera. Ironically, Terri said that she last talked with Bruce on October 3, the same day O.J. Simpson was acquitted. In discussing the famous case, Terri made the comment to Bruce that O.J. was not the only criminal to have gotten off the hook. Bruce agreed and said that in his opinion Mark was one as well.

"What, if anything, do you know about Mark Morgan?"

Terri said she had little firsthand knowledge of the man. "I only met him once."

"What about Janice?"

Terri had worked with Janice and they had gotten along okay. At one time Terri was Janice's supervisor. "One night Janice told me a story about how her parents were wealthy and had given her anything she wanted." Also, Janice told Terri that her father was cruel and she hated her mother because she did nothing about it. Another strange incident that Terri reported occurred when Janice learned of her grandmother's death. "She started screaming and then became catatonic. She had to be put on medication." Janice was living with Bruce at the time and Bruce was present for this episode. When Terri asked Bruce about what happened, Bruce replied, "You don't want to see the movie when it comes out." Bruce seemed embarrassed by the whole situation. Terri did not believe Bruce drank, smoked cigarettes or marijuana or did anything like that. "Bruce was always giving me a hard time about smoking. He seemed to live a clean life."

Unsure what to make of Janice's stories or the strange incidences, Terri felt that Janice was "different."

"In what way was she 'different'?"

Terri sighed then said that Janice could be manipulative.

"Do you feel that Janice could harm Bruce?"

Terri paused a few moments then said softly, "If there was money involved, I would have my concerns."

As Terri collected her final thoughts, she disclosed that she last saw Janice on October 3 at dinnertime, when Janice showed up at the hospital. Bruce and Janice sat at a rear table in the cafeteria. "Janice was fawning over Bruce like a high school girl would." Terri noticed Janice kept scanning the cafeteria to see if others were watching the affectionate display.

Was it, as we thought, a pretense for what she planned next or was there a possibility this was merely normal behavior for an extroverted woman in love? We were pretty sure we knew the answer, but as we knew a future jury would have to be absolutely certain, we pressed on.

= chapter 17 =

Detecting Lies

Approximately three months later, on Tuesday, January 16, 1996, at around 9:00 A.M., Ron Finley received a phone call from the woman who provoked so much controversy. Janice Dodson said she wanted to meet with Finley in reference to some property the Mesa County Sheriff's Department had that belonged to her. She wanted to take possession of it. Janice indicated she would be in town at 1:00 P.M. and requested that he meet with her at that time. Finley told her that would be fine with him.

At 1:05 P.M., Janice Dodson arrived with her friend, Susan Keith. When she came to Finley's office, she requested the film that was in a camera the police had confiscated from her VW Van the day of her husband's death. Finley thanked Janice for coming in. "I've been trying for some time to get in touch with you."

She indicated that she had been out of town for the past three weeks and had called as soon as she returned. "I would like to have the film from my camera," she reiterated. "It is very personal to me and my deceased husband." She stated that if they would develop the film and give her the negatives she would be happy with that arrangement. Finley told her the police would do that.

Finley leaned over. "I'd like to speak with you in private, without your friend being present."

"Susan is like a sister to me," Janice replied. "There is nothing you need to say to me that Susan can't hear."

"Well," Finley said, "The subject matter will be of a personal nature and it would be better if just you and I could talk."

Christie Blake walked into the office and, upon seeing Finley, Janice and Susan Keith, approached the group. "I need to speak with you, Mrs. Keith," Blake said.

Susan agreed saying, "It would probably be better if Detective Finley spoke with Janice privately anyway." She and Investigator Blake left Finley's office to talk in a private room.

Finley asked Janice to sit down and paused a moment before starting. "There are several questions I still need to ask you to clarify some of the things you've told us," he explained.

Janice paled and put her hand up to her face. Finley could see her hand was shaking. She seemed embarrassed or scared or both. "I can't recall some of our prior interviews," Janice said in a quivering voice. "I was too upset over my husband's death." Finley hesitated a moment to let her compose herself, but before he could ask her any questions, she asked him one first.

"Have you seen my insurance policies?"

"No, I haven't," Finley said looking right in Janice's eyes. "I wasn't sure you had any policies."

She stammered, "Yes, I do have insurance policies. I have several at work and private insurance and Bruce had some investments." Nervously, she added, "But if you would look at the insurance policies, you would see that I didn't have to marry him to get the dividends." She explained that she was the named beneficiary before she married Bruce. "I did not have to marry Bruce to get the money," she said adamantly.

All this was interesting, but Finley needed to get to get down to his main reason for contacting her again. Finley had a request to make of Janice. "We can't yet rule you out as a suspect and it would be really helpful to the investigation if you would submit to a polygraph examination."

Janice immediately responded, "Yes, I will. What type of questions will you need to ask that you have not already asked?" Finley told her they would need some more details about the hunting trip and the day of her husband's death.

She nodded but said nothing for a few moments. Finley waited tensely. Gradually, her words came. "I'm the hunter in the family, not him. I was going hunting and really didn't want him to go, but he told me he wanted to go, because he wanted to get a bigger deer than the big one I shot some years back."

Finley nodded then told her gently that she needn't go into the details now. He knew she'd have plenty of time to tell her story to the polygraph examiner. He arranged for her to return the following day to take the polygraph.

The next day, Janice arrived sometime after 10:00 A.M. and met with Finley. He took her into the room where the polygraph examination would be done. She met John Hakes, the polygraph examiner, who hooked her up to the machine and began asking her questions. Nearly nine grueling hours later, Hakes finished administering the examination. He immediately wrote up a report and submitted it to me. His findings were quite interesting.

POLYGRAPH EXAMINATION REPORT
Subject: Janice Morgan Dodson
Date: January 17, 1996
Issue: Homicide

Examiner: John Hakes
Start time: 11:00 A.M.
End time: 7:45 P.M.

On January 17, 1996, I administered a polygraph examination to Janice Dodson concerning whether or not she was involved in causing the death of her husband, Bruce Dodson, on October 15, 1995 during a hunting trip.

After Mrs. Dodson signed a polygraph release form, I explained that I would not ask her any questions we had not reviewed and agreed upon prior to the instrumentation phase of the process. I told her she could ask questions at any time. Mrs. Dodson told me that her health was good and that she had taken her prescribed medication within the past twenty-four hours. She reported she had taken 0.5 mg of Klonopin the night before to help her sleep and half of her prescribed dosage of Prozac at 8:00 A.M. that morning. She told me she had slept more than five hours soundly the previous night.

Pre-Test

Mrs. Dodson told me she wanted to take the polygraph examination, because she wanted to "get to the bottom of this" situation and she "wants this solved." She said, "Bruce was the best thing that ever happened to me." She related that Bruce died on the third month anniversary of their marriage. Mrs. Dodson told me she was an avid hunter and had been hunting ever since she was seven or eight years old. She and her previous husband, Mark Morgan, had hunted every year. However, she had broken her back two years ago and the doctor told her not to go hunting for a while, so she did not hunt again until October 1995.

She told me that Bruce had three degrees and a photographic memory. He had good self-esteem and was self-sufficient. She said Bruce had been an army medic. She also said he had parachuted into places to rescue other personnel.

Mrs. Dodson and Mark Morgan were divorced in 1990 or 1991. She told me Mark had been both physically and mentally abusive during their marriage. Mrs. Dodson told me that Bruce had never been married before and he would have been forty-nine years old next November. To her knowledge, he had never been big game hunting before. When he married Janice, he saw his opportunity to hunt big game since she owned several rifles. She did not want Bruce to go hunting with her. She liked to hunt alone since she could walk up on game easier. Mrs. Dodson had hunted in the same area for many years with her ex-husband and her children. She taught her children gun safety. She said that her family in Texas was wealthy; the smallest family ranch was 6,000 acres. Mrs. Dodson said she grew up with money but no love. "When I found Bruce, money was immaterial; I would have someone to be responsible for me." She said the hospital where Bruce worked provided two years salary as life insurance. Insurance is a fact of life for her: "It is an investment." She said there was no reason for her to kill Bruce since he made her the beneficiary to his

insurance prior to their marriage. Mrs. Dodson said
Bruce was a good cook. She said she would be
changing the oil in a vehicle while he was preparing
dinner.

On October 13, 1995, she and Bruce arrived
at their camp just as it was getting dark. She and
Bruce were going to stay until the following
Wednesday. She noticed there was another camp
close by "to the left and back." She did not see people in the other camp until Sunday. Saturday morning she got out of bed before Bruce. She had told
Bruce where to go and sit to watch for animals.
Bruce left camp Saturday afternoon at about 1:00
P.M. Later he told her he had shot at two deer, but
missed with both shots. Mrs. Dodson had stayed in
camp to read and nap while he was gone. After he
returned to camp, Bruce started to cook dinner and
she went out to hunt before dark. She walked to a
nearby pond. At one point she saw movement in her
peripheral vision and thought it was an animal, so
she brought her gun up, sighted at the movement
and discovered it was a man wearing "camo." She
said there was not a round in the chamber of her
gun. When she saw it was a person, she brought her
gun down. She told me she was a sure shot because
she did not like to watch animals die. She said, "One
shot, they go down—they never move." She told me
she did not shoot an animal and did not shoot at all
this trip. She said Bruce had read an article that said
to use 7 mm magnum ammunition in a .270 rifle to
get extra power. She told me she put the shells in
from the bottom. She said Bruce carried three shells

in his .243 but she didn't know if he had any in his pockets. On Saturday night she was upset at seeing the "camo hunter" and she "coerced" Bruce into wearing an orange hat.

On Sunday morning, while waiting for Bruce to return to camp, she went over and talked with the hunter at the camp next to theirs. At one point, while back at her vehicles waiting, she opened the hood on the Bronco and stood on the bumper to check the engine oil. While standing on the bumper she did not look in Bruce's direction. When she finished she decided to go look for Bruce.

Mrs. Dodson told me the order of events after she returned to camp the first time:

1. She unloaded her rifle using the bottom door dump, removing one shell.
2. She cleaned herself up because of the mud.
3. She got the breakfast stuff out.
4. She took the ice chest out and put it into the Bronco.
5. She put water into the Bronco.
6. Raised the hood on the Bronco—added one quart of oil.
7. While brushing her teeth and holding a cup of water, she went to visit her camp neighbor.

I asked Mrs. Dodson if she had always been faithful to Bruce. She said she had. We had the following exchange:

Hakes: "What about this guy from Texas who lives in Albuquerque? Three days before you were married were you not in a motel room with him?"

Janice: "And Bruce knew about it."

· Hakes: "He knew you were sleeping with this guy three days before you're getting married?"

Janice: "Yes."

Hakes: "And you're telling me that's being faithful to Bruce?"

Janice: "Yes."

Hakes: "How is that being faithful?"

Janice: "We were not married yet."

At one point during the interview, Mrs. Dodson told me that she saw "in a flashback" that Bruce was shot four times in the back.

Relevant Questions — You Phase Test Format

Did you fire the shots that later caused Bruce's death? "No."

Do you know for sure who fired the shots that caused Bruce's death? "No."

Relevant Questions — Exploratory Test

Did you see who fired the shots that caused Bruce's death? "No."

Did you conspire with someone else to cause Bruce's death? "No."

Before the shot was fired that caused Bruce's death, did you know that the shot was going to be fired? "No."

Did you participate in any plan or plot to cause Bruce's death? "No."

After the questions were over and Hakes examined her answers, he explained to Janice that the charts indicated she was attempting deception when she answered the relevant questions during the polygraph examination. Janice adamantly maintained that she was completely innocent and knew nothing about Bruce's death and she had told the truth.

Janice then told Hakes that she was diagnosed as having a multiple personality disorder in 1994. After Bruce was shot she thought about the possibility of a personality switch, but she eventually dismissed that because she believed she would have had flashbacks of her actions. Then, looking more thoughtful, she added, "I didn't have a personality that would harm or kill someone." However, she admitted that when she was in another personality, things would happen that she would not remember later.

Concerned, Hakes asked Janice if there was a possibility that she had a relapse.

Janice replied, "That was one of the reasons I checked myself into a medical facility. I did think about it. I would have killed myself if I had shot Bruce."

When we read the resulting opinion of the examiner: "After a careful analysis of the polygraph charts it is the examiner's professional opinion that deception was indicated to the relevant questions," both Bill Booth and I nodded at the end. We were both aware that this latest indication of Janice Dodson's duplicity, although it could not be admitted in court, was damning. However, because it was inadmissible, we still didn't have enough evidence to charge her with anything. We had to be absolutely sure she, and not someone else, had committed the crime. Soon, though, another intriguing event became known to us. We learned that Janice was already living in Bruce Dodson's house with another man and there were rumors she was talking of marrying him.

Big Powwow

Over the years, I have come to feel that testing of evidence by qualified laboratory technicians is absolutely crucial in a difficult case like this one. Here it was not just one examination that was needed, but rather a long and intertwined string of testing procedures. However, despite these painstaking assessments, it seemed that every time we received a laboratory result it led us to more questions.

Laboratory Agent James Cotter is the forensic firearms and print analyst for the Colorado Bureau of Investigation (CBI) for their division on the Western Slope, which is located in Montrose. I have worked numerous cases with Cotter over the years and have always found his work to be thorough, impeccable and precise. Cotter, a mild-mannered, nice-looking man with a confident demeanor is extremely cautious in providing opinions, as he should be. He was one of the first agents at CBI to examine evidence concerning this case back in October. CBI agents work upon request from local or state law enforcement. In the Dodson case, we called them immediately after the autopsy established that this was a non-accidental homicide. At that time, Cotter examined the various firearms found at the scene of the crime.

Before beginning his work, Agent Cotter asked Laboratory Agent Hank Taube, who was the serology and trace evidence agent at the time, to examine the rifles and the gun case in which Janice had placed the .270 rifle for blood, hairs, fibers and other trace evidence. Taube immediately went to work, but unfortunately his examination turned up nothing significant. There was not the tiniest speck of blood and just a few insignificant hairs and fibers on the gun case and the .270 and nothing at all on the .243. Agent Cotter then conducted a set of examinations and established that the two rifles, the .270 and the .243, were both functioning firearms. Neither revealed latent prints suitable for identification purposes. Each rifle was bolt action and had a capacity of five rounds plus one in the chamber.

On January 24, 1996, Agent Cotter completed his next set of examinations for this case. Again, he found no latent prints suitable for comparison purposes. I find that most people have an unrealistic expectation when it comes to fingerprints. The truth is that a comparable fingerprint is infrequently left behind when an object is handled. I worked for years as a prosecutor before a fingerprint ever made a difference in one of my cases. The metal surfaces of firearms and shell casings are actually good surfaces for retaining decent latent prints, but none were developed in this case.

Agent Cotter is appropriately cautious when stating an expert opinion. He knows that if he is wrong once, every defense attorney in the State of Colorado will find out about it and use it against him every time he testifies in the future. For example, James's stated opinion was that the small piece of copper removed from Bruce's chest is a piece of copper with lead on the surface, not that it is a bullet fragment. It was my job to call it a bullet fragment. It was probably helpful to this opinion that the lead fragment removed from Bruce's left lung was a bullet core that the pathologist located by following the track of a bullet wound. However, it also had the distinctive mushroom shape of a bullet core that has pene-trated a dense object, such as a deer or a human.

Within the agent's notes, was the following note from the laboratory agent who reviewed Agent Cotter's work as a matter of routine for the CBI: "Due to the extremely pointed shape of a rifle bullet, I would expect the entrance hole in the post to be smaller than the diameter of the bullet, especially when considering the pli-ability of wood. The bullet core appears to be of boat-tail design of caliber .25 to .30. The weight of the core is not consistent with a jacketed .22-caliber bullet."

Another CBI agent had the task of testing various items for gunshot residue. What they look for here are elements from the primer compound: lead, barium and antimony. The elements in gunpowder are too common to be of much significance. Primer ele-ments are rarer. Particles from a fired gun form a cloud and con-dense as they land. They may be found resting on skin or embedded in cloth. It is less common to get a positive result when a rifle is used as opposed to a handgun, since more gasses escape the breech of a handgun and may even blow back from the end of the barrel and land on the hands of the shooter. A positive result for the three primer elements in combination indicates that there has been some association with a firearm. A negative result means nothing one way or another. Gunshot residue is extremely fragile and will remain on skin only a few hours on an active person. One washing will get rid of it. We soon learned from the laboratory tests that the results in this case were all negative. No gunshot residue was found on Bruce's hand or face or on any of the clothing items obtained from Bruce or Janice or from their vehicles.

The official armorer for the Mesa County Sheriff's Depart-ment, Sergeant Mike Jones, has been to a number of national firearms training courses and firearms manufacturer's armorer schools. Nick Armand asked Mike to help determine the caliber of the bullet removed from Bruce Dodson's back. Based on his personal observation of the bullet core and his knowledge of its weight and dimensions, Sergeant Jones made inquiring phone calls to four major bullet manufacturers and the three major ammunition manufacturers. Five of the manufacturers refused to provide bullet core weight information based on a claim that this information was a "trade secret." The two manufacturer's representatives who did not refuse to answer the question had similar responses—basically that there were a number of variables to consider, such as bullet deformation and weight loss, but finally said it sounded like the core of a .243-caliber bullet.

Laboratory Agent Simon Starks was assigned to do the hair and fiber analysis in this case. Starks is a forensic expert in areas of discipline including drug identification, arson analysis and trace evidence examination. He has long and incredible experience, having classified hundreds of hairs and fibers. This time he noted that many tiny fibers found at the crime scene came from Bruce's clothing as a result of bullets ripping through cloth with tremendous speed and force. In addition, there was a variety of vegetable material imbedded in Bruce's clothing, an obvious result of spending a few days in the woods and falling bullet-struck to the earth.

Our evidence was tightening up, but we still had a few loose ends to tie together.

In early February, 1996, Ron Finley called me. The sheriff's department investigators working the case wanted a powwow. When he and Nick Armand came over to my office it was clear that Ron's mind was made up. He had decided that Janice shot Bruce using the .243 rifle and that she switched rifles, laying the three shell casings she used next to Bruce. They had worked the case hard for four months and he felt it was unlikely they were going to turn up anything else. He wanted her charged. At our meeting, Armand was pretty quiet, letting Ron do most of the talking.

Bill Booth sat there with me, listening to what they had to

say. We nodded our heads at appropriate times and asked a few questions, such as "What about the .308 shell casing?" "How do you explain Mark's stolen rifle?" "How much of this background information on Janice do you think a judge is going to let the jury hear?" "Don't you think the presence of the ex-husband might be enough to create a reasonable doubt?" After we'd discussed the case a while, I thanked them for coming over. "We need to review what has been done to date before making a decision."

As soon as they left my office, Bill shrugged his shoulders questioningly. I bit my lip, thought for a moment and said, "There are still too many unanswered questions. I want to be sure that we complete all possible forensic testing. If we go with Ron's theory and a defense expert were to come in and prove that the bullet core that killed Bruce was anything other than a .243, we will lose the case. Moreover, there are too many alternate suspects. We have them coming out of our ears: Mark Morgan, Marcy Cleary, Ted Farly, an unknown hit man, some random maniac. We need more. We have to nail down the hard evidence."

Since we were unsure what Bruce was wearing when he got shot, Bill Booth felt we should call in James Cotter and suggest that he dress a mannequin in Bruce's clothing to establish what he had on. We were particularly interested in looking at the red and blue down vest as well as the orange one found at the crime scene. These two vests were located near Bruce's body. The fact that Bruce may not have been wearing the blaze orange vest was troubling, as all hunters are required to wear blaze orange while hunting and Bruce was known to be safety conscious.

Agent Cotter agreed to do the test and examined both vests. His results were revealing. Cotter found that the blaze orange vest had two holes on the back side that tested positive for the presence of lead. "This would be consistent with the passage of a bullet," he reported. He found corresponding holes in the down-filled vest that also tested positive for the passage of a bullet. Because he found no traces of gunpowder residue, he could make no determination of muzzle-to-garment distance. Gunpowder residue typically carries only a few feet, even with a high-powered rifle.

On August 2, 1996, Agent Cotter completed a more involved set of tests. He retested the sweatshirt that Bruce was wearing when shot, which had been soaked by massive amounts of blood.

He also conducted additional testing on the .270-caliber rifle Janice claimed to have been carrying while hunting and the five 7 mm magnum cartridges she had in her pocket.

Results:

7 mm magnum ammunition will fit in the magazine of the .270 rifle but will not chamber. If an attempt is made to chamber a 7 mm magnum cartridge, distinct markings are left on the cartridge case shoulder. Microscopic examination and comparison disclosed no indication of an attempt to chamber the 7 mm cartridges of exhibit 4 into the chamber of the .270 caliber rifle. 7 mm magnum ammunition can be loaded into the magazine of the .270 rifle through the ejection port (in the open bolt position). They can also be removed in this manner, but with difficulty.

With regard to the gray sweatshirt, the examinations disclosed that there were holes in four areas that were positive for the presence of lead, which would be consistent with the passage of a bullet. The report reads:

Area #1 was approximately in the middle of the back; Area #2, located above area #1, consisted of three elongated holes running horizontal, or parallel to the bottom edge of the shirt; Area #3 was located on the right side, toward the front, under the arm; Area #4 was located in the zipper near the top, while the zipper was engaged.

As described in a previous report, there are two holes present in the back of the blaze orange plastic vest of Exhibit 59. These holes are parallel to the bottom edge of the vest.

Examination of the reversible down-filled vest of Exhibit 58 disclosed two holes in the back on the red side, which correspond to the holes in the blaze orange plastic vest. The blue side of the down-filled vest has two holes, which correspond to the holes of the sweatshirt, previously described as Area #2.

No holes were found in the blaze orange plastic vest or the down-filled vest that correspond to the holes described as Areas #1, #3, or #4 in the gray sweatshirt.

Assuming the holes described are the result of bullets passing through the garments and based on these observations, the following conclusions can be drawn:
1. When the first shot was fired, the blaze orange plastic vest was the outer-most garment.
2. The down-filled vest was the second layer of outer clothing with the red side on the exterior.
3. The gray sweatshirt was the third layer of outer clothing and was zipped up.
4. The remainder of the victim's clothing was underneath the sweatshirt.
5. The first bullet passed through the orange vest into the down vest, into and out of the gray sweatshirt,

leaving what resembles a tear, back through the down vest, the blaze orange vest, and then exiting the clothing.

6.   The clothing underneath the sweatshirt was not damaged.

7.   The passage of bullets through holes previously described as areas #1 and #3, through the gray sweatshirt, did not occur when the victim was wearing the orange vest and the down-filled vest.

The report provided eye-opening information. We were now certain there were three shots. Shortly after receiving these reports, Bill and I got together. Again, Bill was animated. "The first shot missed!" I nodded. The first shot had gone across Bruce's back, through his clothing, and missed his skin by a fraction of an inch. It must have been loud.

"It must have scared the heck out of him. He must have instinctively dropped his rifle, torn off his two vests and screamed," I opined. This would explain the yelling heard by Brent Branchwater. I continued laying out the scene. "As Bruce turned toward the source of the shots, perhaps seeing the shooter, he was shot dead center, right through the zipper of his sweatshirt. The force of this shot would have knocked him to the ground where he was then shot in the back. This third shot must have hit the fencepost first, explaining why the lead core had no copper jacket. It was apparent that if the first shot had been two inches to the left, it would have immediately killed Bruce and I probably would have never seen this case. It would have been chalked up as a hunting accident and Janice would have all her money with no more than a few irrelevant, suspicious detractors she would hardly notice." Booth concurred.

This new information also gave us hope of retrieving conclusive evidence. We had never recovered the first bullet. "It must still be up there. It might be in good enough condition to enable us to identify the caliber and something about the rifle that fired it," I said.

By this point, James Cotter was fired up about the case. In the course of his work as a laboratory agent, an area in which he had worked for twenty-nine years, he worked thousands of boring cases. This one was fascinating and it was clearly a case where his work could play an important role. James volunteered to assist in a new search of the crime scene on the Uncompahgre Plateau. I knew we could use his keen intellect, as well as his experience with metal detectors. The search was set for August 19. Ten months had passed since the murder.

On that day, James Cotter and Ron Finley returned to the scene of John Bruce Dodson's death, along with Bill Booth. They arrived at 9:30 A.M. The men went over the scene inch by inch while Agent Cotter operated a metal detector in the area. He was attempting to locate any bullet projectiles or fragments or any evidence that might be connected to the homicide.

The first thing investigators did was run the metal detector over the vicinity where the body was recovered. They found a few rusted nails and pieces of barbed wire, but nothing connected to the case. Then they took a roll of thin orange plastic string and stretched it from the area where the .308 shell casing was recovered to where the body was found. Bill stood in the general area where he expected Bruce would have been when the first shot was fired, assuming that Bruce had been walking in the direction of the gate in the fence. Since Bill was approximately the same height as Bruce, they ran the string across Bill's back to mimic the route traveled by the bullet that pierced Bruce's blaze orange and down-filled vests. They continued the string past Bill in a straight line to where a bullet would have struck the ground on the upsloping terrain. "After we cut down some sagebrush, Agent Cotter ran his metal detector across the area in a careful and controlled manner." Three hours later Cotter hit pay dirt. He located a bullet projectile that was in a line consistent with a bullet fired at the victim from the suspected shooter's location. The projectile was found under a small clump of sagebrush, lying just beneath the surface in loamy soil. It was collected as evidence. "If we can match the bullet to the bullet fragments found on and in Bruce's body, we might be able to prove what caliber rifle, and perhaps what make of rifle, fired those deadly rounds," Cotter told Booth and Finley.

"With a little more luck," he added, "we might even identify a specific rifle, based on unique characteristics left on this newly discovered bullet as it sped twisting down the rifle barrel."

The next day a frowning Bill Booth met with me at my office. "It sure was hot and dusty up on the Uncompahgre Plateau yesterday," he said.

"That's pretty typical," I offered. I could tell from Bill's unsuccessful attempt to appear noncommittal that they'd found something of interest.

"So, what do you have?" I asked with slight smile.

"You know me too well," he replied, smiling back. He explained what they found. "Cotter will have test results in a few weeks."

I nodded. "Then we'll really know what we've got."

A month later, Agent Cotter completed his examination of the bullet—found to be a .308-inch bullet—recovered on the Uncompahgre Plateau. Bill Booth hurriedly came to the office with the report in hand. I quickly scanned Cotter's report:

Current American rifle cartridges using a .308-inch bullet are:
    .30 M1 carbine
    .30 Remington

.30-30 Winchester
.300 Savage
.300 Winchester magnum
.307 Winchester
.308 Winchester
.30-06 Springfield
.30-40 Craig
.303 Savage
.300 H&H magnum
.308 Norma magnum
.300 Weatherby magnum

This bullet is further described as weighing 175.6 grains, and having six (6) land and groove impressions with a right hand twist. The bullet has an exposed lead base and a soft-point lead nose.

Through a search of the general rifling characteristics file, it was determined that the following rifles may have fired the bullet:
    .30-06-caliber Remington rifle
    .30-30 Win caliber Savage and Stevens
    .300 Savage caliber Remington rifle
    .300 Winchester magnum Remington rifle
    .308 Winchester Remington rifle

This list may not be all-inclusive as other firearms possessing similar characteristics may not be in the general rifling characteristics file.

Looking up, I caught a look I knew well in Booth's eyes.

Cotter's analysis was bringing the case together. It showed the bullet was consistent with a .308-caliber bullet fired through a Remington rifle. This made it consistent with the single shell casing found in the oak clump where it appeared the shooter was positioned. It was also consistent with having been fired through the rifle Mark Morgan reported stolen. If it were indeed a .308-caliber bullet, the same caliber as the shell casing recovered some fifty-five yards from Bruce, in line with the hole in the fence post, the only make rifle that could have fired it was a Remington. This fact ruled out the two rifles recovered at the scene and placed increased scrutiny on the one which still was missing.

We both knew just how important these findings—possibly the missing link—could be. Then, as we moved closer to making a decision on whether or not to arrest Janice Dodson for her husband's murder, a new announcement about Janice came through from our sources. She had married a man named Bart Hall.

chapter 19

Strange Serendipity

Paralleling the creek through the narrow canyon, one veers right at Saddleback Mountain, staying on I-70 rather than taking Route 6 through Clear Creek Canyon. It is fifteen minutes faster this way. Then it's over the hump and down the last stretch toward Denver. Here and there you get glimpses of the Great Plains that start at the edge of the foothills, just a few miles ahead. Usually you also get a glimpse of the brown pollution cloud that frequently engulfs Denver. Up on the right is a place called Lookout Mountain. It features Buffalo Bill's grave and the Mother Cabrini Shrine. Of course, there are a dozen or so other places in the West that are claimed to be the true grave of Buffalo Bill.

Lookout Mountain is substantially higher than Denver and the view is amazing. At night, stars and planets fill the sky above and the lights of civilization stretch out over the plains as far as you can see. Roads from all directions lead into the city. The brightest spot is the downtown section with its many skyscrapers. From this vantage point, it is easy to look at humanity more as a whole. The spread-out streetlights and headlights punctuating the darkness can seem like strands of one entity leading to the bright center of the city. Although one's first impression is a vision of the glistening beauty and splendor human beings have wrought, one also might ponder the vast pollution caused by this entity, how coal, mined in distant places, is brought here to burn in power plants to feed those lights as though we were eating our planet or how oil is sucked from the earth, further polluting the air with gargantuan refineries, just so we can keep pulsing along the strands that connect city to city. However, it is better to keep in mind that people can be good and are capable of greatness. Nevertheless, it is important to remember this other negative view of misdirected human growth having disastrous consequences.

If we bring this case to trial, several witnesses will have to travel over the mountains from Denver to testify. But before that happens, I have to lay firm ground as to motive. The investigators from the sheriff's department and from my office had tracked down all the assets and insurance they could find for John Bruce Dodson. For a business record to get into evidence, the custodian of records for the business must testify to the validity and accuracy of the documents. I called custodians of records from several cities with skyscrapers like Denver's, including Indianapolis, Minneapolis, Chicago, Omaha and Trenton. Keeping track of these records and the current custodians was like trying to herd cats. Over the four plus years from the murder to the trial, these people changed jobs frequently. My paralegal kept busy keeping track of who could verify what information. Mostly, these prospective witnesses were cooperative and understanding. Some even looked forward to an all-expense paid trip to western Colorado. One fellow, however, appeared to be a problem. Tom Fields, the custodian of records for an investment company, said he would not come out to testify. As it turned out, the company he worked for was small and Mr. Fields was the attorney as well as the records custodian. While it would be possible to get this evidence before the jury through other means, the impact of personal testimony is the most certain road to admissibility. So I called Fields at his office in Indianapolis.

After introducing myself, I could already sense his resistance. Attempting to find common ground, I made some small talk about Indiana and told him that my wife was from there. I mentioned her passion for basketball and the fact that her grandfather was inducted into the Indiana Basketball Hall of Fame. As the conversation progressed, it turned out that Tom Fields was an Indiana basketball history buff, lived near the Indiana Basketball Hall of Fame, knew my wife's family, even dated her aunt and met my wife when she was a baby. While they were still dating, Fields was drawn into the tragedy of the death of my wife's mother. Sadly, she had been only twenty-four years old at the time of her death and was the mother of four. Suddenly the reason for his reluctance to come to Colorado came to light. He was concerned that the trip would bring back troubling memories. However, he eventually agreed to make the trip if he was needed.

Early on in the investigation, we had asked our local Internal Revenue Service investigator, Special Agent Clark Banyon, for assistance in tracking down assets of Bruce Dodson and for help in tracking any possible transfers of funds between the parties involved. I knew I would need Clark, a friendly and hard-working fellow with a boyish face and a confident demeanor who also was a snappy dresser, to testify as an expert witness in forensic accounting, so I could present the jury with a summary of Bruce Dodson's assets, or, to put it crudely, how much Bruce was worth dead.

With his help another important element of our case fell into place. The bottom line was about $465,000. That is what Bruce was worth dead to Janice. That would be like winning over a million dollars in a lottery and taking the cash-out option. Bruce had a $50,000 life insurance policy through work as a benefit, at no cost to him. He changed his beneficiary from his sister, Martha, to Janice on November 2, 1993, a year and a half before he married her. Janice filed a claim to collect the money on October 25, 1995. She would have done it sooner, but she was having trouble getting the death certificate. Records from Commercial Life Insurance Company showed that Janice took out a life insurance policy on Bruce, through her employment, on July 19, 1995, a few days after they were married. This one was for $180,000, which was the highest amount allowable through that policy. Records from Continental Casualty Company showed that Janice also took out a $60,000 accidental death policy on Bruce on July 4, 1995. It was one of those junk mail life insurance applications. The claim was received in Chicago on November 5, 1995. This policy would pay only in event of an accident, not for death from an illness, not for murder. When Janice was interviewed by an investigator for Continental Casualty Company on March 26, 1997, she expressed a belief that Bruce's death was an accident. She also informed this investigator that she had remarried on November 24, 1996 in Las Vegas and was living with her new husband in the house she had once shared with Bruce.

In addition to $290,000 in life insurance, Bruce had a credit life insurance policy on a loan he took out after he married Janice in order to pay off her debts. Bill Booth interviewed the loan officer, Bob Rothman, who remembered the transaction. He recalled asking Bruce over the phone if he wanted the credit life insurance. Bruce asked Mr. Rothman to hold on a minute while he discussed it with Janice. A few moments later Bruce got back on the phone and agreed to make the higher payment that would include credit life insurance. A check for $15,000, the amount of the loan, went to Bruce and Janice on August 28, 1995. The credit life insurance paid off the balance of $15,885.42 upon Bruce's death. Bruce had retirement and other banking accounts valued at around $85,000 and, when the equity in his two homes and personal property were added in, the total net worth was right around $465,000 and that was after all expenses related to the closing of his estate by his personal representative, Janice Dodson, were deducted. These expenses of $8,556.94 included the cost of Bruce's funeral.

Now we could prove that Janice withdrew all cash from Bruce's bank accounts on October 23, 1995, eight days after the murder. This came to just over $11,000. Within a few days of that, she withdrew $20,000 in cash from Bruce's IRA account and had the remainder, some $30,000, transferred to an account in her name.

Among the documents presented to me were Janice's Visa account records. On her last monthly statement before marrying Bruce, her balance was $8,817.25. It crept up to $9,291.03 by August. By September, Bruce had it paid down to $26.91. The records also show that Janice added credit life insurance on Bruce to her Visa account on October 10, 1995. This was three days before the hunting trip. I noted that her Visa account balance was back up near her limit of $10,000.00 soon after Bruce's murder.

= chapter 20 =

Searching for the Murder Weapon

The investigation continued into a second year. One by one the investigators assigned to this case left the Sheriff's Department for other places or lifestyle changes: first Nick Armand, then Christie Blake and finally Ron Finley. Bill Booth was the only one left and the Sheriff's Department, occupied with other investigations, turned the case over to my office—a challenge we gladly accepted. Bill and I had been fascinated with the case. We knew all the players.

In February 1997, I added a new investigator to my staff, a fellow named Dave Martinez. Dave had been with the sheriff's department working most recently as a narcotics investigator. He worked with Bill Booth several years earlier when Bill was on the narcotics task force and Bill highly recommended him for the job.Dave was in his late thirties, an ex-military, clean cut, intelligent and honest man who had grown up in the vicinity and had many local contacts. Like us,Dave found the case provoking and immediately immersed himself in the investigation. He and Bill became just about inseparable.

To shore up our case, Bill and Dave re-interviewed every witness with information relevant to the investigation. They made several trips to Texas to search out information and spent days on the Uncompahgre Plateau. One day they came into my office and asked if I would authorize money so that they could make a three-dimensional mock up of the crime scene, including the location of the camps for Janice, Bruce and Brent Branchwater, the site of the shooting, the apparent position of the shooter and the mud bog Janice stepped in. I gave them the okay.

Several days later, they brought their project into the office, having constructed it in Bill's garage. I was impressed. It looked like the platform for a model train set, complete with hills and trees, a fence line, VW camper, Bronco, tents and a tiny body sprawled out on the ground.

By this point of the investigation, we knew that finding the murder weapon would be helpful, if not crucial, to a successful prosecution. Both Bill and Dave were experienced with weapons, having experience with firearms on a personal as well as professional level. Each is a lifelong hunter, and each had substantial expertise in criminal investigations of violent crime involving firearms. Bill set his mind to either finding the murder weapon or reaching a sustainable conclusion as to what it was.

Bill met several times with agent James Cotter to discuss ways to enhance the investigation. It was something of a concern that the bullet core removed from Bruce's back had no copper jacket. We surmised this was the round that hit the fence post. Unfortunately, the nature of ballistics gets complicated when dealing with bullets passing through objects.

In March 1997, Investigator Bill Booth went to Texas once again to speak with Mark Morgan. Mark's statement was consistent with his earlier statements and Bill clarified a few other things as well. The vehicle Mark had used on the hunting trip was a 1965 Chevy pickup he had owned since he was married to Janice. According to him, he always hunted alone. He said in this meeting with Booth that he did not like hunting with Marcy, because she never does what he asks. He told Bill when two people hunt together there is twice the movement and twice the noise. He said it is less frustrating to hunt alone. He said he remembered seeing a white helicopter over Brush Mountain late on Sunday afternoon and when he was back at the motel in Grand Junction, he and Marcy saw a news report about a hunter who was shot and killed on the Uncompahgre. He said it was only when he was back home in Utah that he found out through a phone call from Marcy that the dead hunter was Bruce Dodson.

"Is there any way you can get me the serial number for the stolen .308 rifle?"

Mark replied, "Before I went hunting that year I had pawned the .308 at Jack's Pawn Shop in Nacogdoches, Texas. They would have a record of the serial number."

This new information came as a surprise to Bill, who asked, "Why didn't you tell this to the investigators who first interviewed you in Utah?"

"I didn't like them," Mark replied. He said he especially had a problem with one guy who he said accused him of murdering Bruce. Mark's response was of interest to the investigators, as the initial reports of Mark's first interview had stated that he was pleasant and cooperative.

We added these new findings to our already bulging files. We knew that the Colorado Division of Wildlife records showed that Mark Morgan purchased a small game license, such as would be required for hunting grouse, on September 2, 1995 and a deer license on October 12, 1995.

During one of many follow-up conversations with Mark Morgan, investigators asked him why Division of Wildlife records showed he had purchased a small game license on September 2, 1995. He said he had a three-day weekend for Labor Day, so he drove from Utah to Grand Junction and bought the license at Gene Taylor's Sporting Goods. He said he hunted grouse in the area of Snipe Mountain on the Uncompahgre Plateau. He recalled camping overnight up there that weekend.

On June 20, 1997, Agent Cotter completed another sets of examinations of all the wood fragments collected from the scene and found no evidence of copper jacket material. A comparison of the thickness of the copper jacket material in the copper jacket fragment recovered from Bruce at the autopsy and the copper jackets of the .243-caliber cartridges recovered from the VW Van indicated that the thicknesses were close enough to be considered similar. Bruce's clothing items were examined for portions of bullet jacket with no additional findings. In discussing where the bullet jacket may have gone, we considered the possibility that it may have gone zinging off in some unknown direction or perhaps Janice saw it and disposed of it.

Agent Cotter also compared the hydrocal casts of the boot prints recovered at the scene with the boots that had been worn by Janice and Bruce on the day of the murder. Janice made one of the boot impressions found near the spot where the shooter lay in wait and Bruce made the other. Since this place is within two hundred yards from the camp and since Janice and Bruce had been hunting the area the day before, I did not feel that this evidence was particularly probative. I knew were I to argue that Janice's boot print indicated she was the shooter, I would invite the reply that Bruce must have shot himself since his print was there too.

Bill, Dave and James Cotter still made frequent trips to the Uncompahgre Plateau. They used metal detectors and carefully examined the area around where Bruce's body was found, looking in particular for the missing bullet jacket. They fanned out in all directions in the rough terrain looking for the murder weapon. They went to several ponds within a twenty-minute walk of the murder scene. They searched hundreds if not thousands of thick clumps of oak brush. They even went up on the mountains with boats and special water-submersible metal detectors. On one of the trips, Bill got stuck in the mud up to his waist and Dave had to rescue him. It seemed to me that Bill, at this point, was coming up with a new idea of where the murder weapon might be on a near-daily basis. I went up there with them one day to get a better feel for the terrain and the locations of various points of interest.

One of Bill's theories was that the reason Janice had fresh mud on her boots and jeans was because she stole Mark's rifle on Saturday, killed Bruce first thing Sunday morning, went back over to Mark's camp, and tossed the rifle into the pond in an attempt to set up Mark before returning to her campsite. The crew went back up to the Uncompahgre Plateau to check for the rifle in the pond by Mark's old campsite. While on this outing, they noticed that this particular pond was lined with bentonite. Bentonite is a dense clay material found in sporadic outcrops in western Colorado. Ranchers use it to line stock ponds. It has the effect of sealing the pond to curtail leakage. It is recognizable as bluish-gray clay and looks different from most of the soil up there. Bill and the others carefully set up a grid with ropes to ensure every part of the pond was searched, but after many hours of navigating through the mud, they hadn't found a rifle. Suddenly, Bill, in chest waders, bumped into a long object. His heart began to race. It felt like it could be a rifle. He reached down through the thick, gooey mud and worked the object toward the surface. As it broke through the surface of the pond, Bill was sprayed with mud and fetid molecules. It was the leg of dead cow. Up until that point he though the stench was just indigenous to the mud. When they had recovered from the shock and humor of the incident, they continued their search.

James, who was a good athlete, timed himself walking from

Mark's camp to the murder scene. It took him close to twenty minutes. Because of the bentonite, they decided to collect dirt samples from the edges of the pond by Mark's camp, from the pond just east of the murder scene and from the bog Janice claimed to have stepped in back by her camp. When we returned, the samples were packaged separately and sent along with a sample of the dried mud that had been scraped long ago from Janice's boots and jeans to the Colorado Bureau of Investigation for analysis. They had to send the specimens to the Denver lab as there were no soil comparison experts in the Montrose office.

Laboratory Agent Jacqueline Battles examined the soil samples. Agent Battles has worked in several fields relating to chemistry and laboratory research since receiving her chemistry degree. Her resume is replete with training courses such as *Industrial Use of Polarizing Microscope, Identification of Small Particles, Forensic Microscopy, Forensic Glass Analysis, Chromatographic Methods in Forensic Science* and *Forensic Soil*. This was the first forensic soil case I had worked and it was an education. Agent Battles placed the samples in a mortar and pestle and reduced them to powder. Then she checked the samples for color variations, using a chart known as the Munsell Color Chart, both with and without added water. She also checked for magnetic components and under a microscope for any similar appearing minerals. She then weighed out exactly two grams of each sample and ran them through a series of six progressively finer sieves, weighing the residue left behind at each level. The result of these examinations was the opinion that the soil samples removed from Janice's boots and jeans was "similar" to the soil sample from Mark's pond and "not similar" to the soil samples taken from the other pond and the mud bog.

Bill was pleased after we received this report on the teletype. It supported one of Bill's theories—that Janice stole the rifle from Mark's tent. I kept telling Bill that the defense would surely find their own expert to poke holes in the theory. However, he was convinced it was key evidence. And, in truth, despite the possibility of the theory being disputed, I thought he'd done very good work.

= chapter 21 =

Calling in the FBI

It was time to get some expert input to add to our cache of evidence. In July 1997, Bill Booth and James Cotter sent the bullet core and copper jacket fragment recovered from the autopsy and the box of .243-caliber ammunition recovered from the Bronco to the Federal Bureau of Investigation and requested their assistance. We asked if they could identify the caliber of the murder weapon based on the bullet fragments and if they could compare the .243 bullets with those fragments. Since we were all losing hope that we would recover the murder weapon, we concentrated on finding another answer to the puzzle.

Meanwhile, we discussed many possibilities about the actual weapon used to kill Bruce Dodson. Despite our conviction that Janice was responsible, we also considered other possibilities. For instance, we threw out the idea that if Mark alone or with one or more of his comrades were responsible, he would have had plenty of time to get rid of the rifle. By the time the investigators contacted him he had traveled hundreds of miles and crossed several rivers. However, if Mark were the shooter, why would he have told us about the stolen rifle? The only way we were aware of it was because he told the two Rons about it when they called on him in Utah. And knowing how much Mark loved guns, especially a beautiful firearm like this near-new Remington model 700, heavy barrel .308-caliber rifle, the same rifle used by military snipers, it was close to impossible to imagine him destroying it. Another possibility was that he gave it to Janice to use in the murder and got it back after the shooting and stashed it. If the first shot had killed Bruce, as the plan certainly must have been, the heat would have been off in a few weeks and the rifle would no longer be of interest to the investigators. On the other hand, if Janice alone were the shooter, and she stole the rifle from Mark's camp, where did it go?

Within the time period Captain Branchwater described, Janice would probably have had no more than an hour or so between the murder and returning to camp. That would mean she could have gone away from camp for approximately thirty minutes in any direction, concealed the rifle and returned. In thirty minutes, she could have covered well over a mile. Moreover, since Janice was released from the hospital within a day, she had time to return to the scene to recover it, although that seems unlikely because of the risk of being seen.

We located a place where a culvert ran under the main road within ten minutes from the camp. This would have been a perfect place, and was just one of a near infinite number of possibilities. "The search is like looking for a needle in a haystack," I told my investigators wearily. If someone other than Mark or Janice were responsible for Bruce's murder, whether or not he or she worked in concert with Janice or Mark, the rifle could have gone just about anywhere. Testing the bullet fragments seemed like a long shot, but compared to the odds of actually finding the murder weapon, those odds were looking good.

Shawn Bertram was the FBI firearms expert assigned to the case. He looks just like you would want an FBI expert to look and his intelligence is readily apparent. Special Agent Bertram has a degree in civil engineering and had been an FBI agent assigned to the laboratory for over twenty years. He has testified as an expert witness hundreds of times in firearms cases. He is handsome in a southern-gentleman kind of way and is a quick thinker. I was impressed speaking with him. He was always willing to do some more research to answer my questions. But that was usually not necessary, because he knows firearms well. Agent Bertram seemed genuinely interested in helping us solve the case and was as cooperative as could be about coming out to Colorado to testify if he was needed. He was hoping the trial would be during ski season so he could make a vacation out of it.

The second FBI agent assigned to our case was Nancy Saunders. She is their lead (as in metal) expert. I was delighted when I saw a copy of her résumé and learned she had a degree in metallurgy. As I spoke with her, I learned a lot about lead. Not all bullet lead is the same. Most of the lead used in bullet manufacture comes from recycled car batteries and the lead in car batteries is frequently recycled to begin with. Bullet lead therefore has various trace elements in addition to the lead. By testing for these trace elements, an expert can compare lead from one source with another, looking for similarities and differences. Like Shawn Bertram, Special Agent Saunders made an ideal witness: attractive, sophisticated and sharp as a tack, albeit a bit of an egghead. I felt she would be unflappable in the face of defense questioning. For instance, when I asked her to tell me about her analytical training experience, she replied, "My analytical training and experience include work with inductively coupled plasma-atomic emission spectroscopy, atomic absorption spectroscopy, scanning electron microscopy/energy dispersive x-ray analysis, x-ray fluorescence spectroscopy and neutron activation analysis."

Adding to our knowledge and documentation, Special Agent Bertram examined and wrote a report on the bullet core.

FBI Laboratory
FEDERAL BUREAU OF INVESTIGATION
Washington, D. C. 20535

Report of Examination

Examiner name: Shawn Bertram
Date: September 8, 1997
Unit: Firearms/Toolmarks

Results of Examinations:
The bullet core of Exhibit 25 is the core portion of a
jacketed bullet and is consistent with having originated from a .243-caliber projectile, such as the bullet core of the cartridges in Exhibit 2. The core of
Exhibit 25 bears no microscopic marks of value for
comparison purposes.

The copper fragment of Exhibit 23 bears no rifling
impressions or microscopic marks of value for comparison with a suspect weapon.

Unfortunately, we still needed more. While they had found
the bullet core to be consistent with the .243-caliber bullets, I knew
it would be pointed out by any smart defense attorney that the bullet core would also be consistent with larger bullets, certainly up to
and including any of the many bullets in the .30-caliber range.

Special Agent Saunders examined this bullet evidence after
Shawn Bertram was through. She completed her first report on September 19, 1997 and another on January 30, 1998. She examined the
lead core removed from Bruce Dodson and the bullets from the box

of .243-caliber ammunition removed from Bruce's Bronco. She analyzed the bullet materials with inductively coupled plasma-atomic
emission spectroscopy to determine the elemental composition. Her
results indicated that the lead core removed from Bruce was "significantly different" from the lead bullets from the box and that therefore they "could not have originated from the same source of lead."
The lead bullets from the box were all the same as each other. She
analyzed the copper jacket fragment found on Bruce's chest at the
autopsy and the copper jacket material in the cartridges in this box
by the use of scanning electron microscopy/energy dispersive x-ray
analysis "to determine their qualitative elemental composition."
Both were determined to consist of copper/zinc alloys, but again,
they were different.

During this period, Bill Booth experienced an epiphany. He
was at home flipping through a copy of *Guns & Ammo* magazine. He
paused at an advertisement for a brand of bullets called Nosler Partition bullets. This ad had a cutaway diagram of the bullet showing
that within the copper jacket were two separate and distinct lead
cores. It had a caption by the diagram: *"Lead alloy dual-core construction provides dependable mushrooming above and total rear core
integrity below the integral jacket cross member."* As he read the ad it
was as though he was in a dream. Time slowed to a standstill as he
read how *"the Nosler Partition bullet delivers a near perfect balance
between penetration and expansion on all game. So you're prepared for
any possible shot. Better keep the skinning knife sharp."* He could
barely comprehend the words. All he could see was one of these perfectly engineered missiles emerging from the barrel of a Remington
model 700 heavy barrel .308-caliber rifle in a silent cloud of smoke
traveling gracefully through the air until it hit the fence post, shat-
tered and partitioned, the top core with the copper jacket flying off
tumbling into space while the bottom core partitioned Bruce Dodson's spine as he desperately crawled away from Janice peering emo-

tionlessly through the rifle's scope. The ad showed availability in .308-caliber, 180-grain bullets. Bill got up, grabbed his coat, got in his truck and drove straight to Gene Taylor's Sporting Goods where he bought some Nosler Partition bullets. He took them home to his garage and cut one in half with a hacksaw. The next day he told me about his discovery and called James Cotter. James was a bit more artful when he cut one of these new bullets. He agreed that this could be it. James packaged the bullet which had been found on the hillside behind where Bruce had been walking on that peaceful morning, and sent it to the FBI for further testing.

Depending upon the results of these tests, we might be able to establish the identity of the murder weapon with a reasonable degree of certainty. Establishing the murder weapon would erase a huge unknown from the case. If the bullet from the hillside was a Nosler Partition bullet and the metals of the jacket and core removed from Bruce at the autopsy match those in the hillside bullet, then we would have proof that the murder weapon was a .308-caliber rifle, of just a few possible makes, including a Remington model 700. We also would have proof that the bullets fired were Federal Premium brand, the same bullets Mark Morgan reported stolen from his tent the afternoon before the murder. Special Agent Bertram received the hillside bullet on March 24, 1998.

Nancy Saunders' examination included analyzing the jacket component and the upper and lower lead of the hillside bullet and the previously submitted copper jacket fragment by scanning electron microscopy/energy dispersive x-ray analysis to determine their general alloy classifications. The jacket components were determined to consist of the same copper/zinc alloy.

The upper lead core and the lead core from the hillside were analyzed with inductively coupled plasma-atomic emission spectroscopy to determine their elemental composition. The lower core was not analyzed in order to preserve the bearing surface of this specimen. The upper and lower cores and the lead core were determined to consist of the same general alloy of lead. The examination showed that the upper lead core of the bullet and the lead core from the hillside were analytically indistinguishable from one another. This was consistent with these specimens originating from the same source of bullet lead.

I was euphoric. After all this time we finally had what we were looking for. I felt I could now prove that all three shots were fired from the same rifle with the same batch of ammunition. I met with Bill and told him, "The waiting game is over; put together an arrest warrant affidavit for Janice Morgan Dodson for the murder of John Bruce Dodson." I hoped we could arrest her on October 15, 1998, the third anniversary of the heinous crime, a crime that I fervently believed had been occasioned by greed in its ugliest manifestation.

= chapter 22 =

Under Arrest

B ill Booth and I set to work on the warrant to bring Janice Dodson Hall to justice. I knew this document would set the prece-
dent for later arguments between the prosecution and the defense. I
wanted to make sure a few issues were visible from the start. My
main worry was that the law in Colorado says a person is liable as a
principal if he or she is a complicitor in the crime. In other words,
you are just as responsible for a crime if you aid, abet, advise or
encourage another to do it, as you would be if you directly committed it yourself. I felt strongly about the evidence against Janice, but
was aware that a good defense attorney could try to use Mark Morgan to create reasonable doubt. He was ideal for that purpose. An
able attorney could try to paint a picture of a jealous and blood-
thirsty ex-husband and Mark was no saint to begin with. The fact
that there was evidence that Mark's rifle was the murder weapon
would add substantial weight to this argument.

Bill favored the theory that a manipulative, vengeful and
cunning Janice concocted a plan to kill two birds with one stone—
in killing Bruce, she reaped his wealth and in trying to pin the crime
on Mark by using his rifle as the murder weapon, she obtained

revenge for being left for a younger woman and saved herself from prison. I was not convinced. "It does not quite fit together," I told him, shaking my head. "We never found the murder weapon. If your theory was the true scenario, one would expect Mark's rifle to have been found, leading the investigation right to him. It looks more to me like the shooting was planned to appear to be a hunting accident."

"It's possible," Bill acquiesced.

I nodded. "How Mark's rifle came into play could have several equally plausible explanations. I'm not planning to cozy up to any one of them." I felt confident that I could prove that Janice was guilty of first degree murder, but I did not feel confident that I could put the murder weapon in her hands. She was 100 percent guilty either way. The problem that I knew would lie in wait for me was the contradictory state case law dealing with complicity. It was crucial to my case to have the judge instruct the jury on the law of complicity. Without this instruction, Janice might walk. The defense could argue there was no evidence that anyone else was involved in this murder and therefore I had to prove that Janice was the one who fired the shot that killed Bruce or she must be acquitted.

As a second line of defense, they could ask the judge to require a unanimity instruction. In this case, the jury would be instructed that all twelve of them had to be convinced beyond a reasonable doubt that either Janice was guilty as principal or that she was guilty as complicitor. Though to me this would be absurd, it would leave the possibility that each juror could be convinced beyond a reasonable doubt that Janice was guilty of first degree murder, but if they did not agree on the same theory, they must find her to be not guilty. I had no way of knowing which of our four District Court judges would wind up with this case. It is my experience that judges in this conservative western Colorado judicial district, who all were appointed by Democratic governors, can be quite liberal. Because I wanted the importance of this issue in the Dodson case to be apparent, Bill and I included a final paragraph in the arrest warrant affidavit:

> We submit that Janice Dodson Hall's motive and behaviors clearly establish probable cause that she is guilty of the crime of first-degree murder, as principal or complicitor. Various factors present the possible involvement of a co-complicitor, including the fact that we never located the actual murder weapon. Pursuant to Colorado law: "A person is legally accountable for the behavior of another constituting a criminal offense, if with intent to promote or facilitate the commission of the offense, he or she aids, abets, advises or encourages the other person in planning or committing the offense." Whether she acted alone or with the help of another, Janice Dodson Hall remains guilty of this crime. Whether or not she personally fired the shot, she intentionally "caused" the death of John Bruce Dodson after deliberation.

A warrant affidavit is a good place to plant a seed of an idea. It is the first document in a court file and it is where judges turn to familiarize themselves with a case they have been assigned. I felt our affidavit set our case on firm ground.

I was disappointed when we could not quite get everything together in time to arrest Janice on the third anniversary of the murder. However, a week later on October 23, 1998, Bill Booth and Dave Martinez traveled to Texas, where Janice was now living, with the warrant. They had previously arranged with the East Texas Regional Narcotics Trafficking Task Force to assist with the arrest. Before going to Texas, Bill, in his usual mode, was positive he would be able to get Janice to confess when confronted with the arrest warrant. Bill is always optimistic about these things. "I bet you won't get a word out of her," I told him wryly. The plan was for the local officers to go in, make the arrest and then call in Bill and Dave.

At ten that morning, when the agents pulled into Baxter Lane, they observed two residences at the end of the road. They had previously identified a camp trailer in the area which was registered to Janice Dodson. Neither house had visible numbers on the exterior. At one of the residences, a man answered the door. He told the officers that Janice was in the place across the way. Walking there, the officers knocked on the door. There was no response. Trying the door, they discovered that it was unlocked and opened it, calling out that they were police officers. There was still no reply. Pulling out their revolvers and badges, they went in. They found Janice Dodson in a bedroom covered with a blanket with a shotgun next to her. The officers quickly handcuffed Janice and escorted her to the living room. Then they radioed Investigators Bennett and Booth to come in.

Once there, Booth walked straight over to Janice Dodson. "Do you remember us?"

"No," she said shaking her head, seeming as if she was only half awake.

"We're the investigators who spoke to you in your attorney's office in Grand Junction," Booth said.

"I don't remember you," she said vacantly, her bleary eyes downcast.

"We're arresting you for the murder of your late husband, John Bruce Dodson."

Janice looked up, her eyes clearer and her voice firmer. "I

didn't kill him."

Booth didn't reply. Instead, he went on, "I will be asking for permission to look through the residence for the murder weapon."

"That gun's not here," she said determinedly. Nevertheless, she consented to their search of her home for the murder weapon. Looking around, they found five firearms in the house. Three were shotguns, one was a .22-caliber rifle and the fifth was a .30-06-caliber Remington semi-automatic rifle. There was no .308-caliber firearm. While Booth was examining the firearms, the phone rang. It was Bart Hall, Janice's new husband. After speaking to him, Janice told the officers she did not want to speak with them further and revoked her consent to search. Nevertheless Booth and the others had what they wanted—the arrest, after a long and involved investigation, of Janice Dodson Hall. It was what I wanted as well.

chapter 23

Other Men in Janice's Life

The first thing I always do before I start in-depth preparation for a trial is to clean out my garage and get a new pair of shoes. When I do not want anything outside the case to distract me, I take care of the mundane things that must be done so I can completely clear my mind of trivialities. Idiosyncratic, perhaps, but it works for me.

In the period before the trial began, my own resolve hardened as I reviewed the evidence. One of the things I revisited was the issue of the many men in Janice's life. A prosecutor cannot introduce evidence of a woman's lack of virtue in order to inflame the moral passions of the jury. So I knew there was no way the jury would find out about Janice hitting on a variety of other men. But there were relationships in which she was involved that formed part and parcel of the case. I felt the jury needed to know about these in order for them to get the full picture of Janice's motivation. The law favors the admission of relevant evidence unless its probative value is substantially outweighed by the danger of unfair prejudice. Therefore, I decided that I was going to include evidence that Janice was sleeping with Ted Farly three days before her wedding to Bruce. Also germane was her odd relationship with her ex-husband, Mark Morgan. Because we wanted to evaluate their relevance, we continued to look into several other gentlemen friends.

One of the men Investigators Bennett and Booth interviewed was Harold Connors, who provided very interesting background on Janice's new marriage. Mr. Connors said he had "house sat" for Janice Dodson at her Cedaredge residence from April 1996 through June 1996. He met Janice in May 1995 when he worked at the same hospital at which she was employed. According to Connors, Janice was friendly, personable and somewhat flirtatious with him. He did not know Bruce, but had heard about him. He had heard Dr. Canfield and other people at the hospital talk about Bruce being a nice guy, a good worker and likeable. Connors confided to Booth and Bennett that when he heard that Bruce had been murdered, he never suspected Janice. He said he had only seen Janice angry once and that was when one of the patients pronounced her name in the more common way. She reprimanded the patient for mispronouncing her name. He heard people talk disparagingly about how Janice was dressed in expensive clothing with a large hat and black veil at Bruce's funeral but Connors thought nothing of it at the time. In March 1996, Janice came to the hospital and spoke to Mr. Connors about his MG convertible that was for sale. Janice wanted to purchase it. She gave him Bruce's Bronco and a goodly amount of cash in exchange for the man's vintage sports car.

When our investigators spoke to him, Connors recalled that in the beginning of April 1996, Janice called and asked him if he wanted to house sit for her as she was going to be in Texas. "Janice told me she needed to get away, because she was stressed out. I saw an opportunity to save some money and I agreed." So on April 4, 1996, Connors went to Janice's house in Cedaredge to get the keys and instructions from Janice. When he arrived, he saw a gray convertible with Texas plates in the driveway. He walked up on the porch and stopped short when through the window he saw Janice and a man standing in the kitchen embracing each other and kissing. When they broke apart, Connors knocked on the door and Janice let him in, introducing him to the other man. "I thought the scene was strange, because Bruce had only been dead for six months." Connors didn't mention what he saw through the window to Janice. However, when she gave him instructions for house sitting things got even stranger. Janice told him to check the mail every day for tampering. She also said she didn't like talking on the phone, because she believed it might be tapped.

Connors moved into Janice's house in early April. He kept the house clean as part of his responsibility. While cleaning he noticed very expensive women's clothing in the closets. All of Bruce's things were in the basement. Only Janice's items were in the upstairs portion of the house.

Periodically, Janice called from Texas and asked him to describe the mail. She had him open some of it and forward it to her in Texas. Janice also asked if he received any strange phone calls or if he saw any strangers on the property. "I remembered receiving a couple of calls from what sounded like an elderly gentleman. This caller always asked for Janice." When Connors told Janice about the elderly caller, she instructed him not to tell anyone where she was.

One day, Janice called and asked Connors to look into a filing cabinet for information regarding Bruce's Leadville home. Connors put down the phone and looked, but soon returned telling her he couldn't immediately locate what she wanted. He told her he would call her back when he found it. While looking through the cabinet, he located an application to reinstate Janice's nursing license in Texas. He noticed the date on the application was August 1995, two months before Bruce's death. He thought this was suspicious, because he never heard anything about Bruce and Janice moving to Texas.

Connors had heard a lot of the people at the hospital gossiping about their suspicions that Janice committed the murder, so he finally asked her point blank if she did it. "Janice was pissed off and insisted she did not kill Bruce." Instead, she told Connors she suspected her ex-husband of the crime, because he not only didn't want their divorce in the first place, but he also wanted to get back together with her because she was so happy with Bruce. Janice also told Connors she suspected one of the doctors where she worked of killing her husband, but she offered no explanation why she thought the man guilty of murder.

After Janice returned from Texas, she told Connors she would call and tell him what he owed for his long distance calls. She finally called in early July and he agreed to come to her house. Connors arrived at sundown. "I remember it was raining. When I pulled into Janice's driveway, I noticed an unfamiliar car with Texas plates. Janice answered the door wearing a bathrobe. Her hair was wet. Janice hugged me tight and I could tell she was not wearing any clothes under the robe." When Janice invited Connors in, he noticed an open bottle of Champagne on the kitchen counter. He started to walk through the kitchen toward the living room to sit on the sofa when she "kind of cut me off" and told him to stay in the kitchen. She told him she wanted to sell the house and asked if he would be interested. Connors told her it would be too long a drive for him to commute to work every day. Suddenly, she got down to business, telling him what he owed her for his long distance calls. He settled up his debt and left.

I mulled over what Connors had revealed, thinking what a strange woman Janice Dodson was. I wondered if the gentle Bruce Dodson had had any idea.

Next I read over a report on Larry Myers, another of Janice's conquests who lived in her residence at one time.

OFFICE OF THE DISTRICT ATTORNEY
21st JUDICIAL DISTRICT OF COLORADO
Investigator Dave Martinez
May 21, 1997
Case: John Bruce Dodson homicide
Interview of Lawrence Alan Myers

We received information that Janice Dodson rented a room in her residence to a Larry Myers after the death of Bruce Dodson. After locating Myers, we interviewed him at his office.

Myers told us not only did he know Janice, but he had lived with her. Myers said he first met Janice at a training class in June 1996. He was the instructor and she was a student. When he first met Janice, he had been married.

"When Janice first arrived, she was driving an MG sports car." Myers commented to her that it was a nice car. Janice responded by asking him if he would like to go for a ride. She later invited him to play golf at a course nearby. Myers accepted and Janice and he subsequently began a friendship. In August 1996, Larry Myers rented the basement apartment of Janice's residence. "As time went by," Myers observed, "Janice became flakier." Myers said he saw what could be dual personalities in Janice. For example, Myers explained, on the anniversary of Bruce's death, Janice became very emotional and did not get out of bed for several days. Myers' perception of her actions was that they were not signs of genuine grief, but the result of guilt. Myers had not spoken with Janice since he moved out in November 1996, as they parted on bad terms. Janice had spoken with Larry's wife and told her about their relationship. That conversation ended his marriage. Up to that point, Myers and his wife were going through a voluntary separation and had been trying to work things out. When he asked Janice why she told his wife about their relationship, she replied with her favorite saying, "Because I cannot tell a lie."

When Myers spoke with Janice about the murder, she told him she did not do it. He asked her if Mark could have done it and Janice said that Mark could not have done it either. In August 1996, Myers said Janice wanted him to go with her to meet Mark. They met Mark at a restaurant. Mark was with his girlfriend, Marcy and was driving a late-model pickup truck. Janice and Mark began a heated discussion about money and their divorce and something to do with an insurance company doing a fraud investigation over some weapons she had reported stolen. Mark was worried about the insurance fraud coming back to haunt him and wanted to know what Janice was doing about it. Myers became increasingly uncomfortable with the discussion and could see that Mark's girlfriend was uncomfortable as well, so the two of them left the table and let Janice and Mark continue talking in private.

Another incident at Janice's house, Myers recalled, occurred with Mark present. "I was on the porch smoking a cigarette and saw Mark out by his pickup. A few minutes later, Janice came out of the house and walked over to Mark." Myers explained that Janice was trying to conceal an object wrapped in cloth, which she then handed to Mark. Myers later confronted Janice about this and told her he thought the object was a weapon. Janice claimed it was a gun that Mark wanted back, so she gave it to him. Myers said, "Mark and Janice seemed to get along well."

While he was living with Janice, Myers told investigators, she became involved with a man named Bart Hall. Bart traveled back and forth between Texas and Colorado to see Janice. "Eventually Bart bought a trailer and set it up on Janice's property. A short while later he moved into the house with Janice." At the time, Myers still lived in the basement. Bart told Myers that when Janice married Bruce it set him back, but he had accepted it.

Soon after this, to Myers' astonishment, Janice married her visitor.

I put down the report on Myers and picked up Bill Booth's interview with Janice's new husband from May 1997. I slowly went over every word, for I felt that Janice's behavior with Hall revealed the avarice I'd identified so long ago.

OFFICE OF THE DISTRICT ATTORNEY
21st JUDICIAL DISTRICT OF COLORADO

Investigator William G. Booth
May 21, 1997
John Bruce Dodson homicide
Interview of Bartlett M. Hall

On May 21, 1997, I received a phone call from Bart Hall. Mr. Hall stated he was in the building and wanted to know if I could speak with him. As I had been trying to speak with him for several weeks, I told him to come up to the third floor of the courthouse. When he arrived, he stated he only had an hour to speak with me due to his work schedule.

Mr. Hall said he had known Janice since he was nine

years old. Bart said, "We went to grammar school together. I have always been in love with Janice, ever since we were children." From 1982 to 1984, Bart had attended nursing school with Janice in Texas. They became good friends but never dated. Janice was married to Mark Morgan at that time. Bart said that his now ex-wife told him she had encountered Janice in the mall in Nacogdoches in the early summer of 1995. His wife told Bart that Janice had announced she was getting married to someone in Colorado. When his wife told him that, Bart wanted to see Janice, but did not know how to get in touch with her. He had already known that Janice was divorced from Mark Morgan. He tried to find a way to contact Janice, but could not find her. He finally found a contact in Montrose who had her number, but when he called her, she had already married Bruce.

I asked Bart when he next heard from Janice after the phone call in the summer of 1995. He said he believed it was November 30, 1995 when he received a phone call from Janice. She called from San Augustine, Texas where she was staying with relatives. She told Bart her husband Bruce had been shot and killed accidentally while hunting in Colorado. She told him he had been shot three times. The next day Bart met with Janice at the San Augustine Inn. Bart then stated, "That's what's bothering me. Remember when we were in the lawyer's office and you told Janice that Bruce was murdered and she broke down and cried and had to leave the room? She knew Bruce was murdered when I met with her in November of 1995. No one is shot accidentally three times." Bart said he couldn't understand why Janice broke down in the lawyer's office. Bart then said he and Janice had married on Thanksgiving Day, 1996 in Las Vegas at the Chapel of Flowers.

I also questioned Bart as to what he knew about Mark Morgan. Bart said a couple of weeks earlier, Janice went out with Mark, without Bart, and when Mark dropped her off, Janice was upset. Janice said she wanted to set up a bank account for Mark to have access to in case something happened to her. Janice told Bart that maybe if she set up this account Mark would stay off her back. Bart said Mark continues to claim that Janice owes him money from their divorce.

At one of Mark and Janice's meetings, Bart Hall was also present. Hall said he overheard Mark telling Janice he thought the Colorado cops were going to arrest him and Janice, place them in separate rooms and play them against each other.

That wasn't a bad idea, I thought, but it was the next revelation which stirred my blood and memory.

Booth had asked Bart if he had any insurance policies on his life. He replied that he had taken a $100,000 policy out since he and Janice were married. The kind gentleman had replied that if anything happened to him, he wanted to leave her well set. It was, I thought with horror, a deadly pattern beginning to be replayed.

chapter 24

Another Dark Surprise

Despite what he told us were his own agonizing questions and insights, while Janice languished in the jail in Nacogdoches in the few weeks before her extradition to Colorado, Bart was a loyal husband. When she appeared in court for her first advisement on November 13, 1998, the judge set bond at $800,000. The long, drawn out process of providing due process began. Justice in our system is not exactly swift. In the period between the arrest and the trial, sixteen or seventeen months intervened. During this time Bill and Dave continued to tie up loose ends and sought additional evidence.

Bart attended all of Janice's court proceedings and made regular payments to the court to help defer the costs of her court appointed lawyers, since his salary put her just over the guidelines for completely free public defender representation. Nevertheless, Janice's character surfaced in a report given to me by one of the jailers about a very friendly visit between her and her ex-husband.

Officer Green came up to booking to ask if I would assist her with a strip search on a female inmate who had been in a contact visit. I entered the visitation area and noticed visitation room #10 had no light on in it. Officer Green stated that inmate Janice Hall was in there on a contact visit. I could not see anyone in the room. I walked over to the door and looked in. I observed Inmate Hall sitting on a male's lap facing him with one of her legs on each side of his. I observed her hips were moving and he was handling her breasts. I observed bare skin on the side of Inmate Hall at around her lower waist/upper hip area; however, she did have all her clothes on still. The male's shirt was unbuttoned, but otherwise he was dressed. I ordered Inmate Hall to turn on the light and to get off of the male. I had to order her several times before she complied. The male touched her breasts several more times before she slowly got off of him. It took approximately two minutes for her totally to get off of him and another minute for her to turn on the light. When they separated, both the inmate's and the male's complexions appeared flushed. The male remained seated several minutes after she stood up. I informed them that their visit has ended and they needed to come out. After telling them this several times they complied. Both were informed of what was acceptable behavior and what was not during a contact visit. They were informed that they had to keep the lights on and both stay in the line of sight of the master control officer.

In early May 1999, the sheriff of Delta County called Dave Martinez and told him that Janice and Bart had not kept up payments on their storage locker. The contents were to be sold at auction pursuant to statute on May 22, 1999. The sheriff contacted the owner of the storage lockers and told her of our interest. She agreed to call when the sale was complete to let us know who acquired the contents. The purchasers were Harry and Gail Parker. Mr. and Mrs. Parker were entirely cooperative. Once they brought the contents of the storage unit to their home garage, they called Bill and invited him to come up and take a look.

Bill and Dave drove up to see the couple on June 2. They soon arrived in Paonia, a lovely mountain town in a rural setting which enjoys a unique cultural cross with coal mining and fruit orchards as its economic base. The economy is depressed compared to most of the rest of Colorado. It was a beautiful, sunny day when they pulled up to the Parker residence and walked to the front door. Gail Parker opened the door before they could knock and ushered the investigators into her home. Her husband introduced himself and led the two men to the garage where he and his wife stored the contents of Janice Dodson Hall's expired storage locker.

After being immersed in this case for so long, the investigators felt a close bond with Bruce Dodson—going through his things was both uncomfortable and enlightening. Many of the boxes from the storage locker contained only Bruce's belongings, including tax records, personal photographs, documents, diplomas, the marriage license from his union with Janice and the like. Bill and Dave were stunned when they discovered a stack of mottled black and white grade school composition books and read the detailed notes Bruce kept of his expenditures. They knew from working the case that Bruce was known for his thriftiness, but they were not aware of the degree of his frugality. He had years of notes regarding his expenditures. For every month, he recorded his bank account balance at the start, his pay for the month and all of his expenditures, down to the penny, such as "17 cents for three screws" at the hardware store, with an entry for the net gain or loss for the month. He was gaining before he hooked up with Janice. He recorded every time he had a meal out, every grocery purchase, all of his utility payments, mortgage payments and the investigators were a bit saddened to see that he spent a significant amount of his budget every month at the liquor store. It brought home the loneliness that Janice exploited for her own greedy purposes. It is hard to imagine how two such different people, one a spendthrift and one a tightwad, could have come together.

When Bill and Dave saw how many of Bruce's personal items were there, they asked the Parkers if they could put together a box of things to give to Bruce's brother and sister. Harry and Gail Parker told them they could take all of the stuff they wanted. When the day was through, Bill and Dave had amassed quite a collection. They began to compile a list of such items as a marriage license, a funeral guest registry, credit card bills, phone bills, Janice's insurance inventory, utility bills, Bruce's finance log, a memo book, carbon copies of checks for Janice K. Dodson from 1994-1996, wedding photos, work evaluations, education certificates, tax records, payroll records, cancelled checks, insurance records, a wedding album and wedding cards, notes to Mark from Janice, a box containing Bruce Dodson's personal documents, photos, diplomas, etc.

The item noted as "Janice's insurance inventory" was a revelation. This consisted of twenty or so handwritten pages in Janice's handwriting in as much detail as Bruce had put into his composition books. It was obviously the inventory of loss that Mark and Janice prepared to submit to the insurance company for their 1987 fire. Besides scores of firearms, they listed things like "two cans of baked beans - $1.58, box of tissues - $ .89," and so on. It went on and on and must have taken days to prepare.

Soon, Dave Martinez found the real prize of the storage locker, the Mesa View Mortuary Funeral Guide. The stiff manila folder with four pages labeled Emergency Record Guide had a sticker appended for Mesa View Mortuary. The second page had two sections titled Vital Statistics Record and Personal History. It was made out in the name of John Bruce Dodson, but the most shocking part was the date: 9/24/95—three weeks before his death. The third and fourth pages had sections for Funeral Service and Information, Immediate Family, Local Emergency Contacts to Be Notified at Need and Important Legal Information for Family Use. There was an Authorization section with the purported signature of John Bruce Dodson. This section read, "I, John Bruce Dodson, have given the preceding information, to be filed in the funeral home of my choice, in order to avoid placing all responsibility on family and loved ones at the time of my death." This was clearly the document Gail Warner saw sitting on Bruce and Janice's kitchen table shortly after the murder. Janice had this document delivered to the funeral home. On the bottom in a distinctly different handwriting was written, "Wants 8 death certificates." This was written by a funeral home employee.

After my investigators returned with the cache from the Parker residence and showed me the funeral guide, I filed a motion with the court to compel Janice to provide samples of her handwriting. The judge granted my motion without much fuss. A CBI handwriting expert came to the jail and instructed Janice on filling out the samples, which we call handwriting exemplars. Then we collected a variety of known handwriting samples for both Janice and Bruce, including letters, signatures, writing on checks and the like. We packed it up and sent it to the CBI handwriting expert in the Denver office for comparison with the Emergency Record Guide section of the Funeral Service Guide. We wanted to establish who filled out the forms.

The CBI expert, Paige Doherty, was a highly qualified handwriting examiner. She holds a degree in Forensic Science and has worked as an agent with the CBI for over fifteen years. She is a diplomate of the American Board of Forensic Document Examiners and I knew she would be an excellent witness before a jury. We had poster-sized enlargements of each page of the Emergency Record Guide for her to use. I asked her to mark in red every word she was able to identify as Janice's handwriting. Her opinion was that Janice

filled out the majority of Emergency Record Guide. Regarding the
purported signature of John Bruce Dodson, she noted:

*No conclusion is rendered concerning the questioned signature
"John Bruce Dodson" present on page four of the Emergency
Record Guide when compared with the known handwriting
specimens. This opinion is limited, in part, due to the following considerations: The questioned signature is illegibly written and contains a wide range of variation in baseline
alignment, pressure, and letter formation. These features may
be an indication of a disguise attempt, a simulation attempt,
the effects of illness, infirmity, medication and other physiological influences, or some other writing abnormality.*

When we spoke, I questioned Paige on the part of her report
regarding the simulation attempt. As she addressed it, I formed a
dark picture in my mind of the night of September 24, 1995 in the
home of Janice and Bruce Dodson. In it, Bruce, with several drinks
under his belt, was sitting in the hot tub when Janice handed him
the paper to sign, saying, "Oh, come on honey; I know you're not
going to die; I just want to take care of all these icky things so we can
get on with our lives."
The vision made me shiver.

The Trial Begins

At long last, after over four years of investigation and preparation opening day of the trial came on February, 22, 2000. The defense team comprised lead attorney Alex Williams, second chair attorney Scott Nolan, private investigator Carl Mason, former CBI agent Wyatt Tate and firearms expert Barry Hart. Alex Williams moved to Grand Junction when he was with the Public Defenders Office. He is not only a good lawyer, but can develop a rapport with a jury because of the dramatic way he presents his arguments. Scott Nolan, the second lawyer for the defense, came to town a couple of years before and is a nice looking, slightly built man from Alabama. He speaks with a folksy southern accent, treating the jury like intimate friends. By the time the jury selection process was over, the jury knew everything there was to know about Nolan—he is nervous just like they are; he doesn't hunt even though his family does; he races bicycles; his new baby just rolled over; he used to be a musician; he enjoys hiking and so on. Grand Junction is a small community and I had been hearing for some time that Alex Williams and Scott Nolan were telling people that they had a great case they were sure they would win. I had a different opinion.

I had been working on my prosecution of Janice Dodson Hall long days and just about every weekend and holiday for the six months before the trial began. I have a staff of fifteen attorneys, but since I was so fascinated and involved in this case from the start, I wanted to prosecute it myself. It was a case easy to be obsessed with. Something new and different had surfaced around every bend. "It's got more twists and turns than a snake," said one investigator at the sheriff's department. I fully agreed.

Trial work is where it all comes together for an attorney. All training, practice, and experience flow into the moment of trial. It is Zen-like. Lawyers have a fraction of a second to make or respond to an objection. I knew I must be completely focused and there in mind, body and spirit. Furthermore, I was determined to get justice because of my sympathy for Bruce Dodson and his family and my belief in Janice's guilt.

The judge appointed was the Honorable Nick Massaro, a fair man and an able judge. In his mid-forties and energetic, he is physically fit and handsome with a shock of thick, curly, graying dark hair. For vacations, he travels the globe seeking out and conquering the world's highest mountain peaks. If he is angry about something, you will know it. He is a former public defender, tends to be liberal and is not a judge prosecutors like to draw when there are close search and seizure issues. However, for a violent crime, he is as good as any. His courtroom is in the newer wing of the courthouse, but due to the large size of the jury pool, the jury selection was to be done in the big old courtroom, which I personally prefer. Here, the acoustics are poor, but there is an aura of justice. It was completed in 1922, has wooden pews for the observers and a magnificent, ornate wooden bench for the judge. The room has a high ceiling with engravings, including gargoyles, all around the upper edges of the walls. Tall, many-paneled windows grace the southern exposure on one long side of the room, which at this time of year affords a full view through old elm branches of the northern edge of the Uncompahgre Plateau. Cool winter light slants in. Snow falling on elms early in the day melts by noon.

One of my jury selection goals was to seat as many jurors as I could who had knowledge of firearms. I try to find law-abiding, intelligent citizens and I knew this trial, more than most, would require jurors who would be able to follow the evidence and put small details together. All those who wanted to be excused by seeking a continuance (one is automatically granted if asked for), by presenting a hardship such as being self-employed or in school, or by claiming to have a bias for or against the prosecution, were excused. The potential jurors left were, to say the least, a mixed batch. One juror had read a newspaper account against the Judge's instructions in order to be excused. I challenged for cause one woman who had brain surgery and a problem with her memory. I was concerned that the medical problem still affected her and I feared she would not be able to keep straight the difficult testimony in this case. I did not think it was too much to ask to excuse her due to her medical problem. The judge denied my challenge and I had to use one of my preemptory challenges to remove her. A preemptory challenge can be used to excuse a juror without the need to establish cause, such as bias. The replacement was a man with a prior conviction who said the cops had no reason to pull him over and who spoke mainly of his interest in science fiction. I convicted the uncle of one potential juror's wife of attempted first degree murder of a peace officer a few years before. He was excused and his substitute was a habitual traffic offender. That day, Alex Williams was using a standup comic approach and the jurors lapped it up. I took a moment to appreciate the skills of my adversary.

On the second day I had my turn and jury selection turned around. We seated two good jurors for the prosecution in a row; one had been on the Air Force rifle team and the other was conservative and knowledgeable about firearms. Since these were the last two jurors seated, they would be the alternates unless another juror ahead of them was removed. At this point, we were left with jurors I thought would be good plus a few neutrals; so I decided to hold pat with five remaining preemptory challenges out of my original thirteen. The defense team looked astonished when I announced, "I will accept the jury as it is constituted." They huddled for about ten minutes before announcing that they also would accept this jury. I knew why they were caught by surprise. I had violated one of the cardinal rules of prosecutorial jury selection by leaving a minister on the jury. Normally, a prosecutor does not want people on the jury whose careers involve forgiving and helping, including teachers, nurses and most of all clergy. Nevertheless, this man impressed me in two ways. First, he seemed extremely perceptive and second, since he was a hunter and a life member of the National Rifle Association, he knew a lot about firearms, which I felt was important to understanding this case. I had the impression that the defense team thought they snuck him by me. But I was satisfied.

Taking a deep breath and preparing to do battle, I walked forward, and began my opening statement. It was my first chance to impress the jury with the weight of the evidence to come that Janice Dodson was guilty beyond a reasonable doubt of the murder of her husband.

"May it please the Court. Ladies and gentlemen of the jury, the evidence will establish an event of unmitigated greed and cold-blooded murder. A murder planned and executed by this woman," I said, turning and pointing accusatorily, "Janice Hall, formerly known as Janice Morgan and Janice Dodson." I took a few moments to make eye contact with the jurors one by one and then I began to reconstruct the day of the murder.

"On October 15, 1995, her husband of ninety days, John Bruce Dodson, age forty-eight, known as Bruce to his friends, was on his first-ever big game hunting trip. He left camp around daybreak and walked about five hundred feet when he heard the loud report of a high powered rifle being fired from fifty-five yards to his left—and being fired at him!

"If that bullet had been two inches to the left, it would have killed Bruce and we would never have seen this case. It would have been chalked up as an unfortunate hunting accident and Janice would have made a profit of almost one-half million dollars, tax-free. It would have been like winning the lottery.

"Unfortunately for the defendant, this shot missed Bruce. It went through his blaze orange vest, through his down vest, cut a crease across his sweatshirt and traveled back out through the vests and into a hillside, all faster than the speed of sound.

"Bruce ripped off his two vests, yelled and waved them in the air. He turned toward the place from which the shot had been fired, yelling more. WHAM! The second shot hit him dead center. Now keep in mind that this was a shot from a high-powered hunting rifle, a .308-caliber rifle, capable of killing a six hundred pound elk at four hundred yards. It hit a man at fifty-five yards, spun him around and knocked him to the ground." My steam and passion were building. "It did not kill him. He tried to crawl away when—WHAM!—a third shot rang out in the crisp, cool, early morning air. This bullet hit a fence post before hitting Bruce in the back, severing his spine and rendering him dead.

"The defendant's first mistake was not killing Bruce with the first shot. Her second mistake was not realizing that there was a witness—not an eye-witness, but an *ear*-witness, just over two hundred yards away. Those two factors led to a massive investigation involving investigators from the Mesa County Sheriff's Office, the Colorado Bureau of Investigation, the Internal Revenue Service, the Federal Bureau of Investigation, the District Attorney's Office of the Twenty-first Judicial District of the State of Colorado and a number of other organizations.

"That investigation was completed when the FBI finished conducting their final lab tests in August of 1998. The arrest warrant was signed in October. The defendant was arrested in Texas and returned to Mesa County to face these charges. The paperwork created in this investigation is more than 11,000 pages."

Pausing and looking around I saw that Bruce's brother, Michael, and his sister, Martha, were in the courtroom for the opening statements. Occasionally I glanced in their direction as I went on laying out the investigation, the background and all of the evidence the jury would hear from the prosecution. I told them about Mark and the stolen rifle, about Ted Farly and also about the rifles Janice reported stolen. Then I hit on the key evidence:

"Janice bought two boxes of ammunition the day before the hunt at Gibson's in Delta — one box of twenty, 7 millimeter magnums and one box of twenty-four .243-caliber cartridges. She was ostensibly hunting with a .270-caliber rifle yet she had five 7 mm magnum shells in her pocket—the other fifteen were in the box in the Volkswagen. Bruce was found with a .243-caliber rifle and no live ammunition in it at all—three spent cartridges were found on the ground next to him. He could not have shot these after being shot in the back because his spine was severed. In the Volkswagen were the rest of the original box of twenty-four—twenty live rounds and one spent cartridge."

Next I picked up a Ziploc bag with three .243-caliber shells marked in large bold type NEAR BODY and a Federal brand ammunition box with twenty-one shells (twenty live and one spent) marked VW VAN. I showed these to the jury and continued expressing my own fervor in our case against the defendant and the horror of her crime:

"Keep your eyes on this evidence. Janice Dodson did not know that she severed Bruce's spine. When Captain Brent Branchwater told her he heard three shots close by, she realized she needed an explanation. She took whatever live rounds Bruce had with him, removed three spent cartridges from the box in the Volkswagen, and placed these three spent shells from the ammunition box on the ground by his body to make it look as though he fired three shots as a distress signal. But Bruce did not fire those shots; he could not have. His spine was severed. Moreover, Captain Branchwater heard *three* shots, not six.

"The evidence will establish beyond a reasonable doubt that Janice Hall is guilty of first-degree murder, that she had the motive, that she was the last to see Bruce alive, that she was the first to find him dead and only she could have planted the three empty .243 shell casings. Thank you."

The judge asked, "Can counsel approach?" A bench conference was held off the record and out of the hearing of the jury. Then the judge announced, "We're going to break until after lunch, ladies and gentlemen. I would be inclined to start up a little bit earlier, but I've got a meeting that I am committed to that won't allow me to be back here until 1:30. So we'll hear the opening statement of the defense after lunch. That way they'll be able to give it uninterrupted. You can go, of course, wherever you like for lunch.

"Let me go over that admonition instruction with you again. I'm sure you'll soon have it memorized. It is important that you obey it during all of the recesses of the court. First, do not discuss the case among yourselves or with anyone else during the course of the trial. In fairness to the parties to the lawsuit, you need to keep an open mind throughout the trial and reach your decision only during the final deliberations.

"Second, do not permit any third person to discuss the case in your presence. If anyone attempts to do that, report that to the Court immediately.

"Third, during the course of the trial, do not talk with any of the witnesses, with the defendant or with any of the lawyers who are involved in presenting this case to you.

"Fourth, do not attempt to gather any information on your own. Do not engage in any outside reading regarding this case. Do not attempt to visit any places that might be mentioned in this case. Do not, in other words, try to learn about the case other than in the courtroom.

"And fifth, do not read anything about this case in the newspapers or listen to any radio or television broadcasts about the trial. As you know, your verdict will need to be based only on the evidence that you hear in the courtroom. I'll see you back here at 1:30. Thank you."

After the lunch recess, the jury returned to the jury box. The judge turned to the defense attorney and said, "Do you want to give an opening statement at this time?"

"Yes, your Honor, please."

"You may go ahead."

"Good afternoon, ladies and gentlemen. This morning the prosecutor basically told you what his theory of the case was and laid out what he thought the evidence was going to show over the next weeks. Mr. Williams and I are going to show you that his theory is wrong. The information he gave you this morning is incorrect."

Nolan looked nervous. He launched into his argument, giving the impression of folksy candor and informality. I listened intently to see where they were going. He talked about the absurdity of the prosecution arguing that Bruce went hunting with no ammunition. He spoke for a long while about how poor the investigation was, calling it a "sloppy and flawed investigation that cannot be relied on." Referring to the three bullets I claimed were fired at Bruce, he said, "You will not hear that these bullet pieces match."

As I listened intently, Nolan continued his opening statement. "This morning, Mr. Daniels was talking to you about listening to the evidence. We ask you to please listen to the evidence and listen to all the evidence all the way through the trial. The prosecution is going to have a significant amount of time here at the beginning to present evidence for you to see. It's going to be a while before we're presenting evidence to you. I want you to please wait and listen to all the evidence.

"Some of the things that I want to hit on right now that you heard this morning that I just want to straighten right out for you are, we need you to use your common sense. You heard about that in jury selection.

"This morning, the prosecution talked to you about Mr. Dodson going out to go hunting in the morning with no ammunition. Use your common sense about that.

"Mr. Daniels spent a large amount of time this morning talking to you about a thorough and complete investigation. We're going to show you that this was a seriously flawed investigation. It was anything but a complete and thorough investigation. The evidence is going to show you the crime scene was not sealed at any time. Evidence is going to show you that investigators returned days later to collect so-called evidence. Investigators returned one-plus years after this incident to collect evidence.

"Other evidence that you're going to hear about was collected as much as two-plus years after this incident. It was not a thorough investigation. As a matter of fact, it was a sloppy, flawed investigation and you're going to hear the evidence about that. We're going to show it to you. You're going to hear us cross-examine witnesses and you're going to see that it was a sloppy investigation, not an investigation that can be relied upon.

"Evidence is going to show you that in the initial stages of this investigation, there were sheriff's officers there, there were Department of Wildlife officers there, there were various different agency people who were there all tramping up and down in this crime scene. They're tramping up and down in a crime scene where they run into the potential of destroying evidence, burying evidence, carrying evidence away.

"You're going to hear about that. You're going to see that and it's important that you pay attention to that. A lot of trace evidence that's been discussed, it's important for you to see what happened with that evidence and what didn't happen with that evidence.

"There's no weapon, no eyewitness and the only so-called witness is somebody that was woken up from sleep by the sounds of gunshots in a hunting area during hunting season. You couple that with a flawed investigation and what you've got is Ms. Hall accused of first-degree murder. Evidence is going to show you that with no weapon, no eyewitness and this so-called ear witness, Ms. Hall became the prime suspect only because she was Mr. Dodson's spouse and only because she stood to gain money from his estate. That's the only evidence that you'll see of that.

"A great deal of time was spent talking about insurance and the fact that Ms. Hall would have gained financially from the death of Mr. Dodson. Evidence is going to show that Ms. Hall is the prime beneficiary of Mr. Dodson's estate. There's nothing unusual about that. There's nothing dark about that. There's nothing sinister about that. Spouses tend to make spouses the persons who are going to be the prime beneficiaries of estates. There's nothing unusual about that."

In a dramatic flourish, he finished. "I want to ask you just a second, can you folks see my hands? But you can't really see my hands, can you, because I haven't turned them around? You haven't seen the other side of my hands. You've got to wait till you've seen both sides of my hands. Very important for you to keep that in mind.

"I think once you've heard all the evidence in this case and you've seen the evidence and the light that's shed by the evidence and the law in this case, you all will realize there's only one verdict you can come back with and that's a not guilty verdict for Ms. Hall. Thank you."

Twisting in my chair to scrutinize their faces, I hoped the jury would be astute enough to tell the difference between good drama and grim reality.

= chapter 26 =

The Prosecution Strikes

It was time for me to call the first of my witnesses. I like to present witnesses in the chronological order of how events unfolded whenever possible. However, the first three people on my list were not in town yet. I called Nick Armand. Nick makes a good witness, because he is good at what he does, is a heck of a nice guy and that plays well with the jury. Even so, his testimony went on and on due to the tedious nature of all the evidence collected for this unusual case. He was on the stand all afternoon. Alex Williams handled the cross examination the next morning. Looking directly at the jurors, exuding confidence, he debated every detail one by one. I hoped he wasn't running away with the jurors' minds and hearts.

But my next witness, one of the brothers from Wisconsin who'd come on the death scene, was a great kid, as American as apple pie. It was clear from his earnest testimony that he thought Janice was a phony and the scene had been staged. The defense hardly asked him any questions on cross. Deputy Patrick was next. I took a deep breath, afraid we were losing the jury's attention when he had to constantly refer to his reports. Next was Captain Branch-water, who also was a strong witness. I felt the cross examination of

Branchwater did not really seem to head in any particular direction and that he had made a lasting impression on the jury.

One by one, day by day, I called witness after witness. Mark Morgan was a pain to deal with. Getting anything out of him was like pulling teeth. I felt he seemed adept at coming across as a boob from the piney woods who could hardly remember his own name, let alone the events of a hunting trip four years earlier.

Next, I tackled the deputies who conducted the search of Janice and Bruce's vehicles to testify about the results of their search. Victor Poste, the former deputy who had left the department to work as an international peacekeeper in Kosovo, had written the reports, but when I was preparing for the trial I figured rather than bring Poste to Colorado from Kosovo, I could just use the other deputy who searched with him. He would simply have to look over Victor's reports to refresh his recollection. However, after I gave him the reports to look at, he came to me scratching his head saying that he must have been there, because the report said so, but he had absolutely no recollection of it at all. In the end, I had to fly Victor back from Kosovo.

After Victor finished on the witness stand, I was set to call a stretch of witnesses from all over America who came to testify as custodians of business records pertinent to the case. On the day before they were to be called, several of the women from out of town got together and went sightseeing. They went over to Utah to Dead Horse Point and Arches National Park. The next morning they drove up on Colorado National Monument, a beautiful place right here in our own back yard. Wind- and water-sculpted cliffs and spires formed over the course of millions of years from sandstone formations at the northern edge of the Uncompahgre Plateau. The views are spectacular. After lunch, when the judge was ready to go, I had no witnesses ready, because the women had not gotten back. We waited almost an hour. The tension was palpable. Finally they arrived.

After the financial evidence, I began to call the prosecution's expert witnesses. Even though the defense attorneys tried to shake them they were cool, collected and confident. When Alex Williams argued with Shawn Bertram that the lead bullet core "was not a lead bullet at all," I wondered what his theory was about how it ended up in Bruce's liver. When Nancy Saunders testified, Williams launched into a long set of questions concerning standard deviations and mathematical formulas. I hoped it was clear to the jury that of the two of them, Ms. Saunders was the better mathematician. I felt confident he got nowhere when he implied that her testimony was intentionally biased in favor of the prosecution.

Next, I called Bruce's brother and sister. The jury had seen them in the courtroom for the past three weeks. Michael, who is distinguished looking, wore a jacket and tie every day. In Martha, who is tall and attractive, I felt the pain of her loss was palpable to everyone in the courtroom. They brought Bruce to life as a real human being with a family who loved and missed him greatly.

As I had anticipated they would, before the start of the trial the defense team had filed a document entitled "Memorandum Re: Complicity." They made the arguments I anticipated and buttressed the position by quoting Bill Booth's testimony from the preliminary hearing where he testified to his belief: "Ms. Hall is the shooter." They wrote, "The prosecution *now* apparently seeks to instruct the jury on complicity...." My prior work on the arrest warrant affidavit made my reply easier. In my "Memorandum of Law Regarding Complicity," I wrote:

"The evidence will establish that the murder weapon was in the possession of her ex-husband, Mark Morgan, the day before the murder, that Mark Morgan was camped less than a mile away from Janice and Bruce Dodson, that Mark

Morgan was in the area at the time of the murder and that he left the area the same day of the murder in order to return to the state of Utah where he was living, even though this was only the second day of a five-day hunting season and even though Mark had not shot any animal for which he had a license. The murder weapon was never found even though the area around the crime scene was thoroughly searched following the discovery that a murder had occurred. There will be no way that a jury can find from the evidence both that someone other than Janice Hall murdered John Bruce Dodson and that Janice was not guilty as a complicitor. Consider the injustice if the jury were to get to the deliberation stage and were convinced of the defendant's involvement, but felt that they could not convict her solely because they could not rule out that she had an accomplice with her who actually fired the killing shots.

"The eighty-eighth paragraph of the Affidavit in Support of Arrest Warrant for the defendant clearly stated the prosecution's theory that a complicity instruction would be needed. It is disingenuous of the defense to claim surprise. The concern here is that Mark Morgan and perhaps others cannot be ruled out as being accomplices beyond a reasonable doubt. No one knows how the evidence will come out at trial. That is part of the reason we have trials. Through the precise engines of examination and cross-examination, the jury will be presented with tested and tried evidence as to what occurred. The People submit that a complicity instruction will be necessary, is appropriate and is completely justified by the state of the evidence as the jury will receive it."

Then I had the uncomfortable task of taking on my own

investigator:

> "The defendant's claims about Bill Booth's personal
> opinions are without any significance regarding this issue.
> Bill Booth did personally interview Mark Morgan, and Bill
> believes that Mr. Morgan is not involved in this murder. Mr.
> Booth's opinion is well-reasoned and may be correct. But
> that is without particular legal significance. He is as entitled
> to his belief as is anyone else. His beliefs do not hamstring
> how the People will present the evidence in this case."

I won this argument and the judge instructed the jury on
complicity. Bill and I still argue about the possible involvement of
Mark Morgan.

There was another set of legal issues that I pondered long
and hard prior to the charging decision. Clearly, no judge in Grand
Junction, or anywhere else, was going to let the jury hear all the
bad things we dug up about Janice. The general rule here is that
people to be tried for the crime with which they stand charged and
is not to be convicted based on their bad character. The rule of evidence is:

> Rule 404 (a) Character evidence generally. Evidence
> of a person's character or a trait of his character is not
> admissible for the purpose of proving that he acted in con-
> formity therewith on a particular occasion.

However, there is more to it. There is section (b) of this rule,
often referred to as "Prior Bad Acts," and a murky, contradictory and
obtuse volume of case law that interprets it. Entire scholarly treatises
deal just with this subsection:

(b) Other crimes, wrongs or acts. Evidence of other crimes, wrongs or acts is not admissible to prove the character of a person in order to show that he acted in conformity therewith. It may, *however*, be admissible for other purposes, such as proof of motive, opportunity, intent, preparation, plan, knowledge, identity or absence of mistake or accident.

It was the *however* part of 404 (b) that provided substance for my arguments. I argued a somewhat novel and rarely employed theory of evidence called The Theory of Improbability in attempting to get into evidence all the prior insurance claims filed by Janice. The Theory of Improbability (or the Doctrine of Chances) recognizes that innocent people can sometimes become entangled in suspicious situations, but it is unlikely that someone would be repeatedly involved in such circumstances. I quoted from a document we received from an insurance company in Texas that handled the 1987 claim for $87,000 filed by Janice and Mark regarding a home of theirs that burned. I noted the fact that this insurance policy was taken out in July and the claim made in October of the same year, identical to the timeframe in this murder. The attorney for the insurance company in 1987 wrote:

It is very suspicious that Mr. Morgan has had three homes burn when no one was home and no one was injured. He has also had two trucks burn with no witnesses other than himself and he has never been injured. He has had numerous insurance claims for vehicles being stolen. It seems unlikely that anyone would break into the house and take all the guns and ammunition and then burn the house. There would be no need to burn the house. It is strange that someone would be able to locate every gun that was in the house, including those hidden under the waterbed and also take the ammunition.

Very strange indeed. I also quoted an example from the leading treatise in this area of law, *Uncharged Misconduct Evidence*, written by Professor Imwinkelreid:

> "Suppose the government is prosecuting the defendant for arson at her warehouse. The prosecution has evidence that in the past four years, the defendant started three other arson fires at other buildings she owns in town. If the defendant claims that the warehouse fire started accidentally, the prosecutor could introduce the evidence of other arson fires to negate the claim of accident."

Unfortunately, the judge did not allow it in. He ruled that I had not established that Janice was responsible for the other arsons. I thought this was a close call (or even a bit of a reach). I also tried to get in evidence of the Montrose car theft where three firearms were stolen along with the car, just three days after Janice had the firearms insured. "No way," said the judge. Next, I tried to have admitted the incident where Janice reported stolen the very rifles she and Bruce carried on the deadly hunting trip. She even blamed the theft on Bruce. The judge went for this one. He found the circumstances sufficiently linked with the murder and allowed it as proof of motive and intent.

However, there were two points in the trial that almost caused me to have a heart attack. One was during the testimony of Dr. Canfield, the pathologist who conducted the autopsy. He had said from the day of the autopsy that it was not possible that Bruce could have fired a rifle after having been shot. He reaffirmed that to me on several occasions. I had him on the stand for a while going through the autopsy, describing the location of the wounds and the collection of the copper jacket and the lead bullet core and so on. Just before time for our lunch break, I asked him what I considered one of the most crucial questions of the trial. Pausing I changed the pitch of my voice to signify the importance of this question: "Dr. Canfield," I said, brow furrowed, "considering the wound to the chest and the wound to the back that severed Bruce Dodson's spine, is it possible that he would have been able to fire a rifle after having received those wounds?"

Dr. Canfield cocked his head, rolled his eyes pensively toward the ceiling, and when he answered, "Yes," the blood just completely drained out of my head. I have no idea how I appeared to others in the courtroom, but I could hardly speak. As I fumbled around the lectern, Judge Massaro fortuitously declared the lunchtime recess.

As I made my way down the stairs, I was convinced I would lose the case. If Canfield had told me this before, I could have worked around it. I had staked the case on this one fact in my opening statement. Dr. Canfield followed me to my office. He asked me if I was all right. I confronted him with what he had just said on the witness stand after all these years of telling us it that Bruce could not have fired the rifle. He said, "That's not what you asked. You asked if it was *possible*. Anything is *possible*. It's *possible* that little green men came down from Mars and fired the rifle. If you would ask me if Bruce fired the rifle after receiving those wounds my answer would be an unqualified 'No.'" I was annoyed at myself for making the mistake but very relieved to learn the matter of semantics could be cleared up relatively easily. After the lunch recess I asked Dr. Canfield some additional questions and cleared this up for the jury. I looked pretty dumb, but my evidence was intact. By three o'clock the following morning I had the worst migraine headache of my life.

And I knew my next witness might cause more questions

than answers. Ron Finley was a smart, tough cop but he was more stubborn than a mule. Now, he was sticking to his own theory of how the crime occurred. I considered not calling him at all, but since he was the one who collected the hillside bullet on the Uncompahgre Plateau, I had no choice. Fortunately, I was able to guide him through the direct examination without sustaining too much damage. But Alex Williams had done his homework. Skillfully, he went right to the heart of Ron's experience as an investigator and with firearms. Then he went in for the kill.

"Now, Investigator Finley, based on your considerable experience as an investigator and as a firearms expert, is it not a fact that when you examined that bullet from the hillside you formed the opinion that it was not related to this investigation?" Williams asked sternly.

I was in a tricky position here of having to decide whether to object to my own witness giving an opinion as an expert without having been qualified. I opted to hold off.

Finley nodded. "Yes. It looked to me like it had traveled a long distance and reached the end of its course without hitting anything and just came to rest in that area."

As Don made this statement, Bill Booth who was sitting right next to me jerked his head back involuntarily. Quickly putting his hand up to his eye, he held it there, reacting to the sharp pain. Bill later went to a doctor who told him a blood vessel behind his eye had burst. He would have a bloodshot eye for the next two weeks.

Asking the next question, Williams exuded confidence:

"From your involvement in this investigation as lead investigator, you are aware of the location where a spent .308-caliber rifle casing was recovered. Is that not correct?"

"That is correct," Finley replied.

Williams raised his voice with dramatic effect, "Do you have an opinion as to whether the bullet recovered from the hillside was in such a condition so as to be consistent with having been fired from that spot."

"In my opinion it is not consistent. That bullet traveled far further than that, ran out of steam and landed where we found it."

Williams scanned the jury then quickly turned back to Finley. "Thank you," he said, smiling as if he'd made friends with my witness and walked triumphantly back to the counsel table. I felt my stomach roll, but reassured myself that in a trial a winning streak can quickly end.

However, I was concerned about my next witness, Bart Hall, Janice's current husband, and what might result from his testimony. In general, I avoid calling close family members of the defendant unless I absolutely need them, not so much because of my compassionate heart, but because I think it looks cheap to the jury. Before the trial when I read over the reports of Bart's statements, I was leaning toward not using him. At that point I had not met him, but had seen him at hearings. He always dressed in black; he even wore a black cowboy hat and black rain slicker. He drove a black convertible. I really did not know what to make of him, other than my feeling that he must be a goofy romantic to have been in love with Janice since he was nine years old and to have gotten together with her the way he did. Since Bart lived in Texas, we would have to go through the interstate subpoena process to have him served and this takes several weeks. Just about at the end of the period where I would have to make this decision, I decided not to use Bart and instructed my paralegal not to have him subpoenaed.

At that point, I was in good shape insofar as trial preparation was concerned. It was the end of January, so I slipped down to the Tucson Gem and Mineral shows for a few days to clear my mind and make final adjustments to my plans. I brought along a notebook and tape recorder to work on the case during the trip. Then, as sometimes happens when one steps back for a moment, on the drive down it suddenly hit me. I absolutely had to call Bart Hall as a witness. I couldn't explain why, but I knew it was important. I telephoned Bill Booth from Blanding, Utah and asked him to help my paralegal get Bart served.

Now, as the trial progressed, I still felt hesitant about calling Bart to the stand and saved him until late in my case. It may have been instinct and it may be have been luck, but he turned out to be a strong witness and very important to our case. The key point in his testimony came when I asked him about what Janice said to him after she came back from meeting with Mark Morgan.

"Janice said she wanted to set up a bank account for Mark to have access to in case something happened to her. Janice told me that maybe if she set up this account, Mark would stay off her back."

I questioned Bart about this. He became quite animated, his voice rising. "Yes, that was what I couldn't figure out. They had been divorced for seven years and I couldn't see why she would want to open a bank account for him."

"How much money did she want to put in it?" I asked.

His answer stunned me. Bart replied, "Everything. Everything we had. She wanted to sell the Leadville house and the Cedaredge house and put all the money plus whatever else we had into this account for Mark."

I practically fell over. I scanned the jury and from the looks on their faces, their amazement was apparent.

After having him testify, I thought Bart to be an honest, decent man who really was in love with Janice. I felt very sorry for him.

Not every witness I called had this effect on me. My next witness, Ted Farly, had refused to cooperate and forced us to use the interstate subpoena process. We first had to get a court order from a judge, stating that the witness was a material witness. Next, we had to send the paperwork to the prosecuting attorney's office in the home jurisdiction of the witness. That office needed to open a court case there and subpoena the witness to attend. The judge there had to find that the witness was a material witness as we claimed and then order him to honor the interstate subpoena. It is an archaic system, but usually it works pretty well. District attorney offices in large jurisdictions have full-time staff investigators who work only on this. However, in this case, when I finally got hold of the DA, he told me that he was running in an election for judge the following week and was consumed with that and, in addition, he and one assistant were handling 400 felony cases. I contacted the Texas Rangers, who wield enormous power down there, just as they are portrayed in *Lonesome Dove*. They got the job done fast. Once Ted Farly was served, we sent him a plane ticket, some money for meals and arranged for his hotel accommodations. I was tempted to put him in the same small motel I had Mark Morgan in, but I resisted that temptation. One of my investigators met him at our airport and brought him directly to the courthouse. Unfortunately, on the witness stand, he claimed not to remember any of what he had told the investigators before about having a relationship with Janice in Montrose. The rule of evidence requires that I ask him about each statement he made. If he says he does not recall, then I can call the person to whom he made the statement to testify about it. Farly said he was there but was an alcoholic and thought he may have had sex with Janice because he had before on several occasions, but he was so drunk that night he had no recollection. I thought the jury got the general gist of the evening from his testimony anyway.

I have to admit I was stunned when one of my most interesting witnesses, Gary Dalton, Mark Morgan's boss, came to Grand Junction to testify at the trial. From everything I had read I was expecting another East Texas Bubba. Instead, Mr. Dalton turned out to be a pleasant and sophisticated businessperson, clean cut, handsome, well-spoken and he looked at home in a business suit. At trial, he seemed to have managed to lose his East Texas country, slow-talking drawl and he came across as being completely honest.

When I called on him, Dalton told the jury that he and Mark had planned their hunting trip for that year months prior to October. He said they had hunted in the area the year prior but did not camp in the exact same place. He described their camp for 1994 as being near the top of the hill above the campsite they used in 1995. This spot would have been closer to Janice and Bruce's camp and would have been very close to where the Flight for Life helicopter landed to take Janice to Saint Mary's Hospital. The 1995 campsite for Mark, Marcy and Gary Dalton was almost exactly one mile as the crow flies northeast from Janice and Bruce's camp. It is probably a mile and a half by jeep roads. Gary also testified that on Sunday morning, Mark left camp well before daylight to go hunting. Gary said he slept late and that he and Marcy were the only ones in camp when he got up. When they returned to camp mid-morning, Mark was already there.

In total, I called seventy-one witnesses, including experts, friends, foes and intimates of the defendant, to prove the prosecution's assertion that Janice Dodson had murdered her husband in cold blood. It had been difficult through this long procession to sustain the momentum, but I had given my best, hoping the sea of faces in the jury box would stay with me.

After a short recess, we returned for the defense's presentation. The courtroom was absolutely still. For a moment, I looked over at the members of the jury as they filed into the room. From out of the corner of my eye, I could see the defense team gearing up for their turn. It was difficult, in this case, to keep the veneer of civility in place, but I knew it was one of the rules of the game.

= chapter 27 =

For the Defense

To prove their theories, the defense attorneys had the crime scene surveyed again in an attempt to show that the prosecution's ballistics results regarding the hillside bullet were flawed. This resulted in several maps and diagrams and ended in me calling a counter-expert to point out that *their* survey was flawed. One of their experts, Wyatt Tate, found another source of dirt that he said matched the dirt on Janice's boots and jeans. Alex Williams attempted to prove her story about where she hunted that morning and stepping into a bog other than the one we tested, even though Janice's original statement was that the bog she stepped in was two hundred yards from her camp and the one the defense found with the matching dirt was a thirty-minute hike. Later, they called Barry Hart, a firearms expert who contradicted everything our firearms experts had concluded. They tried to prove that it would have been impossible for these shots, fired as quickly as reported by Captain Branchwater, to have been fired through a bolt-action rifle such as the rifle reported stolen by Mark Morgan. I watched intently as they argued that the murder weapon could have been a .243-caliber rifle based largely on the fact that Ron

Finley put so much effort into trying to prove this. Experts like these have in recent years dominated criminal cases and I knew their diverse opinions often could be confusing and muddy the waters. I felt the defense spent an inordinate amount of time on the fact that no one for the prosecution had measured or diagrammed the location of the footprints. They had photographs, a videotape and a PowerPoint presentation, where they attacked the prosecution's evidence.

One of our critical points during the prosecution phase of presenting evidence was the heavy insurance on Bruce's life for which Janice was the primary beneficiary. To contradict this Scott Nolan called Tony Taylor, a local insurance agent who they qualified as an expert witness. I know Tony Taylor and he is as honest as the day is long. We lived in the same neighborhood up until a few years ago.

Nolan queried, "You said you'd sold health insurance and you also sold life insurance. Do you sell both individual and group policies?"

"I do," Taylor said quietly.

"Are you involved in selling group policies to employers?"

"Yes, I am."

"Is that both for life insurance and health insurance?"

"Yes."

"And have you been selling life insurance and health insurance for the same amount of time in Colorado?"

Taylor nodded. "Yes, I have."

"Now, I want to ask you some questions about selling life insurance. When you sit down with a couple to discuss purchasing life insurance, are there some rules of thumb or guidelines on how much life insurance to purchase that you talk to them about?"

Taylor leaned a bit toward the microphone. "Rule of thumb in the industry is usually as a starting point, it's ten times income. So, for example, if someone made $40,000 a year, $400,000 worth of life insurance would be a good starting point because it's ten times their income. In the industry, the reasoning behind such a strategy is that if you can get ten percent interest on that $400,000, it replaces the income of the individual who has died. It's as if he or she hadn't died at all in terms of income. So that the family could still go on and pay their bills, pay their debts, those type of things without touching the principal."

"So, it's looked at from the point of income replacement, right." Nolan looked at Taylor thoughtfully. "If you had a couple where each was making approximately $30,000 sit down to discuss this type of situation with you, what type of amounts would you recommend then?"

"Well," Taylor replied, "usually it's, again, a good starting point would be ten times each of their incomes."

Nolan went on to try to show that the insurance the Dodson's had was not excessive.

"Did you also get a chance to look at some of the information on the Dodsons' insurance policies?"

"Yes, I did."

"And in looking at those, were you able to make any kind of determination as between Mr. Dodson and Ms. Hall, who would have been Ms. Dodson at the time, which one of them actually had the higher amount of insurance on them?"

Taylor responded, "Janice had the higher amount of life insurance on her."

"Do you remember the monetary difference?" Nolan probed.

"I believe she had one policy that was for $300,000 and he was—if he should die, she would get 60 percent of that and on the $100,000 policy, I believe that was also the case."

"And if she were the one to die, the payoff would be...," Nolan trailed off.

"Greater for her death, yeah," Taylor nodded.

"In looking at these policies and that information, did you see anything untoward or improper in those policies?"

"No, actually, I did not."

Nolan thanked the witness who politely did the same. Then the judge looked over at me.

"Cross-examination, Mr. Daniels."

I stood up and cleared my throat. Looking directly at Tony Taylor, I asked him, "How long have you been selling life insurance?"

Taylor replied, "Nineteen years."

"How many times in those nineteen years have any of your life insurance policies been collected on?"

After pausing to reflect, Taylor answered, "Once."

Then I queried, "What is the one thing that the insured must do to enable a beneficiary to collect on a life insurance policy?"

This time he answered immediately. "He or she has to die." His comment brought laughter to the courtroom. I thanked him and sat down.

Janice's cousin, Leah Brown, lives in a small town near Beaumont, Texas. Janice's relatives on her mother's side hail from there. The courtroom stirred as Leah walked slowly and somberly to the witness stand, glancing over at Janice with a loving smile. She described knowing Janice as a small child and adult, Janice's unhappy early marriage and Janice's excitement over her wedding to Bruce Dodson. Then Leah sadly detailed the day she helped Janice pick out an outfit to wear at the funeral service for Bruce.

In her opinion, Janice was truly distraught over her husband's untimely and unfortunate demise. As I watched her there was no doubt in my mind that Leah was a sympathetic witness. As she spoke, tears poured out of her eyes. Alex Williams carried a box of tissues to the witness stand and presented them to Leah with deepest sympathy, a sad grimace and a furrowed brow.

Williams knew he had a strong character witness and he made the most of it.

"What was Janice like at the memorial service?"

"Devastated, very emotional."

"Have you seen her when she's been that way before?"

"Yes, sir."

"Have other family members?"

"Yes, sir."

"Was there anything outlandish or fake about the way she was acting?"

"No, sir," Leah said softly.

Williams nodded, empathizing. "After that, was there a time period when Janice came to stay with you in Texas?"

"Yes, sir."

"Do you remember when that was?"

"I'm not very good on dates. I would probably say the end of October to the first week of November."

"And that's when she arrived at your house?"

"She arrived at my house."

"And how long did she stay at your house?"

"Until January 7, the day before my birthday."

"What was she like while she was staying at your house with you?"

"It was a nightmare. She was just devastated."

"Can you tell me in what way?"

"She cried. She wouldn't eat. It was just an emotional up and down everyday."

"Was she able to participate in any of your family functions with you?"

"That was about the only thing, either church or something that she came to the family. Only time we ever—pertaining to families—only time we ever left the house."

"Did you feel like any part of that was a put-on or fake?"

"No, sir."

Williams looked at the judge. "I don't have anything else."

The judge gestured in my direction. "Cross-examination, Mr. Daniels."

By the end, I knew that I had to be very careful cross examining her. I was not about to hammer a lovely old lady, but somewhere in the eleven thousand pages of reports in this case, I had seen Janice's bank records. These showed that Janice had made two ATM withdrawals at a casino in Lake Charles, Louisiana during the period about which Leah was testifying. I had sat stoically during questioning by the defense, but, poker-faced now, I asked Leah about the ATM withdrawals.

"Isn't it true that Janice was well enough to go gambling at a casino in Lake Charles, Louisiana, during this time?" The question seemed to confound her. She stumbled around for a while before saying that it was her idea to go over there to try to cheer up poor Janice.

At her reply, murmurs grew in the courtroom. I looked over in their direction; the jurors were alert. Their eyes were fixed on the witness. Wanting the jurors to hold fast to their newly acquired insight and not to feel that a hard-nosed prosecutor was preying on a sweet gray-haired lady I said, "No further questions." Sometimes it's best to stop when you've won your point.

The defense endorsed thirty-six witnesses. They called seven to testify; six were qualified as experts and the seventh, Janice's cousin Leah from Texas, was a character witness. Their experts testified that the investigation was flawed; the forensic work done for the prosecution was poorly done; it is not unusual for a couple in the financial situation of Bruce and Janice to have as much insurance as they did; and Janice truly was a grieving widow.

Janice did not testify. This disappointed me as I had an extensive cross-examination planned for her.

= chapter 28 =

The Prosecution Rests

The courtroom was filled with reporters, lawyers, assorted friends, neighbors and the usual collection of curiosity seekers, as well as the by now familiar family members. I did not want to miss anything in my closing arguments. The prosecution goes first; then the defense presents their argument; then the prosecution has the opportunity to rebut the defense argument. The first phase of my argument would be to go over the evidence, tracking my opening statement. I often do this to stress the fact that I have kept the promise of what I said I would prove. I looked squarely at the jury and began by going over the testimony of the bevy of witnesses we had called in this difficult case.

"Two of the first witnesses were hunters, Captain Brent Branchwater and Larry Coller, who just happened to be caught up in this situation because they were hunting in the same area. They came across as reasonable persons presenting their truthful account of what they saw and heard. It is clear from the testimony that these two reasonable people were not taken in by the irrational, theatrical antics of Janice Hall." I stressed the first name Janice and affected Hall, raising my voice slightly. The courtroom had become silent.

The only sounds were those of the court reporter dutifully transcribing each word. Now I continued recreating our picture of the period before the crime occurred.

"Brent Branchwater and his friend, Ryan, arrived at the campsite on October 12 in the afternoon. Friday they went out scouting. In the evening, they noticed the vehicles driven by Janice and Bruce Dodson coming in and camping close to their campsite. On Saturday, they got up around 5:00 A.M. and headed out to a canyon for their hunt. They hunted the entire day, getting back late. On Sunday, Ryan left around the same time and took their only vehicle out of the campsite. Brent Branchwater stayed in camp, having the luxury of sleeping in a bit since he had filled his license the previous day. About 7:00 A.M., while lying in bed in his tent, he heard a shot. This awakened him. The shot was followed by hollering. He recalls checking the time and believing it was shortly after 7:00 o'clock. In a moment he heard another shot—then another, followed by the thump of a bullet strike. The shots were clearly close and coming from an area in front of the Volkswagen camper and the Bronco."

I caught the eye of the pastor on the jury and held it for a moment. Then I continued.

"After getting out of bed around 7:30, he saw the defendant walking up the tree line in front of the Volkswagen camper to go to the vehicles. He went on skinning his deer, glanced over at the Bronco and noticed the person he saw was a woman dressed in blue jeans, a sweater jacket, an orange vest and sandals with white socks. He saw her put a gun into a gun case. The next he sees of her, she is right behind him, toothbrush in hand, saying, 'That's a nice forky you have there.' They had a conversation concerning their hometowns and other small talk. He told her he heard three shots and hollering and asked if one of her group killed a deer. She said she had not heard any shooting or hollering from the area. She started talking about her husband being on the mountain, this being his first deer hunt. She asked where his friend was and he told her. She asked if they would get some water for them when they went into town and, after a while, she said that her husband should be back by now and she was going to go look for him. She said his name was Bruce and she introduced herself."

Now it was time to set up the moment when the forces of good and evil tangled. I paused and then went on.

"As Captain Branchwater was finishing boning his deer, he heard what he thought at first was the sound of an elk bugling. He turned off the radio to listen and could hear it was a person screaming for help from the direction in front of the Bronco and the Volkswagen. He ran up to the front of the sleeping tent and looked over the rise where he could see the defendant standing by a body. She had an orange vest in her hand and when she saw him, she started hollering and beating the vest on the ground screaming, 'Why didn't you have your orange on?' She then picked up a rifle laying there, holding it out in front of her and threw it on the ground near the body."

I lowered my voice, walking to an intimate distance from the jury. The tension in the room was evident as I continued. "Brent went over to help, meeting her about halfway. He asked if the man had a bad heart. She said, 'No, you've got to help him.' He went over and it was obvious to him that Bruce was dead. He could see the hole in the back of the jacket with the bloodstains. Bruce was lying on his stomach with the palms of his hands down and his head facing the fence to his left. He had an orange cap partially on his head and was wearing glasses. The rifle lay by Bruce's left hand and was parallel to the fence. There were two empty shell casings lying between his left hand and his head. Bruce's face was blue, his eyes were glazed over and he had no pulse. He was not breathing. As Brent was checking Bruce, Janice picked up the two empty shell casings and threw them, hitting Brent in the leg. He went to get help. After being gone for some time trying to get law enforcement to respond to the scene, Brent came back with a deputy and found that two boys from Wisconsin were standing by the body with Janice. He was able to get her away from the body so that the deputy could examine the situation.

"During their conversation, she told him that day was Bruce's and her three-month wedding anniversary and they were supposed to have a date that night. She mentioned she had taught her children to shoot by using a .22-caliber rifle, she reloaded her own ammunition and that she and her ex-husband had run hunting camps in the area for twenty years. As each vehicle arrived with other law enforcement personnel, she would ask if this was the paramedics. She kept asking when the helicopter was going to get there to help Bruce." I paused a moment, scanned the jurors' faces and, feeling they were with me, I went on. "As Shakespeare said, 'Me thinks thou dost protest too much.' She talked about what a great relationship she and Bruce had, that he was loving and punctual."

Janice had seemed to ramble on, touching first on one subject then another. I tried to show her nervousness and yet her ability to hold center stage. "She talked about his mother and how she sent money to Bruce, mentioning $10,000. She said Bruce's dad had been an executive with a tobacco company and spoke of how he had bought stock in the company all along and when he died he left it all to Bruce's mom and about how she had invested the money and had done well with it. She talked about how she and Bruce improved Bruce's home and doubled the value. She talked about guns and hunting and how she had not missed a hunting season and was going to come with or without Bruce. Then Janice told him Bruce asked her if she was going whether or not he came along. She said she was. She said Bruce wanted to use a shotgun but she borrowed a rifle for him. She said that she would get up first and warm the camper and make coffee for him while he lay in bed and then she would leave first and get a head start and go low on the mountain and push up through the draws trying to run deer up to him. At one point she digressed, 'You did tell them I threw the gun there, didn't you?' Brent was present when the officers were removing the guns from the defendant's vehicles. When they told Janice they were going to take the guns for testing and wrote her a receipt, she began to faint." I could not help smiling ruefully.

Purposefully, I moved back to the morning of Bruce's death. "Captain Branchwater said he heard the first shot at about 7:30, then heard some hooping and hollering and then a minute or two later he thought he heard two quick gun shots. He thought someone had shot a deer, it had gotten up and then the shooter fired two more rounds. He said that around 8:30 he saw the woman entering behind her camp." I spent a short while discussing the discrepancies in attributing the exact time of the shots pointing out, "This is just the way memories work with time."

Commenting on the testimony of Larry Coller, the young man from Wisconsin who was hunting that day with his brother, I described how they were headed back to camp at 10:00 A.M. when they saw the defendant, out of breath, running up the road with sandals hanging around her ankles. "They took her back to the murder scene, and Larry stayed with her while his brother went to find some help. It was obvious to Larry that Bruce was dead; his hand and wrist were cold, he had no pulse, his cheeks were white, his ears and forehead were blue, his eyes were open and his pupils were dilated." Now I began to recount the dynamics between Larry and Janice and his feeling about her expressed in his testimony. "Janice told Larry that she and her husband had only been married for three months and that day was their anniversary. She said Bruce was her 'Honey Bunny.' Larry said the gun with the bolt open, three spent shell casings, and a hat looked as though they were placed there rather than having been dropped. Janice told Larry she was old-fashioned and would not live with her husband prior to the marriage. She talked about how she was good with a rifle and only carried one bullet. She said that Bruce paid off her debts and they were pretty well off, that he had some land and assets. She talked about shooting grouse with a .22 by shooting them in the head. She never told him that anyone else had gone for help. She must have forgotten—or perhaps she did not know she was doing it when she was doing it. Janice told him that she and Bruce were going to hunt in different directions and meet in camp and that she was going to give him a Swiss Army knife as a present for their three-month anniversary. Janice showed him the ridge where Bruce was going to be hunting and showed him the direction she had come back to camp." I brought in Larry's thought: "It was pretty fishy that she did not see the body that you could so obviously see from where she said she had been walking and from her camper." I finished going over the testimony of this witness and I pointed out, "Larry Coller is obviously a reasonable person with no ax to grind and he was clearly not fooled by the defendant's story."

Next I turned to Nick Armand who had provided a great amount of important testimony. I touched on Nick's outstanding credentials in the area of crime scene investigations and the meticulous efforts he used to see that the crime scene was properly handled, that measurements were taken and that all relevant evidence was collected. "Nick spoke to the defendant after the body was removed, which was after five o'clock in the afternoon. She asked how Bruce was doing and he explained that Bruce was deceased. She responded, 'No, the paramedics took him away.' He explained to her that he would be taking the rifle and other weapons for safekeeping and as he prepared to fill out an inventory sheet, she collapsed."

One by one I went through the major witnesses and highlighted the evidence they added to Janice's guilt. I knew I was risking losing the jury's attention but, on the other hand, I didn't want to take a chance that the cumulative effect of each piece of evidence would be lost.

"The chief from the Palisade Police Department was the witness who found the .308-caliber shell casing with his metal detector. It had been concealed from view in some grass. Carl Todd and Victor Poste found the .243 caliber ammunition box in the Volkswagen camper contained twenty live rounds and one empty shell casing; the remaining three .243-caliber shell casings were found near the left hand of John Bruce Dodson in a pile, obviously having been placed there by Janice Hall because she wanted to make it look like Bruce had fired three shots as a distress signal."

Then I spoke of Dan Faed, who talked of his long and extensive history as a tracker. I reminded the jury that, "Dan has worked for twenty-six years as a professional tracker for outfitters and has volunteered his time for search and rescue and he testified that he found a footprint matching that of the defendant twenty feet behind where the .308 shell casing was found."

The next set of witnesses I needed to bring to the jurors' minds was the Morgan clan and friends—Marcy Cleary, Gary Dalton, Terence Morgan, Carla Morgan and, of course, Mark Morgan. "Mark, Marcy and Gary were camped in an area where they had camped previously and just a short distance from where they had camped the year before. Their campsite from the previous year is even closer to the spot that Janice Hall chose to set up her camp in 1995. In fact, it's just a few minutes walk. Ironically, the spot pointed out on the aerial photograph by Gary Dalton showing where they camped the year before is very nearly the same exact spot pointed out by witnesses showing where the Flight for Life helicopter came in to whisk Janice Hall to St. Mary's Hospital. The issue of Mark Morgan's stolen .308-caliber rifle is a key element to this case. The rifle he reported stolen is a bolt action, Remington Model 700 Varmint rifle with a heavy barrel in .308 caliber. The ammunition he reported stolen is .308-caliber Federal Premium brand. He reported that the rifle was loaded with the same ammunition."

Carefully and meticulously I went over Mark's testimony pointing out Janice's several calls to him asking questions about ammunition and how he had discovered upon his return to Utah that he was missing his .308 heavy barreled rifle loaded with five Federal Premium hunting bullets.

I reminded the jury that Mark had also determined that his firearm and other items were stolen between 3:00 and 7:30 P.M. on the afternoon of Saturday, October 14, because when he returned at 7:30 he noticed that someone had messed around with his tent. I zeroed in on Mark's words: "Janice could shoot in a two-inch circle at 100 meters from a bench rest." He told how in shooting competitions, sometimes Janice would get the upper hand on some of the men. I pointed out that he was helpful in obtaining the serial number for his missing .308 rifle by checking with a pawnshop in Texas.

Turning to Terence Morgan and his wife, Carla, I told the jury my assessment, that they came across as being truthful. I reminded the jury that through Carla Morgan, it came out that Janice did know that Mark was going to be hunting in the area, at least close to the time in question. "Janice even admitted at one point that she knew Mark was going to be up there that same week. Marcy Cleary testified that she and Mark camped in the exact same spot in 1992 or 1993. Gary Dalton testified that he and Mark camped just up the hill in the 1994 season." I went into the fact that Marcy Cleary recalled a time when Janice told her that if she caught any woman with Mark, she would kill her.

I emphasized the testimony of Dr. Thomas Canfield, my expert witness in forensic pathology, saying that his credentials were impeccable and spanned several decades. Then I went into his findings in the autopsy of John Bruce Dodson, who, coincidentally, was a person he knew and who worked for him in the laboratory. "He described the entry wound in the chest as being 51 ½ inches high, 1 ¼ inches right of midline, with an exit wound at 49 inches in height.

That is a difference of 2 ½ inches. He described the wound as being consistent with a high caliber, high velocity jacketed hunting bullet. He recovered a piece of the jacket from about the entry wound in the chest. With regard to the shot in the back, he described this as being 48 ½ inches in height and 2 ¾ inches right of midline. It deflected up into the left lung. There was no exit wound. Dr. Canfield removed a piece of lead bullet core from Bruce's left lung. He stated that Bruce was otherwise a healthy man. He said that the shot to the spine pulverized the bone and essentially 'pole-axed' Bruce. The bullet wound in the chest fragmented as it hit the zipper of Bruce's sweatshirt. He said that Bruce had fresh grass stains on the knees of his bib overalls. He said there was a small injury to the shoulder about the time of death and that, in his opinion, Bruce would not have been able to fire a rifle after receiving those wounds. He marked the bullet core at its base, TMC105. He noted that the shot to the chest collapsed the right lung and fractured three ribs. He ruled the cause of death to be the gunshot wound to the back and the manner of death to be homicide."

Continuing, I talked about the two Division of Wildlife officers who testified. "Harvey James picked up a hat in the ditch just outside the campsite which was the only item we sent to CBI that came back positive for gunshot residue. Bill Johanson introduced records from the Division of Wildlife pointing out that Bruce never before had a big game license and Janice had not had one for several years. Also in evidence from Bill Johanson are 'Rules and Regulations for Hunting in Big Game Season.' One rule," I pointed out, "is that some of the fluorescent orange must be worn on the head, a rule that John Bruce Dodson assuredly would have followed without having to be lectured by Janice."

The next set of witnesses I brought up were members of the Delta County Sheriffs Department plus the representative of an insurance company. "These witnesses deal with an episode wherein Janice Hall reported three firearms, with two scopes and cases, stolen in March of 1995. She blamed Bruce for stealing them. This report was made after she broke up with Bruce. Two of these firearms were the firearms Janice and Bruce had on the hunting trip where Bruce was murdered." I commented that the whole situation was especially fishy. "Janice reported that she put the guns up when she moved into the house in August and noticed that they were missing on March 7, 1995." I reminded the jury, "She told the sheriff's deputies that her boyfriend, Bruce Dodson, said he noticed they were gone on February 24, 1995. She said she was house-sitting for a friend. She said that the two rifles had hard cases and scopes. She said that the .357 was in a case. She said she believed Bruce had her guns. She said she had a .22-caliber semi-automatic target pistol, a 12-gauge shotgun, a .22-caliber rifle and a .38-caliber pistol that belonged to Mark Morgan. She said Bruce was having problems with consumption of alcohol. She said she looked in Bruce's vehicles for the guns and could not find them. A deputy asked her about Mark Morgan because she mentioned him during the conversation. As soon as the deputy arrived back at the sheriff's department, Mark Morgan was there waiting for him. Janice denied having the guns or of having left them somewhere else. The deputy contacted Janice after it was learned that two of the guns were recovered. Janice just said she did not recall leaving the guns at Skip Kay's house. She mentioned a memory loss. She said, 'It is not really a memory loss. What it is, I can be doing something and not know I am doing it, so I don't remember doing it.' She explained this as the situation that existed when she used her credit card in Denver and ran her bill up. She said she did not know she was doing it while she was doing it. Janice collected an insurance payout of $1,665 that included $400 for the .243-caliber rifle and $575 for the .270-caliber rifle. The remainder of the money was for a .357 magnum handgun, cases, and scopes. Here it was just four months before the wedding and she was accusing

Bruce Dodson of having stolen her firearms. She obviously persisted in this claim since she collected the insurance. Only when she realized she needed some firearms to finalize a much larger and more lucrative insurance fraud did she get the guns back from Skip Kay." I further reminded jurors, "Skip said he was surprised when Janice and Bruce were getting married since she had told him previously that she did not want to marry Bruce."

I didn't want the jury to forget that even Janice's own attorneys had elicited from Skip Kay, as well as from another witness, the opinion that "'Sometimes Janice exaggerates things a little bit.' That is the opinion that her friends had of her truthfulness—that she exaggerates things." After this I touched on the testimony of other witnesses who brought damaging aspects of Janice's personality or actions into evidence, including those who could establish the ammunition she'd bought.

Then I came to Ron Roberts, the officer who took the most detailed statements from Janice. She pointed out to Investigator Roberts where she came back to the camp on Sunday through the trees to the rear of the van.

"There are a number of witnesses whose sole role was to offer evidence from a variety of banks, businesses and insurance companies. By and large, these exhibits establish the financial records that were used later by our expert witness in forensic accounting."

Going on, I reminded the jurors of the testimony of Investigator William Booth of the District Attorney's Office who had added his expertise as a law enforcement officer all during the investigation.

When I turned again to Investigator Nick Armand, I reported that he "did much of the preliminary work with his thorough crime scene investigation and subsequent examinations and tests. Later, Investigator Ron Finley took over as lead investigator. Investigator Booth worked with Nick Armand and with Ron Finley as they attempted to piece together the case. Bill was always actively involved in the investigation, including the trip to the Uncompahgre Plateau in the summer of 1996 when they found the .30-caliber bullet in the hillside. When Ron Finley retired approximately a year and a half into the case, Investigator Booth and the Investigations Division of the District Attorney's Office took over." It should be clear, I pointed out, that Booth, who'd devoted so many hours to this case, was seriously invested in bringing justice to John Bruce Dodson and to his family." I hoped my next words would later echo in their minds. "Justice for John Bruce Dodson is justice for Janice Hall."

I reminded the jurors that Ron Finley had reported variances between his early interviews and the testimony presented at trial. "He established that Janice was told that Mark and Marcy were going to be hunting on the plateau around the same time. He brought out that Bart told him that Janice had a 7 mm magnum firearm stored with him at some point. He also took the statement from Skip Kay that when Janice was asked, shortly before marrying Bruce, if she loved him, she replied, 'Yeah, I think so. He's been after me for years and he will take care of me.'"

I backtracked for a moment. "Ron Finley and Ron Roberts were the two investigators who traveled to Layton, Utah, to speak with Mark Morgan a few days after the murder. While in his apartment, they noticed a pad that had some names and a list of items. When they asked about it, Mark told them that some items were stolen from his tent and he was putting together a list in order to file a report. Prior to this time, no investigator involved in this case had any knowledge that Mark Morgan owned or had brought a .308-caliber rifle on the mountain during that trip.

"It was obvious," I said, "from Ron Finley's testimony and from the various requests for further testing he submitted, that he was of the opinion that the murder weapon was the .243. He discounted the .30-caliber bullet found in the hillside but was proven wrong by subsequent testing. He is not a firearms expert and was not qualified by the court as a firearms expert. Upon questioning from the defense about any and all issues involved in this case, his memory of details was often vague at best. Instead of asking Bill Booth these questions, Alex Williams asked an investigator who retired three years ago. Instead of asking a clearly competent and highly qualified firearms expert about firearms questions, Alex Williams asked Ron Finley. Here is a good time to make a point about direct questions and leading questions. A leading question is a question that suggests an answer. On cross-examination, leading questions are permitted. It is important to keep in mind that a leading question that provides information that is answered by 'no' or 'I don't know' does not establish in any way that the subject matter of the question is true. When the defense has had a theory they wished to forward, they have done so in the form of leading questions. They have used hundreds if not thousands of leading questions in this trial. There is nothing improper with doing this; however, it is important for the jury to keep in mind that only the answer provided by the witness is evidence."

Next, I went into the statements of witnesses who had shown Janice's financial stake in the death of her husband Bruce. Getting to the heart of Janice's motive, I showed again how Bruce's murder was worth $457,475.22 to her.

Recounting the testimony of the parade of witnesses who appeared on behalf of the state to lay bare the complicated and tangled web of assets and insurance that cast such a suspicious shadow over Janice's motivations, I went over many of the assets in question.

Peter Thorenson of the American United Insurance Company testified that Bruce's pension from St. Vincent's Hospital was valued at $20,902.93, all but $2000 of which had been cashed out by Janice.

Christine Werner, a representative of UNUM Life Insurance Company testified as to the $180,000 life insurance policy taken out on Bruce's life in July of 1995, only two short months before the fateful hunting trip. Having been held by the courts, the balance of that policy was in excess of $233,000.

Allianz Insurance Company provided documentation of a $50,000 policy, taken out by Bruce during his employment at Delta Memorial Hospital, with Janice Dodson as his beneficiary.

Suzanne Tramell testified that paperwork to collect the monies of Bruce's IRA account, which was valued at $51,235.78, had been filed only eight days after Bruce's death by Janice Dodson. She had been listed as beneficiary a year before the murder, replacing Bruce's siblings.

A representative of the Dodson's local bank had testified to Bruce's frugality, and recounted financial events in the months surrounding the fateful hunting trip. Janice withdrew two certificates of deposit and a money market account on October 23, 1995, walking from the bank with approximately $11,000. He also discussed the loan taken out by Janice and Bruce in late October in the amount of $15,000. They opted to take credit life insurance, which payed the entire debt remaining on the day of Bruce's death. All told, this credit life insurance policy was the sixth insurance policy benefiting Janice Dodson in the event of her husband's death.

Most telling, though, was the testimony of the expert in forensic accounting. I reminded the jury that prior to their marriage Janice had a net worth of negative $5,150 and Bruce had a positive net worth of $167,475.22. His testimony established that before marrying Bruce, Janice had been in debt, and ninety days later, she was sitting on a pile of money worth nearly one-half of a million dollars.

I reminded the jury, "Before marrying John Bruce Dodson, Janice was in debt. Ninety days later, she was looking at close to a half million dollars tax-free. If the Colorado lottery has a million dollars in it, and if you take the cash option and if you win, you get $400,000 and you are still taxed on it. This was better than winning a one million dollar lottery. And the contest was rigged."

Turning to Bruce's family, I went on. "You also heard from Michael and Martha, Bruce's brother and sister. They told you a little about the person that their brother Bruce was. He was an intelligent man, a lover of the outdoors, honest, sensitive and well read. Their father was a salesman, not an executive. They were raised in a row house in Baltimore. Their mother lives in a modest apartment and is not a wealthy woman. His siblings talked about their feelings of grief and how they would like to see justice served for Bruce and for his murderer."

Then I discussed how some of Janice's friends had seen signs of her deadly plans. "Susan Keith said Janice told her that she and Bruce were getting things ready insofar as their financial affairs were concerned prior to the hunting trip and asked her something about singing at the funeral. Beth, another friend, testified that the week following the murder she was with Susan Keith who was a coworker of hers at the hospital. Beth said they were talking about Bruce's death on Susan's way out and Susan said to her, 'What a coincidence, just last week Janice told me that Bruce wanted me to sing at his funeral.' Beth, who was a friend of Bruce's, remembered this clearly and she almost fell over when she heard it."

I spoke of those deadly plans being re-echoed when it came to Bart Hall, Janice Hall's third husband. Bart had said that he has been in love with Janice since he was nine years old. They were married on November 24, 1996, about a week after the divorce from his wife of twenty-one years was final. "Bart was present when Bill Booth was interviewing Janice in a lawyer's office on May 21, 1997, here in Grand Junction. Bart later came to this courthouse to talk to Bill Booth. He told Investigator Booth that something was bothering him about that interview. He said, 'Remember when we were in the lawyer's office and you told Janice that Bruce was murdered and she broke down, cried and had to leave the room? She knew Bruce was murdered, because she told me when I met her in San Augustine in November of 1995 he was murdered. No one is shot three times accidentally.' He said he could not understand why Janice broke down at the lawyer's office. Bart Hall comes across as being completely honest. He does not seem like a man capable of deception. He is like Bruce Dodson in the same vulnerable sort of way."

I went on, "In fact, what is eerily similar is that Bart has taken out insurance policies at Janice's request, making her the beneficiary."

I also went into the testimony of Gail Warner, who had quite a bit of insightful information on Janice for the prosecution. "'Bruce was tight with money,' she had said. 'Janice loved to spend money. Bruce had money and Janice wanted it.' After breaking up with Bruce, Janice talked about suing him for palimony. She was going to sue him to make him pay her money for the work she had done on his house as a spouse. Gail and Lauren Winters, another friend, talked her out of it, but clearly Janice felt that Bruce had money and she should get her share. Keep in mind that at this point whatever security blanket Bruce had offered was evaporating. Janice knew that she was on Bruce's life insurance policy and was the beneficiary of his IRA account and several certificates of deposit. If he were to die right then, she would benefit to the tune of a little over $100,000. Obviously, after it became clear to him that they were not getting back together, Bruce would take her off his policies and put his brother and sister back on." I outlined Janice's motive. "She wanted some of his money, so she first considered suing him for palimony. She later developed a better idea, an idea developed with or without the help of Mark Morgan during their meeting in Texas in June of 1995. When she came back from Texas and decided to marry Bruce, she knew he would marry her. She knew he loved her.

"The most telling part of Gail's testimony," I told jurors, "came when she told about how after Bruce's death they took Janice back to Lauren's house where Janice asked Gail if she would go up to Cedaredge and pick up her funeral arrangement plan. Gail did so, but was stunned when she got there to realize that Janice had made funeral arrangements prior to the hunting trip. Gail was further stunned to find the funeral planner sitting out on the kitchen table, all ready to go."

Next I highlighted the testimony of the three women criminalists at the Colorado Bureau of Investigation in Denver. Jacqueline Battles had told of her examination of some dirt. "What is important here is that the dirt on Janice's overalls and boots was inconsistent with and even not similar to the soil from the bog Janice claimed to have stepped in as her alibi."

Another of the criminologists, Deborah Chavez, was the expert witness on gunshot residue. The bottom line was that she found no gunshot residue on anything except for one hat. That hat was found near the camp the day after the murder. I told them it was not unusual to find gunshot residue on the hat of a hunter. "Where that hat came from, we do not know. Although we do know that Janice's hat was missing."

After this I reminded the jury that the last of the criminologists, Paige Doherty, discussed the procedures used by forensic documents examiners. She talked about the materials she had for comparison purposes, including known handwriting exemplars of Janice as well as normal course-of-business handwriting for both John Bruce Dodson and Janice Dodson. "The questioned document was the Emergency Record Guide collected from the storage unit by Bill Booth and Dave Martinez. Paige Doherty examined the known handwriting of Janice Dodson and of Bruce Dodson and could find no handwriting of John Bruce Dodson on this document. Most of the handwriting was identified as that of Janice Dodson. When it came to the signature of John Bruce Dodson, Ms. Doherty noted, 'The questioned signature, John Bruce Dodson, present on Page 4 of the Emergency Record Guide submitted in Exhibit 230 is illegibly written and contains a wide range of variation in baseline alignment, pressure and letter formation. These features may be an indication of a disguise attempt, a simulation attempt, the effects of illness, infirmity, medication and other physiological influences, or some other handwriting anomaly.' In other words, either Janice forged it or she had him sign it when he had been drinking. The efforts this woman went through to get all these details taken care of prior to Bruce's murder are simply astounding."

Step by step, I showed how we built the prosecution's case against Janice Dodson. The last three witnesses whose testimony I went over were the three forensic firearms experts, James Cotter, Shawn Bertram and Nancy Saunders. "This is perhaps the most important evidence in this case. Cotter first examined the .243 and the .270-caliber rifles. He checked for latent prints and found none suitable for comparison purposes. He found that both weapons were functioning firearms and explained for us how they worked. The capacity of each is six cartridges, five in the magazine and one in the chamber. They are both bolt-action rifles. He later examined some other firearms evidence in this case, including the three .243-caliber shell casings found by Bruce's body, the five 7 mm magnum cartridges from Janice's belongings at the hospital and the remainder of cartridges in the two ammunition boxes, as well as the .308 cartridge casing found in the oak brush. He established seven important facts." I emphasized each one:

"1. When the first shot was fired, the orange vinyl vest was the outermost garment.

"2. The down vest was the second layer of outer clothing with the red side on the exterior.

"3. The sweatshirt was the third layer of outer clothing and was zipped up.

"4. The remainder of the victim's clothing was underneath the sweatshirt.

"5. The first bullet passed through the orange vest into the down vest, into and out of the sweatshirt leaving what resembles to be a tear, back through the down vest, the orange vest, and then exited the clothing.

"6. The clothing underneath the sweatshirt was not damaged.

"7. The shots to the middle of the back and to the chest did not occur when the victim was wearing the orange vest and the down vest. There was no presence of any gunpowder residue on any of these bullet-hole areas."

I went on. "When he later examined the fifteen unfired cartridges in the 7 mm magnum box to attempt to determine if they had ever been loaded into a firearm, he found that five of the fifteen had markings similar to those he previously observed in connection with running a cartridge through the action of a firearm. This indicates that they may have been loaded, extracted and ejected from a firearm. Yet no 7 mm magnum rifle was located in Janice's camp.

"When Cotter received the .30-caliber jacketed bullet recovered from the hillside in the summer of 1996, he found this to be a .30-caliber jacketed bullet which had been fired from a rifle barrel with six lands and grooves, right twist, with extremely limited microscopic marks of value for comparison purposes should a suspect weapon be located. He noted that Remington, Savage and Stevens manufacture rifles producing rifling impressions such as those. He examined this bullet and compared it with a .308-caliber, 180 grain, jacketed, soft-point, Nosler Partition bullet such as those commercially loaded into cartridges of Federal manufacture. He found the questioned bullet to be identical in all its physical characteristics to the Nosler Partition bullet. He further found that the previously submitted bullet core, removed from John Bruce Dodson's left lung, could have originated from the lower core of such a bullet. I will submit here, that based on his testimony, the only logical conclusion to be drawn is that the .30-caliber bullet recovered from the hillside is a .308-caliber, 180 grain, jacketed soft-point, Nosler Partition bullet. There can be no question of that. It is identical, based on every characteristic, including base design, caliber and weight, the cantelor—everything. Based on his photographic comparison, which is in evidence, it appears that this core from Bruce Dodson's lung is the lower core of the Nosler Partition bullet from a 180-grain bullet such as those loaded into Federal Premium Ammunition. The work of Nancy Saunders confirms this."

I paused to be sure the technical information was sinking in, then I continued. "Nancy Saunders, a physical scientist at the Federal Bureau of Investigation, was qualified by the court as an expert witness dealing with analysis of bullet leads. She conducted a series of tests on exhibits forwarded to her by the CBI regarding this case. Her first series of tests established that the lead bullet core and the copper fragment recovered at the autopsy of Bruce Dodson were not consistent with the lead or copper in the .243-caliber cartridges. Likewise, her examination of January 30, 1998, indicated that a random selection of cores from other bullets in the box of .243-caliber cartridges recovered from the Dodson Volkswagen camper were of the same general alloy of lead as was the previously submitted sample and these were all inconsistent with the lead bullet core removed from Bruce Dodson's left lung.

"The August 14, 1998 series of tests resulted in conclusions most important to this case. Now Ms. Saunders had the .30-caliber bullet recovered from the hillside. She determined that the jacket component of the bullet from the hillside and the jacket fragment recovered from Bruce Dodson's chest were the same copper/zinc alloy. She cut the .30-caliber bullet and found that the upper and lower lead cores of this Nosler Partition bullet and the lead core from Bruce Dodson's lung consist of the same general alloy of lead. She further analyzed the lead of the upper core of the .30-caliber bullet and the lead core from Bruce Dodson's left lung by using inductively coupled plasma-atomic emission spectroscopy to determine the elemental composition. The result: the upper lead core of the .30-caliber bullet and the lead core from Bruce's left lung were analytically indistinguishable from one another.

I began to sum up by asserting my faith that the jury would bring justice to Bruce Dodson. "I have summarized most of the key points from the seventy-one witnesses called in our case. Please also rely on your notes, your collective memory and your collective judgment, which will be far more precise than the memory, judgment or argument of any one individual. This is why the jury system works. The jury system has been described as being the most powerful engine ever constructed to determine the truth. I believe this to be true."

Reaching the summit of our case, I didn't hesitate. I plunged on. "Janice Dodson had the motive. She went from a former bitter girlfriend of sorts, wanting to sue Bruce for palimony to a sudden bride. She went from a woman with a credit card balance of $9,000 plus in debt to potentially a wealthy woman with assets of close to one-half million dollars in ninety days."

I could tell from the response of spectators I'd touched a

nerve. I took a deep breath and emphasized my next telling evidence.

"She had the means, the motive and opportunity and there's more. She's the only one who could have planted the three spent shell casings. Branchwater heard three shots, not six. There were only three shots. Even if Bruce's spine had not been severed, he did not fire his rifle. He was not even holding his rifle by the time of shot number three.

"Without doubt, Bruce did not fire those .243 caliber bullets. Bruce was a careful man and most likely sighted in on the way up to the hunting camp or perhaps he did shoot at some deer the day before. Four shots would have been enough for sighting in or to shoot at some deer.

"The defense said in opening you would not hear that those bullet pieces match the one from the lung and the one from the hillside. Well, you have heard that they match. Yes, they do match. Why would Mark Morgan report the rifle stolen? As I mentioned briefly before, if he was supposed to get it back but Janice panicked and stepped into a mud bog, he'd have a motive to report it stolen and perhaps it was stolen. You decide.

"The concept of one bullet, one animal, being certain of a kill with one shot is entirely not consistent with hunting with a rifle that has only been bore sighted and another that has not been sighted at all. When you shoot an elk or a deer, you have an area to aim for. You do not want to shoot it in the ear or in the leg or in the gut.

"When you go through all the evidence and see how it all fits together, the conclusion is easy to reach. Janice Hall is guilty beyond any reasonable doubt. There's no way around it.

"The beauty of the evidence in this case is that there is overwhelming evidence of the human type, that is, proof of motive, the plan, the insurance money, the palimony, the prenuptial agreement, sleeping with another man three days before the wedding, the guns reported stolen, the unmitigated greed, the patently false theatrics.

"On top of that, here you have indisputable scientific evidence to back it up. The scientific evidence alone would be enough to prove the case beyond a reasonable doubt." I stood perfectly still before the jury placing my passion and belief in my last words. "What you have here is proof beyond any doubt. Thank you."

chapter 29

In Retaliation, In Defense

Alex Williams looked spitting mad as he strode up and down during his closing argument for the defense. Several times, he came right up to my table scowling and wagging his finger at me accusatorially. Among his main points were: that the hole in the fencepost was made by a .22-caliber bullet and had nothing to do with this murder; that it was just a coincidence the lead core from Bruce's lung came from the same batch of lead as the hillside bullet; that Bruce shot three shots at a deer, picked up the shell casings and had them in his hand when he was shot; and that it was Bruce's idea to get the insurance. This was just his warm up...

"Ladies and gentlemen, I don't want to insult your intelligence, but let me tell you something I think you all already know," Williams paused his voice rising. "The prosecution's case against Ms. Hall is nothing but speculation and garbage."

With difficulty, I kept my face immobile as I listened to him chew out me and the prosecution team with impunity. I have a temper and I was personally enraged at what he was saying, but I knew I had to keep cool.

Williams continued. "Remember in opening statements, he told you that he was going to show you a thorough and complete investigation, remember that?

"Well, what's the evidence shown? The evidence has shown that from day one, literally day one, the investigation in this case has been through tunnel vision, literally tunnel vision. Think about it. Nick Armand, first he's the lead investigator. He gets up here, up here near where the body is. He told you, well, he considered the crime scene forty-five feet either side of the body, that's it, that's it.

"This whole thing about Ted Farly, well, let's talk about that. She's known Ted for years. At one point in time, yeah, they had been intimate several years before. He came up to Montrose, and they decided to go out to dinner. It was late. She had had a few drinks, not as much as Farly, apparently. Farly told you he had up to half a gallon of whiskey." I watched his eyes come up twinkling with baleful humor and hoped the jury wasn't buying it. "And we don't know what he had there at the restaurant."

Williams went on. "Frankly, ladies and gentlemen, I don't know if Mr. Farly could have had sex, but I do know that he doesn't remember and that's what he came in here and said, he doesn't know what happened. And Janice has always been adamant they didn't have sex that night. She's always freely admitted they did a couple years before.

"Oh, but if we can try to buy that, then again, maybe that means she didn't love Bruce. Well, that's garbage. Same with Skip Kay. Both Skip and Janice have repeatedly said they did not have sex. Yeah, they ended up in bed one time together with no clothes on years ago. Does that have anything to do with anything here?" He shook his head and spat out, "No."

"Oh, but we can paint her, make her look like a bad person. This whole thing with the guns, they keep trying to say that Janice blamed Bruce for these missing guns in March of 1995. That's not true. That's not true at all. She moved out. They decided that they needed some time apart and we'll talk a little bit about that."

I felt antsy listening to these far-fetched theories. I wished I could object but sat back and let the defense spin their web.

"But after she had left, she discovered she couldn't find these two rifles and actually there was another missing. She couldn't find them and she thought they were over at Bruce's, but she had looked and couldn't find them. Bruce thought Janice had them. She thought he probably had them. They end up reporting them as stolen and months later turns out when she tries to borrow some guns or a gun from Skip, turns out he still has those.

"Well, he's had those for five years now. He's had numerous firearms that belong to her over the years and she thought she had got them all back. Once she realized she made the mistake, she did what an honest person is supposed to do: notified law enforcement, notified the insurance company, made arrangements to pay the insurance company back.

"Oh, but the prosecutor comes in and says, oh, it's insurance fraud. Well, no, it's not. It's not even close, but when you don't have a case, you start trying to twist things that way." He went on and on. My ears prickled as I listened and tried to sit still. I told myself to sit back and relax.

"Let's just talk in general for a second about cops and how things get recorded. Think about Nick Armand. He interviews Janice on the fifteenth of October, that very same day and he told you he's taking notes, but they're not verbatim, but he's taking notes. Sometime later he dictates his notes or puts them in a computer. Then he destroys his notes." After this comment, I took a very deep breath and slowly let it out. Williams didn't let up. "Well, I guarantee you, just like all of us during this trial, we're not writing things down verbatim. Anytime Bruce's name is mentioned it's V for victim. Every time Janice's name is mentioned, put a little triangle for defendant. It's called shortening it. Cops do the same thing."

My eyes wide now, I leaned forward as Williams continued his attack on me, my investigators and the prosecution's evidence.

"Nick Armand came in here and said that, although it wasn't in his report, it was his understanding that she was referring," Williams paused and pointed to a map of the hunting campsite, "to this area up here as being the ridge and this area down here as being the draw. Well, that's garbage. I mean, think about it. You might well sit out here on your tailgate," he gestured, frowning and began pacing again, "and go here, deer, deer. It's ludicrous. You've got a whole mountain over here.

"When she talked about going down into the bottom of the draw and she explains it's fifteen minutes from camp, you're not talking over here," Williams gestured to the right and to the left. I wondered if the jury was growing dizzy trying to follow him. "The aerial photograph helps explain that. It's just mind-boggling to me that she explains in detail where she went.

"She comes up out of camp. She goes up to the pond. She circles. She goes to the northeast. She zigzags the ridge. She gets into a mud bog at the bottom of the draw. Then she goes to the west. Then she goes to the southwest and then she comes back east to camp. She explained to them so graphically where she was, and yet, four and a half years and they've never done anything about it. Think about why."

I wanted to get up and tell Williams off. I was incensed by the fabrications, the implications and insults, but held myself in check as he continued.

Williams emitted another humorless laugh. "You can't begin to pinpoint on here anything, but by God, they heard what they wanted to hear. They believed what they wanted to believe. Anything that was to the contrary, they totally disregarded and it's been that way from day one.

"The prosecutor told you in his closing that Brent Branch-water testified that 8:30 or 8:45 was the latest that Janice came in to camp. In fact, that's not what he testified to. He told you that nine o'clock was the latest that he could recall her coming into camp and, in fact, that's what she told law enforcement. Now, have there been times when she said maybe between 9:00, 9:15? Yeah, yeah."

His comments were ruffling my feathers. He went on. "They're trying to make a big deal out of this whole thing with the .270 and her having seven millimeter mag ammo. On the one hand, they're wanting you to believe that she's this expert in firearms and so it wouldn't make sense for her to have seven millimeter mag ammo. Well, but on the other hand, they're wanting you to believe that she committed this murder.

"Why in the world would anybody take ammunition that wouldn't fit in her gun, that she wouldn't be able to use, because all that's going to do is cast suspicion on her. It's just—it doesn't make sense. What does make sense is that she doesn't know the difference. You heard from numerous people that she doesn't understand all these things. You give her a gun. It's loaded. You tell her where to shoot. She's a good shot. She's even won some competitions before, but is she by any means any sort of an expert on different types of calibers and ammunition and so forth? No."

I felt my eyes burning into Williams and found it increasingly hard to remain silent.

"Well, it's clear she had been wanting to either borrow or buy a seven millimeter. She had been up to the Freedom Gun Shop a week or so before going in and having the scope put on the .270 and having it bore sighted, asking about seven millimeter.

"Bruce was just starting to kind of get into, you know, big game hunting and so forth and he mentioned to her that he thought he had read somewhere that you could use seven millimeter magnum ammo in a .270. Now, do I personally think that there was probably an article that actually said that? No, but is that the way he interpreted it? Apparently so. Janice doesn't know that. It's like, okay, fine, you get more power with seven millimeter."

Next, Williams tried to bolster Janice's character while he hammered away at the prosecution's case.

"Janice has been amazingly consistent with everything that she has told them with one exception and actually I'll just tell you the one exception and that is how she loaded the .270. At one point, she was saying she loaded it in from the top and, at one point, she was saying she loaded it from the bottom. Fine.

"It's kind of like we talked about in jury selection, me going to the Shed in Santa Fe and I either get a number ten or eleven plate and I can't always recall which, but it's kind of the same here. Done it both ways, don't know, but the important thing is she has been amazingly consistent about what she did that morning.

"I need to get back to mud slinging here for a minute. This whole thing about multiple personality disorder, she's not the one that brought this stuff in. That's Lieutenant Hakes, who brought up this whole thing. Well, is it possible that, you know, you were in a different personality or something? No, she repeatedly said no, no, no, it's not possible. And she explained to them, and this is hard to understand on that tape, but she explained to them that she had been integrated or cured in 1994.

"I don't know if you all believe in multiple personality disorder or not. I don't care, because it doesn't have anything to do with this case, but the prosecutor brings it out, kind of slinging mud at her, let's see if something will stick. Janice made it abundantly clear that she had no memory loss until the time that she sees Bruce's body and she's made it abundantly clear from that point on she can't recall a whole lot.

"If she was under a different personality, she wouldn't know what she did that morning. She knows exactly what she did that morning. She knows exactly where she went and she's told them over and over and over again.

"Flashbacks, oh, well, she had flashbacks. Well, flashbacks must mean that she—that it refers to reality. No, let's look at how flashbacks come into the conversation here. She's talking about post-traumatic stress disorder, which, given that her husband of three months is killed and she's the one who finds him, is not too surprising she would have some disorder from that.

"The person who loved Bruce the most is Janice. Now, he can come in all he wants and try to say that she didn't love him, but he doesn't know that. All indications are she did. Now, have they had some trouble? Yeah. We're not disputing that, but by the time they decided to get married, to make that commitment, they were both so happy.

"You can see the wedding pictures. I mean, you can just see it. Both of them, they are so happy. Bruce is happy. She did, she made the comment Bruce can take care of her and part of that had to do with finances. I'm not trying to hide that from you because it's true. She would like to spend money and Bruce was kind of just the opposite. Bruce really did keep track of just about everything.

"You have his journal here, Number 239. He did keep track of things even after they were married. He was their financial planner. He's the person that does all this stuff. The prosecutor tries to say, well, we don't even know if Bruce knew about his life insurance policies. Get real. Get real. He's the one that's instigating all this.

"They're trying to say that Janice wants Bruce to quickly prepare a will. That doesn't even make sense because with or without a will, she's the beneficiary. She's the one who needs the will and quickly, because of her kids. If something were to happen to her, her property would go to her kids and not to Bruce

"The prosecutor keeps talking about, oh, all this insurance. Well, you've heard it was not a large amount of insurance. In fact, Janice had more insurance on her than she did on Bruce. I mean, the only thing here really is that they'd only been married three months.

"Now, if they had been married for ten years and they had never had any insurance and shortly before one of them gets killed, all of a sudden, there's this massive insurance that's purchased, that might mean something; but that's not the case here. We've got two people who are in their forties. Janice has two kids. Bruce is—I don't want to say compulsive, but he's very detailed about his finances and so forth.

"It makes sense that he would do this. This thing about Janice planning the funeral, well, that's garbage. The literature from the mortuary, who is that sent to? It's sent to Bruce, because Bruce sent away for it. That's the sort of person that he was. Did Janice fill out the paperwork? Yeah. So the prosecutor coming in here and saying, well, either she forged it or Bruce was drunk at the time, that's just garbage. No one can tell you if that's Bruce's signature or not.

"That's not surprising. I mean, look at what—and I can't remember her name, but from CBI. You know, she's looking at checks and so forth and, you know, yeah, you have a certain type signature. Then on this form you've got this great big spot. It's on floppy paper. I mean, who knows, who knows?

"But why in the world would Janice do that? I mean, it does not make sense. It doesn't make sense." Gesturing toward me, Williams went on, "He's trying to make this whole thing sinister about her sending pictures to Bruce's siblings from the wedding. Okay. If you're going to go out and commit a murder, it's just kind of like the last thing you would do."

Williams paused for a breath then continued. "I mean, ladies and gentlemen, I guess what it comes down to is I'm asking you all to apply your common sense. This case is all speculation, all of it, every single bit and the saddest thing here is a good man lost his life. I don't know if he was murdered. I don't know if it was an accident. I don't know, but neither do you."

"Objection to the attorney's statement about his own

beliefs," I said.

The judge nodded. "Sustained."

Williams nodded back. Walking over to the map of the hunting area he said, "None of us know whether this was an accident or not. If the shooter is up in here somewhere," Williams says pointing to the map, "and Bruce is walking back to camp, shooter sees some movement and fires. Bruce—one thing that's always been puzzling is why he takes off his vest. Probably he wasn't sure if he had been hit. I mean, he's taking off his vest to see.

"Well, at that point, he no longer has his orange on." Again Williams pointed to the map. "The shooter is up here. There's still movement going on down here and he fires two more times before realizing what has actually happened. That makes perfect sense. Who knows? That's the point."

Moving away from the map, Williams approached the jury box. "The one thing that is abundantly clear is that Janice loved her husband and she was devastated. I don't care how many people you bring in here to talk about, oh, it didn't seem real to me and the clothing was excessive, whatever, at the funeral, that's garbage. The people who know her saw a grieving widow. The people who know her saw her drop to under one hundred pounds, because she couldn't stand to eat. She couldn't stand to get out of bed for months.

"Yeah, that really sounds like somebody who just wants to go out and kill people for insurance money, doesn't it? It's garbage. That's all it is." A ripple of nervous laughter broke out in the courtroom. Ignoring it, Williams plunged on. "The only fair and just verdict in this case is not guilty. One man has already lost his life. That's tragic enough. What would compound it, make it so much worse is for you all to come back with a guilty verdict just to try to make things better, because it doesn't. It makes this so much worse.

"The person who killed Bruce is still out there. Now,

whether it's someone he knew or someone who we never heard from at all in this trial, we'll probably never know. Thank you."

The judge looked over at me. "Are you ready with your rebuttal closing?"

"Yes, your Honor," I said grimly.

"You can go ahead."

In my rebuttal I went after the fallacies in Williams' argument. Turning to face the jury, I began. "Was Mr. Williams at the same trial as the rest of us? As Cicero said, 'If you don't have the evidence, abuse the plaintiff.' Well, Mr. Williams is pretty good at that. The hole in the fence post was not shot with a .22. Shawn Bertram talked about the elasticity of wood and there's nothing inconsistent with a .30-caliber bullet having cause that hole. A .308 was considered as a weapon being involved since day two when the casing was first found. It's never been excluded and it's always been in the mind of the investigators.

"This idea that Bruce took three shots at a deer and he had the cartridges in his hands to explain how they wound up next to his body is about in the same category as 'Martians came down and put those shell casings next to him' because the person that put the shell casings next to him is sitting right here. It was Janice Hall.

"We never said that Bruce was out hunting without ammunition. He had some ammunition. She switched it for the three spent casings to explain the three shots that Brent Branchwater heard. Mr. Williams says they would have found the bullets. Well, you heard Shawn Bertram. These things can splinter into a zillion pieces and particles that wouldn't get picked up by a metal detector and Bertram never said you'll lose weight in a bullet just by going out the barrel. He never said that.

"And with regard to the .30-caliber bullet, remember it also passed through about this much cloth," I said, indicating with my hands, "and documenting the location of the .30-caliber bullet, that stringing that they did was the best way to do that. It went right from the area of the shooter, right by Bill Booth, across his back, right to where the bullet was in the ground.

"The core is, indeed, the bottom core of a .30 caliber Nosler Partition bullet. This argument by Mr. Williams about Nancy Saunders' testimony just makes one thing clear. He said, 'Hope I'm not confusing you.' Well, he didn't understand what she said and that is clear. She was not ambivalent at all about her testimony. I should say ambiguous. It was clear as a bell, not ambiguous.

"So under their theory of who shot Bruce, someone just randomly committed cold blooded murder at dawn on the day of October 15, 1995. That's without any basis in fact whatsoever. He said I'm riding two horses. Well, those were the only two horses that work. It's either one or the other and either way Janice Dodson is guilty one hundred percent." I felt that in the grip of strong emotion, I had to assert the voice of reason.

"There's no evidence either that Bruce instigated the insurance. There's no evidence that he knew about the insurance. There's a form in there from Janice's work where she went down on July 19 and added John Bruce Dodson on there. He didn't sign it. There's nothing to indicate he even knew about the insurance. The wills were to protect her property? What property did she have to protect with these wills? She didn't have any property.

"The mortuary documents, Bruce asked for them, Mr. Williams says, because they were sent to him. Well, you could call up—I could call up a mortuary and say, 'Would you please send this to John Bruce Dodson at such and such an address?' Why would Janice have forged this funeral stuff? Well, Bruce wasn't particularly interested in dying at the age forty-eight, that's why."

I approached the jury box. I felt I had to make it completely apparent that Janice Dodson Hall was evil, plain and simple. "It's time to turn the case over to you. You have all the evidence. You've heard all of the witnesses discuss it. Look at everything, come back with a just verdict which has to be guilty as charged to first-degree murder for this woman."

= chapter 30 =

The Verdict

The jury went out to deliberate on Wednesday afternoon. We were all exhausted. I lay awake that night thinking of all I should have argued that I forgot or that I should have argued differently. I could not focus on anything else the next day. To occupy my mind, I reorganized my desk. The jury was out all day Thursday. Towards the end of the day on Friday, I was getting worried. Surely, they would come back with a verdict before five. They did not. Now I was really worried. I agonized through the weekend until we started up again Monday. Finally, late Monday afternoon the call came in—the jury had a verdict. My heart was pounding.

The judge announced, "Before I bring the jury in, I just want to caution everyone before I do so, though I want to acknowledge that everyone who has watched and participated in the trial has, I think, every day conducted themselves with a great deal of class." He wanted those in the courtroom not to show emotion when they heard the jury's verdict. "I don't expect any outbursts no matter what the jury verdict. So no screams of anguish or glee out of respect, if for nothing else than the work that the jury has done. So I'll go ahead and bring the jury in."

It took a while for everyone to gather back in the courtroom. The word had gotten out and the room was packed—standing room only. Janice looked confident. She was joking with her lawyers before the jury came into the courtroom. When the jury filed in, I looked to see who was carrying the packet of instructions and the verdict form, which would indicate the jury foreperson. It was the pastor.

When they were all seated in the jury box, the judge said, "I am informed the jury has reached a verdict." The judge looked at the pastor, saying, "I know you must be the foreperson from the notes we've received before. Has the jury, in fact, reached a verdict?"

"We have, your Honor."

"If you can hand those documents to the bailiff, she will bring them up to me." The pastor handed the paper to the bailiff who handed it over to the judge. After spending what seemed to me far too long reading it, the judge announced, "I'll go ahead and read the jury verdict. We, the jury, find the defendant, Janice K. Hall, guilty of first-degree murder, signed by the foreperson. Is that, in fact, your verdict as well as the verdict of the jury as a whole?"

The pastor replied, "Yes, your Honor."

Then, as my heart pounded, the judge polled each juror. Upon hearing each juror affirm that he or she agreed with the verdict, Judge Massaro said, "The jury verdict is received and accepted. Anything else before the jury is discharged, Mr. Daniels?"

I let out a deep breath. "I have nothing else your honor."

"Did you have anything, Mr. Williams?" Judge Massaro asked.

"No, Judge. Thank you."

The jury was dismissed. The judge waited until all of them were gone. He then said, "My understanding is that there's to be a waiver of the presentence report and we can, therefore, go ahead with sentencing today. Did you have anything you wanted to present or argue for sentencing, Mr. Daniels?"

"Your Honor, Bruce Dodson's brother is here and he may want to say a few words to the Court."

The judge nodded at Michael Dodson. "Mr. Dodson, you're welcome to say something if you like. You're not required to, but if you would like to, that's fine."

Michael stood up and cleared his throat. "The only thing I can say is this is all so sad. My brother loved this girl and he was just taken advantage of. It's the saddest day of my life."

"Thank you," the judge said soberly.

I stepped forward. "And, Judge, I know you've heard all the evidence in the case and know exactly what happened and there's only one choice with regard to the sentence since we did not seek the death penalty. I ask you to impose that sentence and to allow thirty days for restitution amounts to be submitted to the Court."

"Thank you," the judge answered. "Anything you'd like to present or argue, Mr. Williams."

"Judge, with due respect to the jury's verdict, Ms. Hall didn't kill her husband. She didn't have anything to do with the death of her husband and, other than that, Judge, the Court has no choice but a life sentence to impose."

"Thank you," the judge said nodding. "Did you have anything you wanted to say, Ms. Hall?"

Hearing murmurs turn to whispers and chatter, I looked over at the spectators who were talking and moving about trying to get a closer look at Janice. The judge banged his gavel and quiet returned.

"Yes sir," Janice replied, her voice angry. "I am not guilty of this crime. I did not kill John Bruce Dodson. I still love this man with all my heart. I am not guilty and I don't understand this, and I don't understand—I don't understand how my God has let this happen, the God that I serve. I'm not guilty." Tears were streaming down her face. She was good, I had to admit, but the truth was now known. She continued. "Michael, Martha, I didn't do it. This is wrong. If I had done this, I would have pled guilty, but from my heart, I'm telling you that you've convicted the wrong person and the guilty person is out there and that person is free. I'm sorry for Bruce's death and many times I have wished that it would have been me. I'm sorry, Bart, and I'm sorry that you have to go through this.

"I'm not guilty. You're sending this person that's an innocent person to prison. Somewhere out there is the guilty person. May God have mercy on your soul. That's all I have to say."

The courtroom was now stonily silent. My heart deconstricted and I could breathe normally again. I heard a thud and looked to my right to see that Janice had fallen over backwards like a lead weight to the floor. Everyone in the packed room stood stock still and just stared at her. The room was in suspended animation. No one moved or said anything for the longest time, until finally one of the deputies on courtroom detail felt obliged to check on Janice. When she regained consciousness, we went directly into sentencing.

The judge's face was stony and his voice had a razor's edge. "Thank you. Judgment of the conviction does enter to first-degree murder, the only count charged in the information. There was sufficient evidence for the jury to reach the decision that they did. Mr. Daniels and Mr. Williams are right, there is only one sentence that can be imposed under Colorado's existing law and that's the sentence I am imposing.

"You, therefore, Ms. Hall, are sentenced to life in the Department of Corrections. I'll hold the issue of restitution open for thirty more days. Mr. Daniels will have within that period of time—he is to, within that period of time, file a statement regarding what the amount of restitution is requested. The defense will then have fifteen days after that within which to file any objections. If there are objections, we'll go ahead and schedule a restitution hearing.

"Ms. Hall, you have the right to appeal from the judgment

of conviction that has just been entered. If you wish to appeal, you need to file a notice of appeal and that has to be done within forty-five days of today's date. If you need a lawyer or a transcript for purposes of the appeal and if you are not able to afford either or both, ask the Court, they'll be provided at no expense to you."

Turning to Alex Williams, Judge Massaro asked, "Will you be perfecting the appellate documents if that's her intention?"

Williams' voice was stern. "Judge, I'll file the appellate packet with the public defender's office."

I knew he would do just that, but as I'd earlier told the jury, I had faith in the system.

Leaving the courthouse, I walked out of the building into the sunlight. I took a deep breath; the air outside smelled of springtime. I felt refreshed by the clean air and redeemed by the jury's verdict and the sentence the judge imposed on Janice Dodson Hall. Moments like these reaffirmed my belief in our great system of justice and I was thankful that justice had been served and that Bruce Dodson's killer had been convicted.

As I drove home, I thought about how during periods of cloudy thoughts, nagging questions of whether there really was some merit to the defense arguments rose to the surface. I felt satisfied that while the trial was going on, all such questions were exposed to the lights of day and reason. We do all that is humanly possible to see that justice is served. We have no interest in prosecuting an innocent person. There was no doubt in my mind that Janice was guilty of the cold-blooded murder of John Bruce Dodson.

The appellate court later addressed the conviction of Janice Dodson Hall. As I had anticipated, a main issue on appeal was the question of jury unanimity. The Court wrote:

"Defendant's primary contention on appeal is that the trial

court erred in refusing to instruct the jury that before she could be convicted, all jurors had to agree unanimously which of the prosecution's alternative theories supported the first degree murder count. Because we conclude the trial court did not err, we affirm." *People of the State of Colorado v. Janice Hall*, Colorado Court of Appeals, April 11, 2002.

Afterword

Although jarring memories of the murder case of Bruce Dodson permeated my journey thus far into my trip, as I cross the border into Louisiana I begin to feel like a kid on an adventure. Having spent so long on the preparation and trial of Janice Dodson, leisure time to travel on a pursuit I love opens a completely new and exciting world for me. Maybe it is because everything is so different from Colorado. There is nothing to see in the distance. It is flat. The air is thick, wet, and hot and smells unusual. Piney woods fence in the highway, cutting off vision after a few hundred feet. Here, your vision goes only to the next low rise. In Colorado, you can see for hundreds of miles. For a while, my distance vision seems stolen as if I'm wearing blinders. Then, directly in front of me are fields of wildflowers—red, yellow, pink—more in radiant abundance than any planted garden. As I approach Shreveport, I am smiling.

I pull off the interstate on the west side of town near the airport to get my bearings. The map I brought does not have enough detail to negotiate a city as big, filled with history and rambling as Shreveport. I stop to get some gas and a better map of the city. The map of the city costs $3.95 and is well worth it to be able to find my way around. I get specific directions from the store clerk and get back on a road named Hollywood, which seems to me an odd name for a street in Louisiana. Hollywood turns out to be a forlorn highway rife with poverty and despair. At some point, the name of the road changes to Pierremont and at a place called Caddo Heights, the poverty disappears. The sudden transition from poor to rich is thought-provoking and startling. There are big brick homes with large verandas on huge properties with expansive green manicured lawns, magnificent old hardwood trees and abundant flowering shrubbery. One popular smaller flowering tree I do not recognize comes in several colors including the loveliest lavender and appears to be at the peak of splendor. I do not recall ever having seen a tree like this before. Driving is dreamlike. I have to check my consciousness to be sure I am staying on the road. I wander off the main road through an older residential section with more beautiful homes and twisting streets. I am lost, but I do not care. It is early enough that I am confident I will find Mr. Akin's home before long. I know I am heading in the right direction. Mr. Akin's neighborhood is not quite as exclusive as the one I just drove through, but it is still nice. Finally, I arrive at his home, a single story brick house, sitting on a large lot and surrounded by huge twisty old live oaks and many flowering shrubs.

After we exchange greetings, Mr. Akin and I stand on the front porch looking at the house's exterior. Mr. Akin tells me he bought the house in 1943, when it was just a few years old. He always wanted a brick house. He was driving by with his wife and saw a man pounding the "For Sale" sign into the lawn. He stopped and asked what the man was asking for the house and the man told him "eleven thousand, five hundred." Mr. Akin said, "I'll take it," without even going inside. Mrs. Akin was miffed about his quick purchase without their seeing the place, but they made it their home and raised a family there. His daughter is now a retired mathematics professor from Louisiana State University. Mr. Akin's wife passed away some fifteen years ago and he has been lonely. He tells me he thinks that the petrified palm wood business has kept him alive. Every year he loads up a trailer and heads out to the Arizona desert for three weeks or a month and sells petrified palm wood in Quartzsite, where the air is dry and the sun shines every day. He thought this year would be the last, though. He has a hard time standing that long now.

Next, Mr. Akin beckons inside the house and shows me to my room. Every room in the house looks like it has not changed for over fifty years, other than by the addition of a new television set. It is a nice home and comfortable for Mr. Akin. At ninety-four years of age, he moves slowly but surely, but has been concerned lately about his health. He tells me it took him seven tries to get out of the bathtub the other night. Although I am anxious to see the palm wood collection, I do not mention it. The home is filled with many beautiful things. There are jade carvings and mineral specimens from all over the world placed in curio cabinets around the living room.

The next day we meet with Mr. Akin's friend who has the collection and lives south of the city on a large, deep lot in the woods. His name is Major Governor. He and his wife, Margaret, are retired and own a modest, well-maintained home. Both have had recent health problems and that is why Major Governor wants to sell his collection. I find Major Governor is a likable man who comes across as being extraordinarily competent. His first name is a nickname, rather than a military rank. He worked as the foreman of a carpentry crew that did fine finish work, such as the interiors of churches. Major Governor tells me he is seventy-two; I guess Miss Margaret to be about seventy.

When the time comes to view the collection, we all rise and head through the back yard toward a large out-building. It is hot and humid and there is no air conditioning. The temperature is hovering close to a hundred and so is the humidity. This out-building is as large as the house. There are boxes, tables and shelves, wall to wall. All available surfaces are packed with the most perfect petrified palm wood in existence. The volume and quality put me in awe. Mr. Akin told me before we came, "You could spend the rest of your life and a million dollars buying and cutting petrified palm wood and not be able to reproduce this collection." I now believe it. As I wander along the edges of the collection, the Major gives me a history. As a young man, he became interested in Louisiana petrified palm wood and eventually acquired saws and polishers. He started into this as a hobby close to fifty years ago. Living in rural central Louisiana put him in the right place and he had the right contacts to obtain the best wood. He bought and sold hundreds of thousands of pounds of palm wood. In the old days, he could get it for five or ten cents a pound. A good portion of the best Louisiana palm wood offered for sale at the Quartzsite and Tucson gem and mineral shows over the past forty years passed through his hands. As is the case with many lovers of fossil wood, he kept the best pieces for his own collection. Until recently, he says, he never considered selling a single specimen from his personal collection.

Most people think of petrified wood as just rocks. I sometimes hear people say, "Oh, petrified wood; my aunt's ranch is covered with it." To collectors such as the Major and me, 99.9 percent of petrified wood is of no interest. However, when certain factors come together, petrified wood is almost miraculous. Petrified *Araucaria* cones from Patagonia and petrified *Hermanophyton* from southwestern Colorado are two examples of fossil plant materials in which everything came together just right; this quality Louisiana palm wood is another. The material is absolutely solid and without fractures. The cellular structure is perfectly preserved. It has the hardness of an amethyst and will ring like a china plate when tapped. The colors range from white to black with a rainbow of

gold, red, blue, yellow and lavender in between. They are gem quality. Every one of these specimens could be cut and made into jewelry, but they really belong in a museum where they can be
appreciated for many years to come. These palm trees grew in a low-
lying, tropical, coastal plain during the Oligocene Epoch of the Ter-
tiary Period, some thirty to thirty-five million years ago. They most
recently reposed within the Catahoula Formation. When you hold
one of these specimens in your hand, you hold a memory of the
geologic and plant history of this planet. Try to imagine what the
world was like when these trees were swaying in the breeze. What
bizarre creatures ate their leaves and fruit? Fossil wood of this quality is extremely rare and can be quite valuable. Collectors from Ger-
many and Japan are especially interested in top quality pieces and
will pay high prices for rare and beautiful specimens.

Major Governor is a perfectionist and a master stone pol-
isher in addition to being a master woodworker. Every piece is perfect and the colors are amazing. It is the best of the best. The
collection includes a number of specimens that are sections of trees
cut and polished on each end. These are generally cylindrical in
shape. There is one small, perfect piece that catches my eye; I pick it
up and heft it. Small fully round tree sections like this are rare. It
weighs about four pounds and is seven inches long with a diameter
of three inches at the widest end; it is about the size of the fat end of
a baseball bat with a creamy ivory color in the center and gold
around the edges. There are some small blue agate inclusions, perfect cell structure and a white rind all around. Miss Margaret has
long since gone back into the house and, as I examine this piece,
Major Governor looks over at me and says, "That's my favorite piece
and it's about as perfect as they get. I found it forty years ago in the
White Ground. What I really like about," he adds with a sly grin, "is
that it's just exactly the same size as my pecker." That gets a chuckle
out of Mr. Akin and me.

After spending hours with the collection and computing the value, I eventually make a deal to buy it. I know if I pass these specimens up, I will never see anything like them again. We tell the Major we are going down south to Flatwoods the next day so that I can see the petrified palm wood country, visit Poor Boy and then I will be back to pack up the collection the day afterward.

My entire stay in Louisiana is dreamlike, pleasant and comforting. For the first time, I am able to distance myself from thinking constantly of Janice, Bruce and the murder. Thankfully, Mr. Akin lets me drive his car down to Flatwoods as he had two places in mind to visit. One is the home of Poor Boy, another collector, and the other is the home of a man named Mr. White. I heard Mr. Akin and Major Governor talk about "The White Ground," a term used with obvious reverence as the source of the most amazing petrified wood. When Mr. Akin mentioned going over to Mr. White's place, I assumed this was it.

We first pay a visit to Poor Boy. This man and his home are amazing beyond words. There is no worry here about over conformity. Unique seems too trivial a word to describe the scene. His house is old and ramshackle. He has petrified palm wood all over. On the porch is a tall petrified palm tree that rises up to and right through the roof. The walls inside are covered with large polished slabs of petrified wood and even the tables are made of petrified wood. The walls of one room boast floor to ceiling shelves filled with small petrified logs, each cut and polished on one end. It is a remarkable sight. Large chainsaw carvings of bears and humanoid figures clutter the yard, another hobby and source of income. Speaking with Poor Boy quickly puts one at ease. He is a gentle man with varied interests and, although not formally educated, wise in the ways of his world. For a moment I think of another gentle man, Bruce Dodson, and how he was unwise. Again, I push the memories aside.

I spend some time questioning Poor Boy about the petrified

wood situation in the area these days. He tells me it is all gone or closed off in private property. He shows me some colorful small pieces of the best quality and remarks reverently that they are from "The White Ground." I asked him where that is and learn it is not far, but is now closed to collecting and trespassing. No one has collected there for many years. I ask why it is called "The White Ground," and he looks at me as though I am an idiot, squinting his good eye, and states, "Because the ground is white."

After leaving Poor Boy's home, we drive over to Mr. White's. As I learned from Poor Boy, this is not the "White Ground." Mr. White has a forty-acre tract. A long dirt driveway snakes from the road back to the home and outbuildings, which all look like they have been left unchanged since the Civil War, other than for the effects of time and weather. At first, it seems that no one is there. We wander around a little and find the aged Mr. White down behind the barn tending to a beautiful crop of red beans. It is truly a rich crop and, weather permitting, should yield a good harvest. He has the same general comments about the petrified palm. It has all been hunted out. On the way back to the main highway, I stop and take some pictures of Lake Rodemacher.

The next day, Mr. Akin and I arrive at Major and Miss Margaret's home early in the morning. I have a lot to pack up and want to get on the road. This is the hottest it's been this early in the morning. However, Major did not want to do any packing before I arrived, because he wanted me to see what was there and to accept responsibility for any damage that might occur. Now, he goes down to a packing shed and brings back dozens of sturdy tomato boxes and a large roll of foam packing material. We start the process of wrapping the palm wood in the foam material and loading each piece into the tomato boxes. Mr. Akin helps by sitting in a chair and telling stories.

When we are nearing the end of the job, a woman I have not

met before sticks her head into the doorway and says, "Hello, Papa," to Mr. Akin in the sweetest Southern voice I have ever heard. He glances up with a broad contented smile and looks at her with love and adoration. This is Camellia, his daughter. He asked her to come over so that she can meet me before I head back to Colorado. Meeting Camellia is comforting, as I can see now that Papa Akin is in loving and caring hands. She is a lovely woman with strawberry blond hair, bright blue eyes and a fair complexion. I can envision in her the young freckled, smiling face of childhood. The grace I came to recognize in Mr. Akin has flowed into this lovely woman.

It takes much of the day to get the job done. By late afternoon, my car is packed full to the brim. I have boxes and rough logs of petrified wood everywhere. Without question, I am over the manufacturer's recommended weigh capacity. In addition to the cargo area, the front passenger side floor and seat are crammed with boxes. I keep a box with some of the more special smaller specimens on top of the pile in the front seat. Since it is late, Mr. Akin invites me to spend another night in his home. I am exhausted from the day's work and gladly accept.

However, that night at Mr. Akin's, I do not sleep well. Perhaps, lodged in my subconscious, is the thought that I will soon be returning to my "other life" and once again the Dodson case slithers through my mind, this time causing a disturbing dream:

I call Brent Branchwater in Marshall, Texas to let him know I will be stopping by for a quick visit on my way back to Colorado. Captain Branchwater tells me to get off the Interstate at Exit 617, call from the service station and he will "come on down and fetch me." When I get there and call, he explains that an emergency just came up and he has to go out and work it. He says there is a barricaded suicidal subject they need to pry loose. He is sorry that he will not be able to meet and show me around. He goes on to tell me that he has asked around for petrified wood places for me and he came across an old-timer who has been collecting all his life. He says the old fellow showed him the collection and he thought it was pretty amazing. Branchwater says he never knew that petrified wood could look like colored glass on the inside. He tells me I can get to this man's house in fifteen minutes from my present location and asks if I would like to see it. I tell Brent I am sorry we could not get together, but I might as well go to see this man's collection, as it might be a long time before I am back in the area. He gives me the directions and I am on my way.

Branchwater tells me the man with the collection is named Jim Smith and he lives out in the woods, but not far off the paved road. I am to take Highway 59, the one I just turned onto from the Interstate and head south toward Carthage. When I cross the Sabine River, I am to look for a dirt driveway to my right, turn there and follow the road as it curves back about a quarter mile to where I'll see a small, run-down house to my left in a stand of tall pine trees. "That is Jim's house. He is usually home," says Captain Branchwater.

When I get to the house, I am somewhat surprised at how much of a hovel it really is. "It is hard to imagine that the owner would have much of a petrified wood collection," I mutter, "but you never know." I grab the small petrified wood log, Major Governor's favorite, from the box in the seat next to me to show Mr. Smith. I figure I will impress him with some really good wood and that way, if he has any to sell, it will pale in comparison, allowing me to make a better bargain. I step up onto the rickety porch and knock. There is no response. I knock again—still no reply. As I am about to give up, I sense a presence to my left, just behind my shoulder. It is a dark, animal-

like presence. I hesitate to look. I turn my head and find myself
staring into the pale, cold blue eyes of Janice Dodson. A rifle is
in her hands and she slowly raises it up. Major Governor's
favorite specimen flies out of my right hand and lands hard
right between her eyes. It seems to have done so of its own voli-
tion. It is as though I am not the actor, but just a prop in the
scene.

Upon awakening in the morning, I say good-bye to Mr. Akin
and am on the road again. It is especially hard for me to leave Mr.
Akin as I know there is a good chance I will never see him again. I
am glad he has Miss Camellia close by. Despite my dream, I do not
stop in Marshall to visit with Brent Branchwater. The trip back to
Colorado is uneventful. I drive straight through, stopping only for
gas and food.

Still, thoughts of the Dodson case continue to intrude on an
otherwise peaceful existence and I cannot help but ponder the
senseless brutality of murder and the ancient motivation of greed.
While my choice of career seems to have painfully dictated to me
that our human tendency towards violence and our susceptibility to
the basest of responses, self-interest and greed are integral and time-
less aspects of the human condition, my job also offers the redemption of serving a higher purpose.

As these traits are forever etched onto too many lives, and
leave their indelible marks on society and the world through the
instrument of people such as Janice Hall and the loss of good men
like Bruce Dodson, I too, backed by the weight and force of justice
and our great system of law, am able to leave a mark. Echoed in the
permanence of the antique and ancient woods all around me, forged
to stone by relentless time and offering a record of ages and events
long past in their delicate hues and markings, justice served in the

name of fairness, equality and truth offers redemption to the belea-
guered and wronged. For without justice, violence and greed escape
across the broad plateaus of our world, only to arise again. By visiting justice upon the guilty, both the misdeeds of violence and greed
are etched into our collective consciousness, and the value of those
lives whose loss we seek to avenge is imprinted into the social
record, made permanent in history and mind and with the bang of
a gavel, marked in stone for all to read.

Janice is serving her sentence of Life without the Possibility
of Parole at the Colorado State Penitentiary. The insurance companies paid all claims to Bruce's family. Martha and Michael are putting the money to good use by paying for Bruce's nieces and
nephews to attend college.

Bill, Dave and I are working on other murder cases, but the
strange, fascinating, unbelievably cold-blooded murder of Bruce
Dodson by his greedy wife is one none of us will ever forget.